Hands-On Explaina with Python

Interpret, visualize, explain, and integrate reliable AI for fair, secure, and trustworthy AI apps

Denis Rothman

BIRMINGHAM - MUMBAI

Hands-On Explainable AI (XAI) with Python

Producer: Tushar Gupta

Acquisition Editor – Peer Reviews: Divya Mudaliar

Project Editor: Tom Jacob

Content Development Editors: Kate Blackham, Alex Patterson

Copy Editor: Safis Editing

Technical Editor: Saby D'silva

Proofreader: Safis Editing

Indexer: Rekha Nair

Presentation Designer: Pranit Padwal

First published: July 2020

Production reference: 1290720

Published by Packt Publishing Ltd.
Livery Place
35 Livery Street
Birmingham B3 2PB, UK.

ISBN 978-1-80020-813-1

www.packt.com

packt.com

Subscribe to our online digital library for full access to over 7,000 books and videos, as well as industry leading tools to help you plan your personal development and advance your career. For more information, please visit our website.

Why subscribe?

- Spend less time learning and more time coding with practical eBooks and Videos from over 4,000 industry professionals
- Learn better with Skill Plans built especially for you
- Get a free eBook or video every month
- Fully searchable for easy access to vital information
- Copy and paste, print, and bookmark content

Did you know that Packt offers eBook versions of every book published, with PDF and ePub files available? You can upgrade to the eBook version at www.Packt.com and as a print book customer, you are entitled to a discount on the eBook copy. Get in touch with us at customercare@packtpub.com for more details.

At www.Packt.com, you can also read a collection of free technical articles, sign up for a range of free newsletters, and receive exclusive discounts and offers on Packt books and eBooks.

Contributors

About the author

Denis Rothman graduated from Sorbonne University and Paris-Diderot University, writing one of the very first word2vector embedding solutions. He began his career authoring one of the first AI cognitive **natural language processing (NLP)** chatbots applied as a language teacher for Moët et Chandon and other companies. He has also authored an AI resource optimizer for IBM and apparel producers. He then authored an **advanced planning and scheduling (APS)** solution that is used worldwide.

> *"I want to thank those corporations who trusted me from the start to deliver artificial intelligence solutions and share the risks of continuous innovation. I would also like to thank my family, who believed I would make it big at all times."*

About the reviewer

Carlos Toxtli is a human-computer interaction researcher who studies the impact of artificial intelligence in the future of work. He completed a Ph.D. in Computer Science at the University of West Virginia and a master's degree in Technological Innovation and Entrepreneurship at the Monterrey Institute of Technology and Higher Education. He has worked for numerous international organizations, including Google, Microsoft, Amazon, and the United Nations. He has also created companies that use artificial intelligence in the financial, educational, customer service, and parking industries. Carlos has published numerous research papers, manuscripts, and book chapters for different conferences and journals in his field.

"I want to thank all the editors who helped make this book a masterpiece."

Table of Contents

Preface

In today's era of AI, accurately interpreting and communicating trustworthy AI findings is becoming a crucial skill to master. Artificial intelligence often surpasses human understanding. As such, the results of machine learning models can often prove difficult and sometimes impossible to explain. Both users and developers face challenges when asked to explain how and why an AI decision was made.

The AI designer cannot possibly design a single explainable AI solution for the hundreds of machine learning and deep learning models. Effectively translating AI insights to business stakeholders requires individual planning, design, and visualization choices. European and US law has opened the door to litigation when results cannot be explained, but developers face overwhelming amounts of data and results in real-life implementations, making it nearly impossible to find explanations without the proper tools.

In this book, you will learn about tools and techniques using Python to visualize, explain, and integrate trustworthy AI results to deliver business value, while avoiding common issues with AI bias and ethics.

Throughout the book, you will work with hands-on Python machine learning projects in Python and TensorFlow 2.x. You will learn how to use **WIT**, **SHAP**, **LIME**, **CEM**, and other key explainable AI tools. You will explore tools designed by IBM, Google, Microsoft, and other advanced AI research labs.

You will be introduced to several open source explainable AI tools for Python that can be used throughout the machine learning project lifecycle. You will learn how to explore machine learning model results, review key influencing variables and variable relationships, detect and handle bias and ethics issues, and integrate predictions using Python along with supporting machine learning model visualizations in user explainable interfaces.

We will build XAI solutions in Python and TensorFlow 2.x, and use Google Cloud's XAI platform and Google Colaboratory.

Who this book is for

- Beginner Python programmers who already have some foundational knowledge and/or experience with machine learning libraries such as scikit-learn.

- Professionals who already use Python for purposes such as data science, machine learning, research, analysis, and so on, and can benefit from learning the latest explainable AI open source toolkits and techniques.

- Data analysts and data scientists that want an introduction to explainable AI tools and techniques using Python for machine learning models.

- AI project and business managers who must face the contractual and legal obligations of AI explainability for the acceptance phase of their applications.

- Developers, project managers, and consultants who want to design solid artificial intelligence that both users and the legal system can understand.

- AI specialists who have reached the limits of unexplainable black box AI and want AI to expand through a better understanding of the results produced.

- Anyone interested in the future of artificial intelligence as a tool that can be explained and understood. AI and XAI techniques will evolve and change. But the fundamental ethical and XAI tools learned in this book will remain an essential part of the future of AI.

What this book covers

Chapter 1, Explaining Artificial Intelligence with Python

Explainable AI (XAI) cannot be summed up in a single method for all participants in a project. When a patient shows signs of **COVID-19**, **West Nile Virus**, or any other virus, how can a general practitioner and AI form a cobot to determine the origin of the disease? The chapter describes a case study and an AI solution built from scratch, to trace the origins of a patient's infection with a Python solution that uses k-nearest neighbors and Google Location History.

Chapter 2, White Box XAI for AI Bias and Ethics

Artificial intelligence might sometimes have to make life or death decisions. When the autopilot of an autonomous vehicle detects pedestrians suddenly crossing a road, what decision should be made when there is no time to stop?

Can the vehicle change lanes without hitting other pedestrians or vehicles? The chapter describes the MIT moral machine experiment and builds a Python program using decision trees to make real-life decisions.

Chapter 3, Explaining Machine Learning with Facets

Machine learning is a data-driven training process. Yet, companies rarely provide clean data or even all of the data required to start a project. Furthermore, the data often comes from different sources and formats. Machine learning models involve complex mathematics, even when the data seems acceptable. A project can rapidly become a nightmare from the start.

This chapter implements **Facets** in Python in a Jupyter Notebook on Google Colaboratory. Facets provides multiple views and tools to track the variables that distort the ML model's results. Finding counterfactual data points, and identifying the causes, can save hours of otherwise tedious classical analysis.

Chapter 4, Microsoft Azure Machine Learning Model Interpretability with SHAP

Artificial intelligence designers and developers spend days searching for the right ML model that fits the specifications of a project. Explainable AI provides valuable time-saving information. However, nobody has the time to develop an explainable AI solution for every single ML model on the market!

This chapter introduces model-agnostic explainable AI through a Python program that implements Shapley values with SHAP based on Microsoft Azure's research. This game theory approach provides explanations no matter which ML model it faces. The Python program provides explainable AI graphs showing which variables influence the outcome of a specific result.

Chapter 5, Building an Explainable AI Solution from Scratch

Artificial intelligence has progressed so fast in the past few years that moral obligations have sometimes been overlooked. Eradicating bias has become critical to the survival of AI. Machine learning decisions based on racial or ethnic criteria were once accepted in the United States; however, it has now become an obligation to track bias and eliminate those features in datasets that could be using discrimination as information.

This chapter shows how to eradicate bias and build an ethical ML system in Python with Google's What-If Tool and Facets. The program will take moral, legal, and ethical parameters into account from the very beginning.

Chapter 6, AI Fairness with Google's What-If Tool (WIT)

Google's PAIR (People + AI Research – `https://research.google/teams/brain/pair/`) designed **What-If Tool (WIT)** to investigate the fairness of an AI model. This chapter takes us deeper into Explainable AI, introducing a Python program that creates a **deep neural network (DNN)** with TensorFlow, uses a SHAP explainer and creates a WIT instance.

The WIT will provide ground truth, cost ration fairness, and PR curve visualizations. The Python program shows how ROC curves, AUC, slicing, and PR curves can pinpoint the variables that produced a result, using AI fairness and ethical tools to make predictions.

Chapter 7, A Python Client for Explainable AI Chatbots

The future of artificial intelligence will increasingly involve bots and chatbots. This chapter shows how chatbots can provide a CUI XAI through Google Dialogflow. A Google Dialogflow Python client will be implemented with an API that communicates with Google Dialogflow.

The goal is to simulate user interactions for decision-making XAI based on the **Markov Decision Process (MDP)**. The XAI dialog is simulated in a Jupyter Notebook, and the agent is tested on Google Assistant.

Chapter 8, Local Interpretable Model-Agnostic Explanations (LIME)

This chapter takes model agnostics further with **Local Interpretable Model-agnostic Explanations (LIME)**. The chapter shows how to create a model-agnostic explainable AI Python program that can explain the results of random forests, k-nearest neighbors, gradient boosting, decision trees, and extra trees.

The Python program creates a unique LIME explainer with visualizations no matter which ML model produces the results.

Chapter 9, The Counterfactual Explanations Method

It is sometimes impossible to find why a data point has not been classified as expected. No matter how we look at it, we cannot determine which feature or features generated the error.

Visualizing counterfactual explanations can display the features of a data point that has been classified in the wrong category right next to the closest data point that was classified in the right category. An explanation can be rapidly tracked down with the Python program created in this chapter with a WIT.

The Python program created in this chapter's WIT can define the belief, truth, justification, and sensitivity of a prediction.

Chapter 10, Contrastive XAI

Sometimes, even the most potent XAI tools cannot pinpoint the reason an ML program made a decision. The **Contrastive Explanation Method (CEM)** implemented in Python in this chapter will find precisely how a datapoint crossed the line into another class.

The program created in this chapter prepares a MNIST dataset for CEM, defines a CNN, tests the accuracy of the CNN, and defines and trains an auto-encoder. From there, the program creates a CEM explainer that will provide visual explanations of pertinent negatives and positives.

Chapter 11, Anchors XAI

Rules have often been associated with hard coded expert system rules. But what if an XAI tool could generate rules automatically to explain a result? Anchors are high-precision rules that are produced automatically.

This chapter's Python program creates anchors for text classification and images. The program pinpoints the precise pixels of an image that made a model change its mind and select a class.

Chapter 12, Cognitive XAI

Human cognition has provided the framework for the incredible technical progress made by humanity in the past few centuries, including artificial intelligence. This chapter puts human cognition to work to build cognitive rule bases for XAI.

The chapter explains how to build a cognitive dictionary and a cognitive sentiment analysis function to explain the marginal features from a human perspective. A Python program shows how to measure marginal cognitive contributions.

This chapter sums up the essence of XAI, for the reader to build the future of artificial intelligence, containing real human intelligence and ethics.

To get the most out of this book

To get the most out of this book, it is recommended to:

- Focus on the key concepts of **explainable AI (XAI)** and how they are becoming mandatory
- Read the chapters without running the code if you wish to focus on XAI theory
- Read the chapters and run the programs if you wish to go through the theory and implementations simultaneously.

Download the example code files

You can download the example code files for this book from your account at http://www.packt.com. If you purchased this book elsewhere, you can visit http://www.packt.com/support and register to have the files emailed directly to you.

You can download the code files by following these steps:

1. Log in or register at http://www.packt.com.
2. Select the **SUPPORT** tab.
3. Click on **Code Downloads & Errata**.
4. Enter the name of the book in the **Search** box and follow the on-screen instructions.

Once the file is downloaded, please make sure that you unzip or extract the folder using the latest version of:

- WinRAR / 7-Zip for Windows
- Zipeg / iZip / UnRarX for Mac
- 7-Zip / PeaZip for Linux

The code bundle for the book is also hosted on GitHub at https://github.com/PacktPublishing/Hands-On-Explainable-AI-XAI-with-Python. In case there's an update to the code, it will be updated on the existing GitHub repository.

We also have other code bundles from our rich catalog of books and videos available at https://github.com/PacktPublishing/. Check them out!

Download the color images

We also provide a PDF file that has color images of the screenshots/diagrams used in this book. You can download it here: https://static.packt-cdn.com/downloads/9781800208131_ColorImages.pdf.

Conventions used

There are a number of text conventions used throughout this book.

CodeInText: Indicates code words in text, database table names, folder names, filenames, file extensions, pathnames, dummy URLs, user input, and Twitter handles. For example; "If the label is 0, then the recommendation is to stay in the right lane."

A block of code is set as follows:

```
choices = str(prediction).strip('[]')
  if float(choices) <= 1:
    choice = "R lane"
  if float(choices) >= 1:
    choice = "L lane"
```

Command-line or terminal output is written as follows:

```
1 data [[0.76, 0.62, 0.02, 0.04]] prediction: 0 class 0 acc.: True R
lane
2 data [[0.16, 0.46, 0.09, 0.01]] prediction: 0 class 1 acc.: False R
lane
3 data [[1.53, 0.76, 0.06, 0.01]] prediction: 0 class 0 acc.: True R
lane
```

Bold: Indicates a new term, an important word, or words that you see on the screen, for example, in menus or dialog boxes, also appear in the text like this. For example: " Go to the **Scatter | X-Axis** and **Scatter | Y-Axis** drop-down lists."

Warnings or important notes appear like this.

Tips and tricks appear like this.

Get in touch

Feedback from our readers is always welcome.

General feedback: If you have questions about any aspect of this book, mention the book title in the subject of your message and email us at customercare@packtpub.com.

Errata: Although we have taken every care to ensure the accuracy of our content, mistakes do happen. If you have found a mistake in this book we would be grateful if you would report this to us. Please visit, http://www.packt.com/submit-errata, selecting your book, clicking on the Errata Submission Form link, and entering the details.

Piracy: If you come across any illegal copies of our works in any form on the Internet, we would be grateful if you would provide us with the location address or website name. Please contact us at copyright@packt.com with a link to the material.

If you are interested in becoming an author: If there is a topic that you have expertise in and you are interested in either writing or contributing to a book, please visit http://authors.packtpub.com.

Reviews

Please leave a review. Once you have read and used this book, why not leave a review on the site that you purchased it from? Potential readers can then see and use your unbiased opinion to make purchase decisions, we at Packt can understand what you think about our products, and our authors can see your feedback on their book. Thank you!

For more information about Packt, please visit packt.com.

1

Explaining Artificial Intelligence with Python

Algorithm explainability began with the first complex machines in the 1940s, the first being the Turing machine. Alan Turing himself struggled to explain how the intelligence of his machine solved encryption problems. Ever since machines have made calculations and decisions, explainability has been part of any implementation process through user interfaces, charts, business intelligence, and other tools.

However, the exponential progress of **artificial intelligence (AI)**, including rule-based expert systems, machine learning algorithms, and deep learning, has led to the most complex algorithms in history. The difficulty of explaining AI has grown proportionally to the progress made.

As AI spreads out to all fields, it has become critical to provide explanations when the results prove inaccurate. Accurate results also require an explanation for a user to trust a machine learning algorithm. In some cases, AI faces life and death situations that require clear and rapid explanations. In this chapter, for example, we will study a case that requires an early diagnosis for a patient unknowingly infected by the West Nile virus.

The term *explainable artificial intelligence* or *artificial intelligence explainability* describes the explanatory process. We will often refer to explainable AI as XAI.

The goal of this chapter is to understand the key features of XAI and apply them to a case study in Python.

We will first define **explainable AI (XAI)** and the challenges we face when implementing explanations. Each profile requires different AI explanations. An AI expert will expect different perspectives than end users, for instance.

We will then explore a life and death case study in which AI and XAI constitute critical tools for a medical diagnosis of the propagation of the West Nile virus in Chicago, Illinois, USA.

The goal of XAI in this chapter is not to explain AI to developers but to explain the predictions of an ML system to a general practitioner enough for the ML decisions to be trusted.

We'll build the components of an XAI solution in Python from scratch using a **k-nearest neighbors (KNN)** algorithm and Google Maps Location History data, among other functions.

This chapter covers the following topics:

- Defining XAI
- The key features of XAI
- Describing a case study from the perspective of various profiles
- An executive function XAI feature chart
- The different forms and methods of XAI
- The XAI timeline from conception to production
- AI accountability
- The XAI timeline from a user's perspective
- k-nearest neighbors in Python
- Reading Google Maps Location History stored in JSON in Python

The first step will be to explore the key features of XAI before building an XAI prototype from scratch.

Defining explainable AI

Explainable AI, or AI explaining, or AI explainability, or simply XAI, seems simple. You just take an AI algorithm and explain it. It seems so elementary that you might even wonder why we are bothering to write a book on this!

Before the rise of XAI, the typical AI workflow was minimal. The world and activities surrounding us produce datasets. These datasets were put through black-box AI algorithms, not knowing what was inside. Finally, human users had to either trust the system or initiate an expensive investigation. The following diagram represents the former AI process:

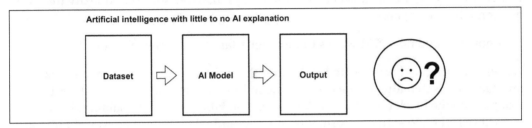

Figure 1.1: AI process

In a non-XAI approach, the user is puzzled by the output. The user does not trust the algorithm and does not understand from the output whether the answer is correct or not. Furthermore, the user does not know how to control the process.

In a typical XAI approach, the user obtains answers, as shown in the following diagram. The user trusts the algorithm. Because the user understands how a result was obtained, the user knows whether the answer is correct or not. Furthermore, the user can understand and control the process through an interactive explanation interface:

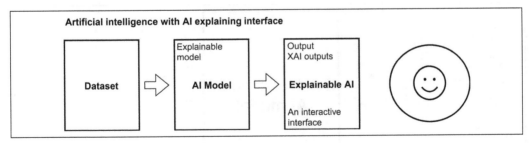

Figure 1.2: XAI process

The typical XAI flow takes information from the world and the activities that occur in it to produce input datasets to extract information from, to build, in turn, a white box algorithm that allows AI explainability. The user can consult an interface that accesses interpretable AI models.

The XAI phase will help the users of AI understand the processes, build up trust in the AI systems, and speed AI projects up. If the developers do not implement XAI, they will encounter the ethical and legal stumbling blocks described in *Chapter 2, White Box XAI for AI Bias and Ethics.*

Understanding the concept of XAI is quite simple, as we just saw. But in AI, once you begin digging into a subject a bit, you always discover some complexity that was not immediately apparent!

Let's now dig into how XAI works to discover a fascinating new area in AI.

We just saw that XAI was located right after the AI black box and before a human interface. But is that always the case? In the following section, we will first start by looking into the black box, then explore interpretability and explainability. Finally, we will see when to extract information for XAI and when to build XAI right into an AI model.

Let's first define what looking into a black box algorithm means.

Going from black box models to XAI white box models

Common sense tells us that XAI should be located right after a black box AI algorithm, as shown in the following diagram:

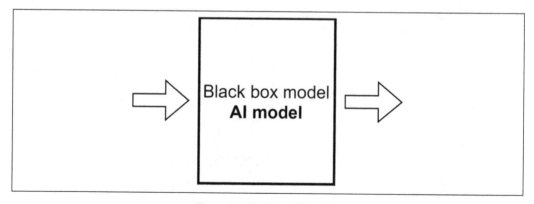

Figure 1.3: Black box AI model

But we must first define what a black box is.

The definition of a black box that applies to AI in mainstream literature is a system whose internal workings are hidden and not understood. A black box AI model takes an input, runs an algorithm or several algorithms, and produces an output that might work, but remains obscure. This definition somewhat fits the expression "black box AI."

However, there is another formal definition of a black box that contradicts this one!

This other definition reflects a conflicting concept, referring to the flight recorder in an aircraft. In this case, the black box records all of the information in real time so that a team of experts can analyze the timeline of a given flight in minute detail.

In this case, a black box contains detailed information. This definition contradicts the algorithm definition! The use of a black box as a way to record important information, as in the case of an aircraft, is similar to software logging.

A log file, for example, records events, messages between systems, and any other type of information the designers of a system saw fit to include in the process. We refer to logging as the action of recording information and the log as the file or table we store the logged information in.

We can use a software log file as the equivalent of an aircraft flight recorder when applying the concept to software. When we talk about and use logs and log files in this sense, we will not use the term "black box" in order to avoid conflicting uses of the expression.

When we use a log file or any other means of recording or extracting information, we will use the term *white box*. We will refer to white box models as ones containing information on the inner working of the algorithms.

Once we have access to the information of a white box model, we will have to explain and interpret the data provided.

Explaining and interpreting

Explaining makes something understandable and something unclear plain to see. Interpreting tells us the meaning of something.

For example, a teacher will explain a sentence in a language using grammar. The words in the sentence are accepted the way they are and explained. We take the words at face value.

When the teacher tries to explain a difficult line of poetry, the same teacher will interpret the ideas that the poet meant to express. The words in the sentence are not accepted the way they are. They require interpretation.

When applied to AI, explaining a KNN algorithm, for example, means that we will take the concepts at face value. We might say, "a KNN takes a data point and finds the closest data points to decide which class it is in."

Interpreting a KNN is going beyond a literal explanation. We might say, "The results of a KNN seem consistent, but sometimes a data point might end up in another class because it is close to two classes with similar features. In this case, we should add some more distinctive features." We have just interpreted results and explained the KNN mathematically.

The definitions of explaining and interpreting are very close. Just bear in mind that interpretation goes beyond explaining when it becomes difficult to understand something, and deeper clarification is required.

At this point, we know that a white box AI model generates explainable information. If the information is difficult to understand or obscure, then interpretation is required.

We'll now see whether the information we want to use in a white box AI model should be designed from the start or extracted along the way.

Designing and extracting

Extracting data from the outputs of an AI model is one way of providing XAI data. Another approach consists of designing outputs at each phase of an AI solution from the start. Explainable components can be designed for the inputs, the model, the outputs, the events occurring when the AI model is in production, and the accountability requirements.

We need an XAI executive function to visualize how explainable models fit into each phase of an AI process.

The XAI executive function

Our executive function in everyday life includes our way of thinking and managing our activities. We can follow directions and focus on certain things, for example, using our executive function.

Our brain uses an executive function to control our cognitive processes. AI project managers use executive functions to monitor all of the phases of an AI system.

A representation of XAI through an executive function will help you make your way through the many ways to implement XAI.

One question that must guide you at all moments when implementing XAI is:

Can your AI program be trusted?

A basic rule to remember is that when a problem comes up in an AI program that you are related to in one way or another, you are on your own. The partial or total responsibility of explaining will be on you.

You cannot afford to miss any aspect of XAI. One omission, and critical errors will go unexplained. You can lose the trust of users in a few hours after having worked for months on an AI project.

The first step is to represent the different areas you will have to apply XAI to in a chart that goes from development to production and accountability, as shown in the following example:

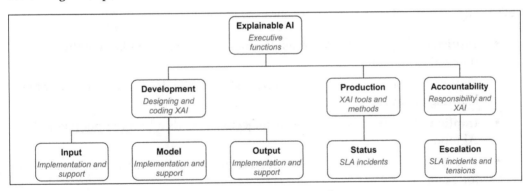

Figure 1.4: Executive function chart

You can implement XAI at every stage of an AI project, as shown in the chart:

- **Development, input**: By making key aspects of the data available to analyze the AI process
- **Development, model**: By making the logic of an AI model explainable and understandable
- **Development, output**: By displaying the output in various ways and from different angles
- **Production**: By explaining how the AI model reached a result with all of the development XAI tools
- **Accountability**: By explaining exactly how a result was reached, starting from the first step of the process to the user interface

Note that in the chart development phase, XAI functions need to be activated by support requests once the AI program is in production for XAI, maintenance, and support.

Also, you can see that a **service-level agreement (SLA)** for XAI can be required in your AI contract with your customer or end user. If your SLA requires you to fix an AI program within an hour, for example, and no developer is present to explain the code, it is recommended to have *intuitive* XAI interfaces!

The word "intuitive" has opened the door to the many profiles of people that will need to use XAI at different times for different reasons.

Let's list a few examples of XAI approaches:

- **Intuitive**: The XAI interface must be understandable at a glance with no detailed explanations.
- **Expert**: Precise information is required, such as the description of a machine learning equation.
- **Implicit**: An expert that masters a subject just needs a hint to understand the AI model.
- **Explicit**: A user might want a detailed explanation but not at the expert level, for example.
- **Subjective**: A manager might just want a group of users to explain how they view an AI model.
- **Objective**: A manager might want the developers to produce XAI to confirm a subjective view.
- **Explaining**: An AI model can be explained using simple natural language explanations.

- **AI to explain**: Other AI models can be used to analyze AI outputs.

Let's sum this up in an executive function table. In this table, each letter has the following meaning:

- *D* stands for a development XAI request.
- *P* stands for a production XAI request.
- *A* stands for an accountability XAI request.

Each XAI request is followed by an alert level from 1 to 10. 1 is a low level, and 10 is a high level of alert. For example, *D*(1) means that a small XAI module is required.

The following table provides a few examples of how to use it in a given situation:

Method/Area	Input	Model	Output	Production	Accountability
Intuitive	D(3)-A(9)				
Implicit		P(9)-D(1)			
Subjective					
Expert					
Explicit					
Objective					
Explaining					A(10)
AI to explain				P(7)	

The following explanations are simply examples to show you the tremendous number of possibilities we can encounter when implementing XAI:

- *D*(3)-*A*(9): A legal team of users of an AI program requests input dataset XAI by a developer.
- *P*(9)-*D*(1): A user rejects a result and asks for a developer to activate the XAI interface.
- *P*(7): A group of users in production requests the XAI interface to be activated to explain results.
- *A*(10): The legal team is facing an investigation into its privacy policy and requires simple Excel type queries to provide the required explanations. No AI is required to perform the XAI tasks.

These examples show the huge number of combinations reached between the different XAI approaches in the eight lines of the table and the five phases of an AI and XAI project. This adds up to more than 10 elements to consider. This represents n possibilities in an average of 10 elements. The number of combinations of 5 elements among 10 already represents 252 scenarios to design and implement. It could be a problem from input to production (4) involving an expert (1) XAI interface for each phase. It is impossible to design all the possibilities separately.

In this chapter, we will dive directly into an XAI project within a medical diagnosis timeline.

The XAI medical diagnosis timeline

We often think we can see a doctor, and we will get a straight explanation of what we are suffering from and what the solution is. Although it might be true in simple cases, it is far from reality in situations in which the symptoms are either absent or difficult to detect. The case study in this chapter describes a case with confusing symptoms and unexpected outcomes.

We can represent such a patient's history, from the diagnosis process to the treatment protocols, in a timeline. A medical diagnosis timeline starts when a doctor first discovers the symptoms of a patient. A simple disease will lead to a rapid diagnosis. When the same symptoms can describe several diseases, the timeline stretches out, and it might take several days or weeks to reach the end of the process and come up with a diagnosis.

Let's introduce a standard AI prototype that will help a general practitioner. The practitioner must deal with a persistent fever symptom that will extend the medical diagnosis timeline over several days. The standard prototype will be a classical AI program, and we will then add XAI once it's created.

The standard AI program used by a general practitioner

In this section, we will explore the basic version of an experimental AI program used by a general practitioner in France. According to the World Health Organization, France is one of the top-ranking countries in the world when it comes to healthcare. Online medical consulting is already in place, and doctors are curious about AI decision-making tools that could help them in making their diagnoses. We will imagine ourselves in a fictional situation, albeit based on real events transformed for this chapter. The doctor, the patient, and the program were created for this chapter. However, the disease we will explore in this chapter, the West Nile virus, is real.

We will begin by exploring a simple KNN algorithm that can predict a disease with a few symptoms. We will limit our study to detecting the flu, a cold, or pneumonia. The number of symptoms will be limited to a cough, fever, headache, and colored sputum.

From the doctor's perspective, the symptoms are generally viewed as follows:

- A mild headache and a fever could be a cold
- A cough and fever could be a flu
- A fever and a cough with colored sputum could be pneumonia

Notice the verb is "could" and not "must." A medical diagnosis remains a probability in the very early stages of a disease. A probability becomes certain only after a few minutes to a few days, and sometimes even weeks.

Let's start by defining our AI model, a KNN algorithm, before implementing it.

Definition of a KNN algorithm

The KNN algorithm is best explained with a real-life example. Imagine you are in a supermarket. The supermarket is the dataset. You are at point p_n in an aisle of the supermarket. You are looking for bottled water. You see many brands of bottled water spread over a few yards (or meters). You are also tempted by some cans of soda you see right next to you; however, you want to avoid sugar.

In terms of what's best for your diet, we will use a scale from 1 (very good for your health) to 10 (very bad for your health). p_n is at point $(0, 0)$ in a Euclidian space in which the first term is x and the second y.

The many brands of bottled water are between (0, 1) and (2, 2) in terms of their features in terms of health standards. The many brands of soda, which are generally bad in terms of health standards, have features between (3, 3) and (10, 10).

To find the nearest neighbors in terms of health features, for example, the KNN algorithm will calculate the Euclidean distance between p_n and all the other points in our dataset. The calculation will run from p_1 to p_{n-1} using the Euclidean distance formula. The k in KNN represents the number of "nearest neighbors" the algorithm will consider for classification purposes. The Euclidean distance (d_1) between two given points, such as between $p_n(x_1y_1)$ and $p_1(x_2y_2)$, for example, is as follows:

$$d_1(p_n, p_1) = \sqrt[2]{(x_1 - x_2)^2 + (y_1 - y_2)^2}$$

Intuitively, we know that the data points located between (0, 1) and (2, 2) are closer to our point (0, 0) than the data points located between (3, 3) and (10, 10). The nearest neighbors of our point (0, 0), are the bottled water data points.

Note that these are representations of the closest features to us, not the physical points in the supermarket. The fact that the soda is close to us in the real world of the supermarket does not bring it any closer to our need in terms of our health requirements.

Considering the number of distances to calculate, a function such as the one provided by `sklearn.neighbors` proves necessary. We will now go back to our medical diagnosis program and build a KNN in Python.

A KNN in Python

In this section, we will first create an AI model that we will then explain in the next sections.

Open `KNN.ipynb` on Google Colaboratory. You can run the program with other environments but might have to adapt the names of the directories and the code required to import the dataset.

We will be using `pandas`, `matplotlib`, and `sklearn.neighbors`:

```
import pandas as pd
from matplotlib import pyplot as plt
from sklearn.neighbors import KNeighborsClassifier
import os
from google.colab import drive
```

The program imports the data file from GitHub (default):

```
repository = "github"
if repository == "github":
  !curl -L https://raw.githubusercontent.com/PacktPublishing/Hands-On-
Explainable-AI-XAI-with-Python/master/Chapter01/D1.csv --output "D1.csv"


  # Setting the path for each file
  df2 = "/content/D1.csv"
  print(df2)
```

If you want to use Google Drive, change `repository` to `"google"`:

```
# Set repository to "google" to read the data from Google
repository = "google"
```

A prompt will provide instructions to mount the drive. First, upload the files to a directory named XAI. Then provide the full default path, shown as follows:

```
if repository == "google":
  # Mounting the drive. If it is not mounted, a prompt will
  # provide instructions.
  drive.mount('/content/drive')
  # Setting the path for each file
  df2 = '/content/drive/My Drive/XAI/Chapter01/D1.csv'
  print(df2)
```

You can choose to change the name of the path to the Google Drive files.

We now read the file and display a partial view of its content:

```
df = pd.read_csv(df2)
print(df)
```

The output shows the features we are using and the `class` column:

	colored_sputum	cough	fever	headache	class
0	1.0	3.5	9.4	3.0	flu
1	1.0	3.4	8.4	4.0	flu
2	1.0	3.3	7.3	3.0	flu
3	1.0	3.4	9.5	4.0	flu
4	1.0	2.0	8.0	3.5	flu
..	...	...	...	...	...
145	0.0	1.0	4.2	2.3	cold

146	0.5	2.5	2.0	1.7	cold
147	0.0	1.0	3.2	2.0	cold
148	0.4	3.4	2.4	2.3	cold
149	0.0	1.0	3.1	1.8	cold

The four features are the four symptoms we need: colored sputum, cough, fever, and headache. The `class` column contains the three diseases we must predict: cold, flu, and pneumonia.

The dataset was created through an interview with a general practitioner based on a group of random patients with a probable diagnosis based on the early symptoms of a disease. After a few days, the diagnosis can change depending on the evolution of the symptoms.

The values of each of the features in the dataset range from 0 to 9.9. They represent the risk level of a symptom. Decimal values are used when necessary. For example:

- `colored_sputum`: If the value is 0, the patient does not cough sputum. If the value is 3, the patient is coughing some sputum. If the value is 9, then the condition is serious. If it is 9.9 then the colored sputum is at the maximum level.

  A patient that has high levels of all features must be rushed to the hospital.

- `cough`: If the value of `cough` is 1, and `colored_sputum` also has a low value, such as 1, then the patient is not acutely ill. If the value is high, such as 7, and `colored_sputum` is high as well, the patient might have pneumonia. The value of `fever` will provide more information.

- `fever`: If `fever` is low, such as level 2, and the other values are also low, there is not much to worry about for the moment. However, if `fever` goes up with one of the other features going up, then the program will use the labels to train and provide a prediction and an explanation if `headache` also has a high level.

- `headache`: For the West Nile virus, a high-value `headache`, such as 7, along with a high level of coughing, is a trigger to send the patient to the hospital immediately to test for the virus and avoid encephalitis, for example. The general practitioner I interviewed was faced with such a difficult diagnosis in January 2020. It took several days to finally understand that the patient had been in contact with a rare virus in an animal reserve.

At the same time, the novel coronavirus, COVID-19, was beginning to appear, making a diagnosis even more difficult. A severe headache with high fever and coughing led away from COVID-19 as a hypothesis. Many patients have serious symptoms that are not from COVID-19.

As I'm finalizing this chapter, the general practitioner I interviewed and a second one I asked to confirm the idea of this chapter, are in contact with many patients that have one or all of the symptoms in the dataset. When the disease is COVID-19, the diagnosis can be made by checking the lungs' respiratory capacity, for example. However, even in the period of the COVID-19 pandemic, patients still come in with other diseases. AI can surely help a general practitioner facing an overwhelming number of incoming patients.

Warning

This dataset is not a medical dataset. The dataset only shows how such a system could work. DO NOT use it to make real-life medical diagnoses.

The model is now trained using the default values of the KNN classifier and the dataset:

```
# KNN classification labels
X = df.loc[:, 'colored_sputum': 'headache']
Y = df.loc[:, 'class']

# Trains the model
knn = KNeighborsClassifier()
knn.fit(X, Y)
```

The output shows the default values of the KNN classifier that we will have to explain at some point. For the moment, we simply display the values:

```
KNeighborsClassifier(algorithm='auto', leaf_size=30,
                     metric='minkowski', metric_params=None,
                     n_jobs=None, n_neighbors=5, p=2,
                     weights='uniform')
```

If an expert requested an explanation, an interface could provide the following details:

- `algorithm='auto'`: This will choose the best algorithm based on the values.
- `leaf_size=30`: The leaf size sent to `BallTree` or to `KDTree`.
- `metric='minkowski'`: The distance metric is the Minkowski metric, which uses a specific tensor for the calculation.
- `metric-params=None`: Additional options.
- `n_jobs=None`: The number of parallel jobs that can be run.

- **n_neighbors=5**: The number of neighbors to take into account.
- **p=3**: Options for the Minkowski metric.
- **weights='uniform'**: All weights have a uniform value.

The first level of XAI in this chapter is not to explain AI to developers. The goal of the experiment is to explain how the program came up with the West Nile virus in such a way that a general practitioner could trust the prediction and send the patient to hospital for treatment.

If an expert wants to go deeper, then a link to the documentation can be provided in the XAI interface, such as this: https://scikit-learn.org/stable/modules/generated/sklearn.neighbors.KNeighborsClassifier.html

We now can now move on and visualize the trained model's output using `matplotlib`:

```
df = pd.read_csv(df2)
# Plotting the relation of each feature with each class
figure, (sub1, sub2, sub3, sub4) = plt.subplots(
    4, sharex=True, sharey=True)
plt.suptitle('k-nearest neighbors')
plt.xlabel('Feature')
plt.ylabel('Class')
X = df.loc[:, 'colored_sputum']
Y = df.loc[:, 'class']
sub1.scatter(X, Y, color='blue', label='colored_sputum')
sub1.legend(loc=4, prop={'size': 5})
sub1.set_title('Medical Diagnosis Software')
X = df.loc[:, 'cough']
Y = df.loc[:, 'class']
sub2.scatter(X, Y, color='green', label='cough')
sub2.legend(loc=4, prop={'size': 5})
X = df.loc[:, 'fever']
Y = df.loc[:, 'class']
sub3.scatter(X, Y, color='red', label='fever')
sub3.legend(loc=4, prop={'size': 5})
X = df.loc[:, 'headache']
Y = df.loc[:, 'class']
sub4.scatter(X, Y, color='black', label='headache')
sub4.legend(loc=4, prop={'size': 5})
figure.subplots_adjust(hspace=0)
plt.show()
```

The plot produced provides useful information for the XAI phase of the project:

k-nearest neighbors
Medical Diagnosis Software
cold
pneumonia
flu
colored_sputum
cough
fever
headache
Class
Feature
0
2
4
6
8
10

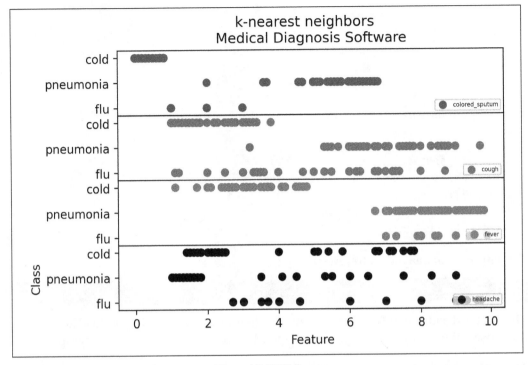

Figure 1.5: KNN figure

The doctor can use an intuitive form to quickly enter the severity of each symptom on a scale of 0 to 9.9:

Evaluation Form
colored_sputum: 1
cough: 3
fever: 7
headache: 5

Figure 1.6: Evaluation form

The form was generated by the following code:

```
# @title Evaluation form
colored_sputum = 1 # @param {type:"integer"}
cough = 3          # @param {type:"integer"}
fever = 7          # @param {type:"integer"}
headache = 5       # @param {type:"integer"}
```

The program uses these values to create the input of the prediction the KNN now runs:

```
# colored_sputum, cough, fever, headache
cs = colored_sputum; c = cough; f = fever; h = headache;
X_DL = [[cs, c, f, h]]
prediction = knn.predict(X_DL)
print("The prediction is:", str(prediction).strip('[]'))
```

The output is displayed as follows:

```
The prediction is: 'flu'
```

The doctor decides that for the moment, the diagnosis is probably the flu. The diagnosis might evolve in a few days, depending on the evolution of the symptoms.

The critical issue we have as AI specialists resides in the fact that, at first, the doctor does not trust AI or any other system to make life or death decisions. In this chapter, our concern was to explain AI to a doctor, not a developer. A user needs to be able to trust the XAI system enough to make a decision. The whole point of this chapter is to use charts, plots, graphs, or any form of information that will explain the predictions made by **machine learning (ML)** to the doctor for the case we are dealing with in this chapter. Doctors are ready to use AI. We need to explain the predictions, not just make them.

However, let's say that in our fictitious scenario, we know that the West Nile virus has infected the patient. Both the AI program and the doctor have made a mistake. The error has gone undetected, although the KNN has run with perfect accuracy.

We are now at the heart of XAI. When the KNN runs with perfect accuracy but does not provide the diagnosis that will save a patient's life, the prediction is either a false positive if it produces the wrong prediction, or a false negative if it missed it! The whole point of people-centered AI, as we will see in the following chapters, is to detect weaknesses in our ML predictions and find innovative ways of improving the prediction.

In our case, the general dataset did not contain enough information to make a real-life prediction, although the KNN was well trained. XAI goes beyond theoretical AI and puts the human user at the center of the process, forcing us to get involved in the field the dataset was built for.

We need to find a better prediction with better data. The core concept of this section is that XAI is not only for developers, but for users too! We need users to trust AI in order for AI to see widespread adoption in decision-making situations. For a user such as a doctor to understand and accept our predictions, we need to go the extra mile!

Let's take a closer look at the West Nile virus, its itinerary, and the vector of contamination.

West Nile virus – a case of life or death

XAI involves the ability to explain the **subject matter expert** (**SME**) aspects of a project from different perspectives. A developer will not have the same need for explanations as an end user, for example. An AI program must provide information for all types of explanations.

In this chapter, we will go through the key features of XAI using a critical medical example of an early diagnosis of an infection in a human of the dangerous West Nile virus. We will see that without AI and XAI, the patient might have lost his life.

The case described is a real one that I obtained from a doctor that dealt with a similar case and disease. I then confirmed this approach with another doctor. I transposed the data to Chicago, used U.S. government healthcare data and Pasteur Institute information on the West Nile virus. The patient's name is fictitious, and I modified real events and replaced the real dangerous virus with another one, but the situation is very real, as we will see in this section.

We will imagine that we are using AI software to help a general practitioner find the right diagnosis before it's too late for this particular patient. We will see that XAI can not only provide information but also save lives.

Our story has four protagonists: the patient, the West Nile virus, the doctor, and the AI + XAI program.

Let's first start by getting acquainted with the patient and what happened to him. This information will prove vital when we start running XAI on his diagnosis.

How can a lethal mosquito bite go unnoticed?

We need to understand the history of our patient's life to provide the doctor with vital information. In this chapter, we will use the patient's location history through Google Maps.

Jan Despres, the patient, lives in Paris, France. Jan develops ML software in Python on cloud platforms for his company. Jan decided to take ten days off to travel to the United States to visit and see some friends.

Jan first stopped in New York for a few days. Then Jan flew to Chicago to see his friends. One hot summer evening during the last days of September 2019, Jan was having dinner with some friends on Eberhart Avenue, Chicago, Illinois, USA.

Jan Despres was bitten by a mosquito, hardly noticing it. It was just a little mosquito bite, as we all experience many times in the summer. Jan did not even think anything of it. He went on enjoying the meal and conversation with his friends. The problem was that the insect was not a common mosquito — it was a *Culex restuans*, which carries the dangerous West Nile virus.

The day after the dinner, Jan Despres flew back to Paris and went on a business trip to Lyon for a few days. It was now early October and it was still the summer. You might find it strange to see "October" and "still the summer" in the same sentence. Climate change has moved the beginning and the end of our seasons. For example, in France, for meteorologists, the winters are shorter, the "summers" are longer. This leads to many new propagations of viruses, for example. We all are going to have to update our season perceptions to climate change 2.0.

In our case, the weather was still hot, but some people were coughing on the train when Jan took the train back from Lyon. He washed his hands on the train and was careful to avoid the people that were coughing. A few days later, Jan started to cough but thought nothing of it. A few days after that, he came up with a mild fever that began to peak on Thursday evening. He took medication to bring the fever down. We will refer to this medication as *MF* (medication for fever). On Friday morning, his body temperature was nearly normal, but he wasn't feeling good. On Friday, he went to see his doctor, Dr. Modano.

We know at this point that Jan was bitten by a mosquito once or several times at the end of September, around September 30th. We know that he flew back to Paris in early October. During that time, the incubation period of the infection had begun. The following approximate timeline goes from the estimated mosquito bite in Chicago to the trip back to Paris:

Figure 1.7: Timeline of the patient

Jan was tired, but thought it was just jetlag.

Jan then traveled to Lyon on October 13-14th. The symptoms began to appear between October 14th and October 17th. Jan only went to see his doctor on October 18th after a bad night on the 17th. The following timeline shows an approximate sequence of events:

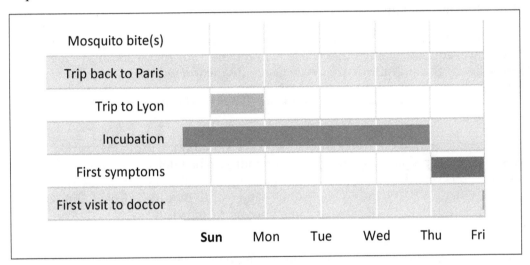

Figure 1.8: Timeline of the patient

We have Jan's itineraries in natural language. We will use this information later on in this chapter for our XAI program.

Let's now meet the West Nile virus and see how it got to Chicago.

What is the West Nile virus?

As for Jan's itinerary, we will be using that data in this section for our XAI program. Being able to track the virus and inform the doctor will be critical in saving Jan's life.

The West Nile virus is a zoonosis. A zoonosis is one of the many infectious diseases caused by parasites, viruses, and bacteria. It spreads between animals and humans.

Other diseases, such as Ebola and salmonellosis, are zoonotic diseases. HIV was a zoonotic disease transmitted to humans before it mutated in humans. Sometimes swine and bird flu, which are zoonotic diseases, can combine with human flu strains and produce lethal pandemics. The 1918 Spanish flu infected 500+ million people and killed 20+ million victims.

The West Nile virus usually infects animals such as birds that constitute a good reservoir for its development. Mosquitos then bite the birds to feed, and then infect the other animals or humans they bite. Mosquitos are the *vectors* of the West Nile virus. Humans and horses are unwilling victims.

West Nile virus usually appears during warmer seasons such as spring, summer, warm early autumn, or any other warm period depending on the location—the reason being that mosquitos are very active during warm weather.

The West Nile virus is known to be transmitted by blood transfusions and organ transplants.

The *incubation* period can range from a few days to 14 days. During that period, the West Nile virus propagates throughout our bodies. When detected, in about 1% of the cases, it is very dangerous, leading to meningitis or encephalitis. In many cases, such as with COVID-19, most people don't even realize they are infected. But when a person is infected, in 1% of cases or sometimes more, the virus reaches a life or death level.

Our patient, Jan, is part of that 1% of infected humans for which the West Nile virus was mortally dangerous. In an area in which hundreds of humans are infected, a few will be in danger.

In 80% of cases, the West Nile virus is asymptomatic, meaning there are no symptoms at all. The infection propagates and creates havoc along the way. If a patient is part of the 1% at risk, the infection might only be detected when meningitis or encephalitis sets in, creating symptoms.

In 20% of cases, there are symptoms. The key symptom is a brutal fever that usually appears after three to six days of incubation. The other symptoms are headaches, backaches, muscle pain, nausea, coughing, stomachaches, skin eruptions, breathing difficulties, and more.

In 1% of those cases, neurological complications set in, such as meningitis or encephalitis. Our patient, Jan, is part of the approximately 1% of those cases and the approximately 20% with mild to severe symptoms.

We now know how the West Nile virus infected Jan. We have first-hand information. However, when we start running our XAI program, we will have to investigate to find this data. We have one last step to go before starting our investigations. We need to know how the West Nile virus got to Chicago and what type of mosquito we are dealing with.

How did the West Nile virus get to Chicago?

It puzzles many of us to find that the West Nile virus that originally came from Africa can thrive in the United States. It is even more puzzling to see the virus infect people in the United States without it coming from somewhere else in 2019. In 2019, the West Nile virus infected hundreds of people and killed many of the infected patients. Furthermore, in 2019, many cases were neuroinvasive. When the virus is neuroinvasive, it goes from the bloodstream to the brain and causes West Nile encephalitis.

Migratory birds sometimes carry the West Nile virus from one area to another. In this case, a migratory bird went from Florida to Illinois and then near New York City, as shown on the following map:

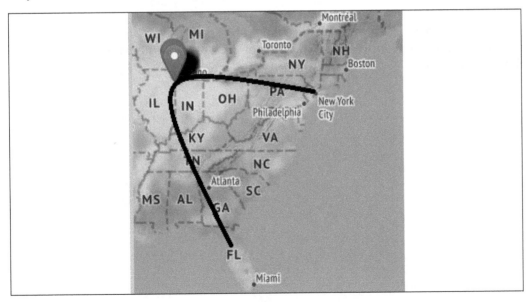

Figure 1.9: Migratory map

During its stay in Illinois, it flew around two areas close to Chicago. When the bird was near Chicago, it was bitten by a *Culex pipiens* mosquito that fed on its blood. The authorities in Chicago had information provided from mosquito traps all around the city. In this case, a Gravid trap containing "mosquito soup" attracted and captured the *Culex pipiens* mosquitos, which tested positive for the West Nile virus:

SEASON YEAR	WEEK	TRAP	TRAP_TYPE	RESULT	SPECIES	LATITUDE	LONGITUDE
2019	33	T159	GRAVID	positive	CULEX PIPIENS/RESTUANS	41.731446858	-87.649722253
2019	36	T159	GRAVID	positive	CULEX PIPIENS/RESTUANS	41.731446858	-87.649722253
2019	37	T159	GRAVID	positive	CULEX PIPIENS/RESTUANS	41.731446858	-87.649722253

Our patient, Jan, was visiting Chicago at that time and was bitten on Eberhard Avenue while visiting friends during the period. In that same period, the Gravid traps produced positive results on mosquitos carrying the West Nile virus on Eberhart Avenue:

SEASON YEAR	WEEK	TEST ID	BLOCK	TRAP
2019	27	48325	100XX W OHARE AIRPORT	T905
2019	29	48674	77XX S EBERHART AVE	T080
2019	31	48880	50XX S UNION AVE	T082

The following map provides the details of the presence of *Culex pipiens/restuans* mosquitos at the same location Jan, our patient, was, at the same time, as shown by the following map:

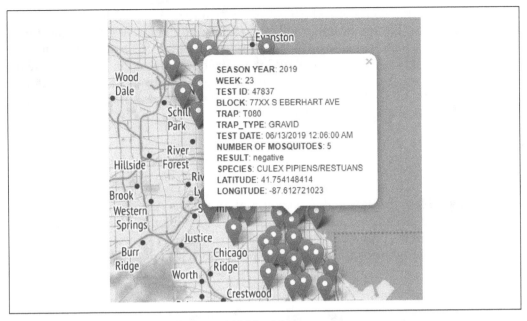

Figure 1.10: Mosquito traps map

Our patient, Jan, is now infected, but since he is in the incubation period, he feels nothing and flies back to France unknowingly carrying the West Nile virus with him, as shown in the following map (the flight plan goes far to the North to get the jet stream and then down over the UK back to Paris):

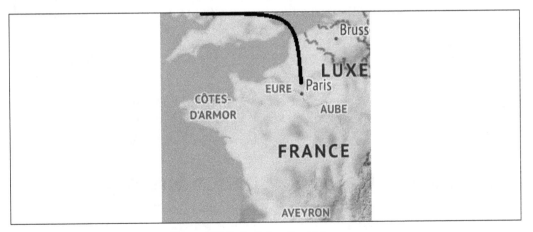

Figure 1.11: Patient's location history map

The West Nile virus does not travel from human to human. We are "dead-ends" for the West Nile virus. Either our immune system fights it off before it infects our brain, for example, or we lose the battle. In any case, it is not contagious from human to human. This factor indicates that Jan could not have been infected in France and will be a key factor in tracing the origin of the infection back to Chicago. Location history is vital in any case. In the early days of COVID-19, it was important to know which patients arrived from China, for example.

Jan, our patient, traveled with his smartphone. He had activated Google's Location History function to have a nice representation of his trip on a map when he got home.

We will now explore the data with Google Location History, an extraction tool. The tool will help us enhance our AI program and also implement XAI, which will allow us to explain the prediction process in sufficient detail for our application to be trustworthy enough for a doctor using its predictions to send the patient to the emergency room.

XAI can save lives using Google Location History

The protagonists of our case study are the patient, the doctor, the AI, and the XAI prototype. The patient provides information to the doctor, mainly a persistent fever. The doctor has used the standard AI medical diagnosis program, seen previously in this chapter, which predicts that the patient has the flu. However, the fever remains high over several days.

When this situation occurs, a doctor generally asks the patient about their recent activities. What did the patient recently eat? Where did the patient go?

In our case, we will track where the patient went to try to find out how he was infected. To do that, we will use Google Location History. We start by downloading the data.

Downloading Google Location History

Google Location History saves where a user goes with a mobile device. To access this service, you need to sign in to your Google account, go to the **Data & personalization** tab, and turn your **Location History** on:

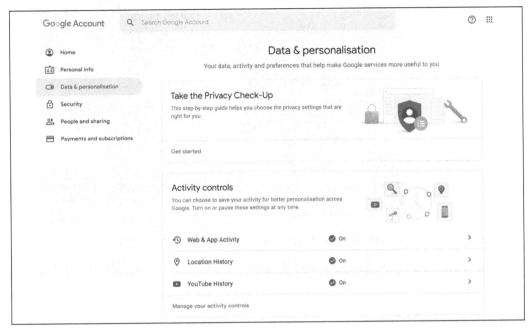

Figure 1.12: Google account

If you click on **Location History**, you will reach the option that enables you to activate or deactivate the function:

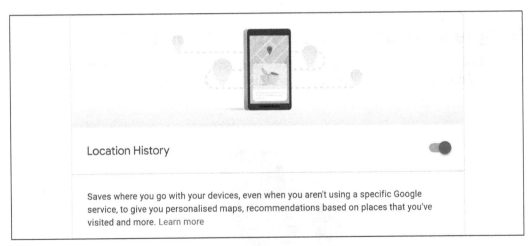

Figure 1.13: Turning on Location History

Once activated, Google will record all the locations you visit. You can then access the history and also export the data. In our case, we will use the data for our XAI project. If you click on **Manage activity**, you can access the history of your locations on an interactive map:

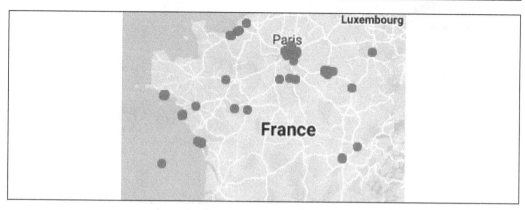

Figure 1.14: Location History map

The interface contains many interesting functions we can use for XAI:

- Locations a user visited
- Dates
- Location maps
- And more!

We will now move forward and explore Google's Location History extraction tool and retrieve the data we need for our XAI prototype.

Google's Location History extraction tool

We first need to extract data and make sure our hypothesis is correct. For that, we will use a data extraction tool designed by the Google Data Liberation Front:

Figure 1.15: Google Data Liberation Front logo

The Google Data Liberation Front was started by a team of Google engineers, whose goal is to make Google data available. They developed many tools such as Google Takeout, the Data Transfer Project, and more. We will focus on Google Takeout for our experiment.

The tool is available through your Google account at this link: https://takeout.google.com/settings/takeout

Once you have reached this page, many data display and retrieval options are available. Scroll down to **Location History**:

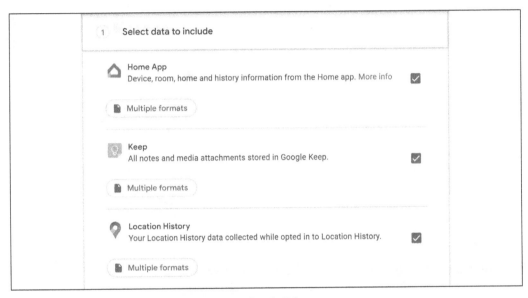

Figure 1.16: Google Takeout page

Make sure **Location History** is activated as shown in the preceding screenshot, and then click on **Multiple formats**.

A screen will pop up and ask you to choose a format. Choose **JSON** and press **OK**. You will be taken back to the main window with JSON as your choice:

Figure 1.17: JSON selected

Go to the top of the page, click on **Deselect all** and then check **Location History** again. Then, go to the bottom of the page and click on **Next step** to reach the export page. Choose your export frequency and then click on **Create export**:

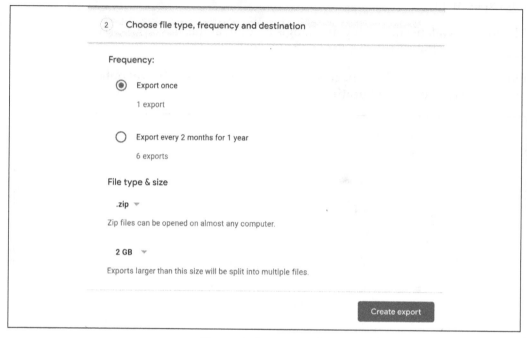

Figure 1.18: Report options

You will be notified by email when you can download the file:

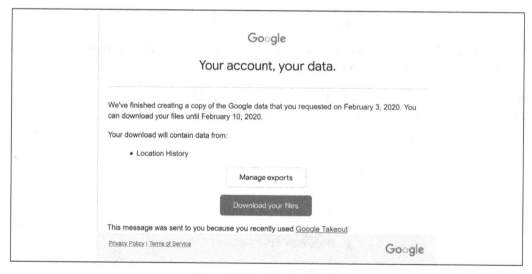

Figure 1.19: Archive download

When you click on **Download archive**, you will reach a download window:

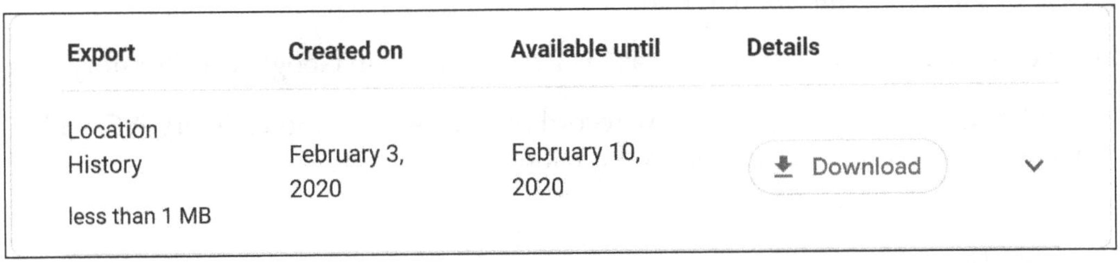

Export	Created on	Available until	Details
Location History less than 1 MB	February 3, 2020	February 10, 2020	⬇ Download ⌄

Figure 1.20: Download window

The file will only be available for a certain period. I recommend you download it as soon as it arrives.

The downloaded file is a ZIP archive. Unzip the file, and now we can read it. Find the `Location History.json` file and rename it to `Location_History.json`.

We now have access to the raw data. We could just rush, parse it in memory and add some features, in memory as well, to the data we loaded for `KNN.ipynb`. In just a few lines of code, our program could run in memory and make predictions. But a user will not trust a prediction from a black box decision-making process.

We must make our process visible by reading and displaying the data in such a way that the user understands how our AI program reached its prediction.

Reading and displaying Google Location History data

We could take the raw data of the location history provided and run an AI black box process to provide a quick diagnosis. However, most users do not trust AI systems that explain nothing, especially when it comes to life and death situations. We must build a component that can explain how and why we used Google's Location History data.

We will first address an important issue. Using a person's location history data requires privacy policies. I recommend starting the hard way by logging in and downloading data, even if it takes an online service with humans to do this for a limited number of people when requested. In a data-sensitive healthcare project, for example, do not rush to automate everything. Start carefully with a people-centered approach controlling the privacy and legal constraints, the quality of the data, and every other important aspect of such critical data.

When you are ready to move into a fully automatic process, get legal advice first, and then use automatic data extraction tools later.

That being said, let's open `GoogleLocationHistory.ipynb` in Google Colaboratory.

We will now focus on the data. A raw record of a Google Location History JSON file contains the structured information we are looking for:

```
{
  "locations" : [ {
    "timestampMs" : "1468992488806",
    "latitudeE7" : 482688285,
    "longitudeE7" : 41040263,
    "accuracy" : 30,
    "activity" : [ {
      "timestampMs" : "1468992497179",
      "activity" : [ {
        "type" : "TILTING",
        "confidence" : 100
      } ]
    }, {
      "timestampMs" : "1468992487543",
      "activity" : [ {
        "type" : "IN_VEHICLE",
        "confidence" : 85
      }, {
        "type" : "ON_BICYCLE",
        "confidence" : 8
      }, {
        "type" : "UNKNOWN",
        "confidence" : 8
      } ]
```

We must transform the input data to run our AI models. We could just read it and use it, but we want to be able to explain what we are doing to the expert in our case study: the doctor.

To do so, we need to read, transform, and display the data to convince our expert, the doctor, that the KNN algorithm provided the correct output. That output will ultimately save our patient's life, as we will see once we have gone through the process of explaining AI to our expert.

We first need to display the data and explain the process we applied to reach our unusual but correct diagnosis. Let's start by installing the `basemap` packages.

Installation of the basemap packages

basemap is part of the Matplotlib Basemap toolkit. basemap can plot two-dimensional maps in Python. Other mapping tools provide similar features, such as MATLAB's mapping toolbox, GrADS, and other tools.

basemap relies on other libraries such as the GEOS library.

Please refer to the official Matplotlib documentation to install the necessary packages: https://matplotlib.org/basemap/users/installing.html

In this section, we will install the basemap packages on Google Colaboratory. If you encounter any problems, please refer to the preceding link.

On Google Colaboratory, you can use the following code for the installation of the necessary packages for basemap:

```
!apt install proj-bin libproj-dev libgeos-dev
!pip install https://github.com/matplotlib/basemap/archive/v1.1.0.tar.gz
```

To be sure, update once the two previous packages have been installed:

```
!pip install -U git+https://github.com/matplotlib/basemap.git
```

We can now select the modules we need to build our interface.

The import instructions

We will be using pandas, numpy, mpl_toolkits.basemap, matplotlib, and datetime:

```
import pandas as pd
import numpy as np
from mpl_toolkits.basemap import Basemap
import matplotlib.pyplot as plt
from datetime import datetime as dt
import os
```

We are now ready to import the data we need to process the location history data of our patient.

Importing the data

We will need `Location_History.json`, which exceeds the size authorized on GitHub.

Upload `Location_History.json` to Google Drive. The program will then access it. You will be prompted to grant an authorization to your drive if it is not mounted. The code is set to only read Google Drive:

```
# @title Importing data <br>
# repository is set to "google"(default) to read the data
# from Google Drive {display-mode: "form"}
import os
from google.colab import drive


# Set repository to "github" to read the data from GitHub
# Set repository to "google" to read the data from Google
repository = "google"


# if repository == "github":
# Location_History.json is too large for GitHub

if repository == "google":
  # Mounting the drive. If it is not mounted, a prompt will
  # provide instructions.
  drive.mount('/content/drive')
  # Setting the path for each file
  df2 = '/content/drive/My Drive/XAI/Chapter01/Location_History.json'
  print(df2)
```

We now read the file and display the number of rows in the data file:

```
df_gps = pd.read_json(df2)
print('There are {:,} rows in the location history dataset'.format(
    len(df_gps)))
```

The output will print the name of the file and the number of rows in the file:

```
/tmp/nst/Location_History.json
There are 123,143 rows in the location history dataset
```

A black box algorithm could use the raw data. However, we want to build a white box, explainable, and interpretable AI interface. To do so, we must process the raw data we have imported.

Processing the data for XAI and basemap

Before using the data to access and display the location history records, we must parse, convert, and drop some unnecessary columns.

We will parse the latitudes, longitudes, and the timestamps stored inside the location columns:

```
df_gps['lat'] = df_gps['locations'].map(lambda x: x['latitudeE7'])
df_gps['lon'] = df_gps['locations'].map(lambda x: x['longitudeE7'])
df_gps['timestamp_ms'] = df_gps['locations'].map(
    lambda x: x['timestampMs'])
```

The output now shows the raw parsed data stored in `df_gps`:

```
                                          locations  ...   timestamp_
ms
0        {'timestampMs': '1468992488806', 'latitudeE7':...  ...
1468992488806
1        {'timestampMs': '1468992524778', 'latitudeE7':...  ...
1468992524778
2        {'timestampMs': '1468992760000', 'latitudeE7':...  ...
1468992760000
3        {'timestampMs': '1468992775000', 'latitudeE7':...  ...
1468992775000
4        {'timestampMs': '1468992924000', 'latitudeE7':...  ...
1468992924000
...                                                    ...   ...
...
123138  {'timestampMs': '1553429840319', 'latitudeE7':...  ...
1553429840319
123139  {'timestampMs': '1553430033166', 'latitudeE7':...  ...
1553430033166
123140  {'timestampMs': '1553430209458', 'latitudeE7':...  ...
1553430209458
123141  {'timestampMs': '1553514237945', 'latitudeE7':...  ...
1553514237945
123142  {'timestampMs': '1553514360002', 'latitudeE7':...  ...
1553514360002
```

As you can see, the data must be transformed before we can use it for `basemap`. It does not meet the standard of XAI or even a `basemap` input.

We need decimalized degrees for the latitudes and longitudes. We also need to convert the timestamp to date-time with the following code:

```
df_gps['lat'] = df_gps['lat'] / 10.**7
df_gps['lon'] = df_gps['lon'] / 10.**7
df_gps['timestamp_ms'] = df_gps['timestamp_ms'].astype(float) / 1000
df_gps['datetime'] = df_gps['timestamp_ms'].map(
    lambda x: dt.fromtimestamp(x).strftime('%Y-%m-%d %H:%M:%S'))
date_range = '{}-{}'.format(df_gps['datetime'].min()[:4],
                            df_gps['datetime'].max()[:4])
```

Before displaying some of the records in our location history, we will drop the columns we do not need anymore:

```
df_gps = df_gps.drop(labels=['locations', 'timestamp_ms'],
                     axis=1, inplace=False)
```

We can display clean data we can use for both XAI purposes and `basemap`:

```
df_gps[1000:1005]
```

The output is perfectly understandable:

	lat	lon	datetime
1000	49.010427	2.567411	2016-07-29 21:16:01
1001	49.011505	2.567486	2016-07-29 21:16:31
1002	49.011341	2.566974	2016-07-29 21:16:47
1003	49.011596	2.568414	2016-07-29 21:17:03
1004	49.011756	2.570905	2016-07-29 21:17:19

We have the data we need to display a map of the data to make it easy to interpret for a user.

Setting up the plotting options to display the map

To prepare the dataset to be displayed, we will first define the colors that will be used:

```
land_color = '#f5f5f3'
water_color = '#cdd2d4'
coastline_color = '#f5f5f3'
border_color = '#bbbbbb'
meridian_color = '#f5f5f3'
```

```
marker_fill_color = '#cc3300'
marker_edge_color = 'None'
```

- land_color: The color of the land
- water_color: The color of the water
- coastline_color: The color of the coastline
- border_color: The color of the borders
- meridian_color: The color of the meridian
- marker_fill_color: The fill color of a marker
- marker_edge_color: The color of the edge of a marker

Before displaying the location history, we will now create the plot:

```
fig = plt.figure(figsize=(20, 10))
ax = fig.add_subplot(111, facecolor='#ffffff', frame_on=False)
ax.set_title('Google Location History, {}'.format(date_range),
             fontsize=24, color='#333333')
```

Once the plot is created, we will draw the basemap and its features:

```
m = Basemap(projection='kav7', lon_0=0, resolution='c',
            area_thresh=10000)
m.drawmapboundary(color=border_color, fill_color=water_color)
m.drawcoastlines(color=coastline_color)
m.drawcountries(color=border_color)
m.fillcontinents(color=land_color, lake_color=water_color)
m.drawparallels(np.arange(-90., 120., 30.), color=meridian_color)
m.drawmeridians(np.arange(0., 420., 60.), color=meridian_color)
```

We are finally ready to plot the history points as a scatter graph:

```
x, y = m(df_gps['lon'].values, df_gps['lat'].values)
m.scatter(x, y, s=8, color=marker_fill_color,
          edgecolor=marker_edge_color, alpha=1, zorder=3)
```

We are ready to show the plot:

```
plt.show()
```

The output is a Google Location History map with history points projected on it:

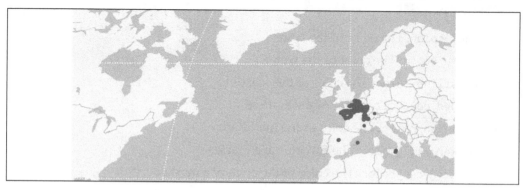

Figure 1.21: Location History map

In our case study, we are focusing on our patient's activity in the USA and France, so for those purposes we'll add some data points in the USA, as follows:

Figure 1.22: Location History map (with added U.S. data points)

We can either read the data points in numerical format or display a smaller section of the map.

To show how to zoom in the map, we will focus on the patient's location history in his home city, Paris.

Let's select a traverse Mercator around Paris:

```
map_width_m = 100 * 1000
map_height_m = 120 * 1000
target_crs = {'datum':'WGS84',
              'ellps':'WGS84',
              'proj':'tmerc',
              'lon_0':2,
              'lat_0':49}
```

Then define how to display the annotations:

```
color = 'k'
weight = 'black'
size = 12
alpha = 0.3
xycoords = 'axes fraction'
# plotting the map
fig_width = 6
```

We now plot the map:

```
fig = plt.figure(figsize=[fig_width,
    fig_width*map_height_m / float(map_width_m)])
ax = fig.add_subplot(111, facecolor='#ffffff', frame_on=False)
ax.set_title('Location History of Target Area, {}'.format(
    date_range), fontsize=16, color='#333333')

m = Basemap(ellps=target_crs['ellps'],
            projection=target_crs['proj'],
            lon_0=target_crs['lon_0'],
            lat_0=target_crs['lat_0'],
            width=map_width_m,
            height=map_height_m,
            resolution='h',
            area_thresh=10)

m.drawcoastlines(color=coastline_color)
m.drawcountries(color=border_color)
m.fillcontinents(color=land_color, lake_color=water_color)
m.drawstates(color=border_color)
m.drawmapboundary(fill_color=water_color)
```

Once the map is plotted, we scatter the data, annotate a city, and show the map:

```
x, y = m(df_gps['lon'].values, df_gps['lat'].values)
m.scatter(x, y, s=5, color=marker_fill_color,
          edgecolor=marker_edge_color, alpha=0.6, zorder=3)

# annotating a city
plt.annotate('Paris', xy=(0.6, 0.4), xycoords=xycoords,
             color=color, weight=weight, size=size, alpha=alpha)

# showing the map
plt.show()
```

The target area is now displayed and annotated:

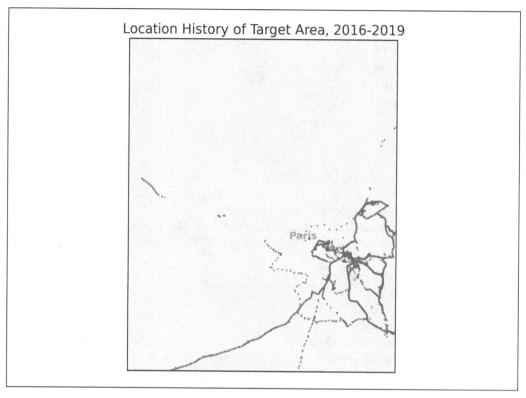

Figure 1.23: Target area

We took the location history data points, transformed them, and displayed them. We are ready to enhance the AI diagnosis KNN program:

- The transformed data can be displayed for XAI purposes, as we will see in the following section.
- The transformed data can enhance the KNN dataset used for the medical diagnosis.
- The maps can provide useful additional XAI information to both the software development team and the doctor.

We have the information we need. We will now transform our AI program into an XAI prototype.

Enhancing the AI diagnosis with XAI

In this section, we will enhance the KNN.ipynb model we built in *The standard AI program used by a general practitioner* section of this chapter. We will use the location history of the patient and the information concerning the presence of the West Nile virus in places they both were in at the same time during the past few weeks.

We will focus on XAI, not the scripting that leads to proving that the patient and the West Nile virus were not in the same location at the same time when the location is Paris. However, they were in the same place at the same time when the location was Chicago. We will suppose that a preprocessing script provided information with two new features: france and chicago. The value of the location feature will be 1 if both the virus and the patient were at the same location at the same time; otherwise, the value will be 0.

Enhanced KNN

Open KNN_with_Location_History.ipynb in Google Colaboratory.

This program enhances KNN.ipynb to make it explainable.

We will take D1.csv, the original file for the KNN, and enhance it. The dataset file we will use is now renamed DLH.csv and contains three additional columns and one additional class:

```
colored_sputum,cough,fever,headache,days,france,chicago,class
1,3.5,9.4,3,3,0,1,flu
1,3.4,8.4,4,2,0,1,flu
1,3.3,7.3,3,4,0,1,flu
1,3.4,9.5,4,2,0,1,flu
...
2,3,8,9,6,0,1,bad_flu
1,2,8,9,5,0,1,bad_flu
2,3,8,9,5,0,1,bad_flu
1,3,8,9,5,0,1,bad_flu
3,3,8,9,5,0,1,bad_flu
1,4,8,9,5,0,1,bad_flu
1,5,8,9,5,0,1,bad_flu
```

Warning

This dataset is not a medical dataset. The dataset only shows how such a system could work. DO NOT use it to make a real-life medical diagnosis.

The three additional columns provide critical information:

- days indicates the number of days the patient has had these symptoms for. The evolution of the symptoms often leads to the evolution of the diagnosis. This parameter weighs heavily in a doctor's decision.

- france is the conjunction of the location history of the patient and the location of a specific disease. In our case, we are looking for a serious disease in a location. The month of October is implicit in this dataset. It is implicitly a real-time dataset that only goes back 15 days, which is a reasonable incubation time. If necessary, this window can be extended. In this case, in October, no serious flu is present in France, so the value is 0 although the patient was in France. The patient and the disease must be equal to 1 for this value to be equal to 1.

- chicago is the conjunction where the location history of the patient, and the location of a disease, the West Nile virus, occurred at the same time. Both the patient and the disease were present at the same time in this location, so the value is 1.

A new class was introduced to show when a patient and a virus were present at the same location at the same time. The name bad_flu is an alert name. It triggers the message for the doctor for the immediate need for additional investigations. There is a probability that the flu might not be a mild disease but might be hiding something more critical.

We will use the GitHub repository to retrieve a data file and an image for this section:

```
# @title Importing data <br>
# repository is set to "github"(default) to read the data
# from GitHub <br>
# set repository to "google" to read the data
# from Google Drive {display-mode: "form"}
import os
from google.colab import drive


# Set repository to "github" to read the data from GitHub
```

```
# Set repository to "google" to read the data from Google
repository = "github"

if repository == "github":
  !curl -L https://raw.githubusercontent.com/PacktPublishing/Hands-On-
Explainable-AI-XAI-with-Python/master/Chapter01/DLH.csv --output "DLH.csv"
  !curl -L https://raw.githubusercontent.com/PacktPublishing/Hands-On-
Explainable-AI-XAI-with-Python/master/Chapter01/glh.jpg --output "glh.jpg"

  # Setting the path for each file
  df2 = "/content/DLH.csv"
  print(df2)
```

Then, `DLH.csv` is opened and displayed:

```
df = pd.read_csv(df2)
print(df)
```

The output shows that the new columns and class are present:

	colored_sputum	cough	fever	headache	days	france	chicago
class							
0	1.0	3.5	9.4	3.0	3	0	1
flu							
1	1.0	3.4	8.4	4.0	2	0	1
flu							
2	1.0	3.3	7.3	3.0	4	0	1
flu							
3	1.0	3.4	9.5	4.0	2	0	1
flu							
4	1.0	2.0	8.0	3.5	1	0	1
flu							
..	...	...	...	...	...	...	...
...							
179	2.0	3.0	8.0	9.0	5	0	1
bad_flu							
180	1.0	3.0	8.0	9.0	5	0	1
bad_flu							
181	3.0	3.0	8.0	9.0	5	0	1
bad_flu							
182	1.0	4.0	8.0	9.0	5	0	1
bad_flu							
183	1.0	5.0	8.0	9.0	5	0	1
bad_flu							

The classifier must read the columns from `colored_sputum` to `chicago`:

```
# KNN classification labels
X = df.loc[:, 'colored_sputum': 'chicago']
Y = df.loc[:, 'class']
```

We add a fifth subplot to our figure to display the new feature, days:

```
df = pd.read_csv(df2)
# Plotting the relation of each feature with each class
figure, (sub1, sub2, sub3, sub4, sub5) = plt.subplots(
    5, sharex=True, sharey=True)
plt.suptitle('k-nearest neighbors')
plt.xlabel('Feature')
plt.ylabel('Class')
```

We don't add france and chicago. We will display that automatically in the doctor's form for further XAI purposes when we reach that point in this process.

We now add the fifth subplot with its information to the program:

```
X = df.loc[:, 'days']
Y = df.loc[:, 'class']
sub5.scatter(X, Y, color='brown', label='days')
sub5.legend(loc=4, prop={'size': 5})
```

We add the new features to the form:

```
# @title Alert evaluation form: do not change the values
# of france and chicago
colored_sputum = 1 # @param {type:"integer"}
cough = 3           # @param {type:"integer"}
fever = 7           # @param {type:"integer"}
headache = 7        # @param {type:"integer"}
days = 5            # @param {type:"integer"}
# Insert the function here that analyzes the conjunction of
# the location History of the patient and location of
# diseases per country/location
france = 0  # @param {type:"integer"}
chicago = 1 # @param {type:"integer"}
```

The title contains a warning message. Only days must be changed. Another program provided france and chicago. This program can be written in Python, C++ using SQL, or any other tool. The main goal is to provide additional information to the KNN.

The prediction input needs to be expanded to take the additional features into account:

```
# colored_sputum, cough, fever, headache
cs = colored_sputum; c = cough; f = fever; h = headache; d = days;
fr = france; ch = chicago;
X_DL = [[cs, c, f, h, d, fr, ch]]

prediction = knn.predict(X_DL)
predictv = str(prediction).strip('[]')
print("The prediction is:", predictv)
```

The prediction is now displayed. If the prediction is bad_flu, an alert is triggered, and the need for further investigations and XAI is required. A list of urgent classes can be stored in an array. For this example, only bad_flu is detected:

```
alert = "bad_flu"
if alert == "bad_flu":
    print("Further urgent information might be required. Activate the XAI
interface.")
```

The output is as follows:

```
Further urgent information might be required. Activate the XAI
interface.
```

XAI is required. The doctor hesitates. Is the patient really that ill? Is this not just a classic October flu before the winter cases of flu arrive? What can a machine really know? But in the end, the health of the patient comes first. The doctor decides to consult the XAI prototype.

XAI applied to the medical diagnosis experimental program

The doctor is puzzled by the words "urgent" and "further information." Their patient does not look well at all. Still, the doctor is thinking: "We are in France in October 2019, and there is no real flu epidemic. What is this software talking about? Developers! They don't know a thing about my job, but they want to explain it to me!" The doctor does not trust machines—and especially AI—one bit with their patient's life. A black box result makes no sense to the doctor, so they decide to consult the prototype's XAI interface.

Displaying the KNN plot

The doctor decides to enter the XAI interface and quickly scan through it to see whether this is nonsense or not. The first step will be to display the KNN plot with the number of days displayed:

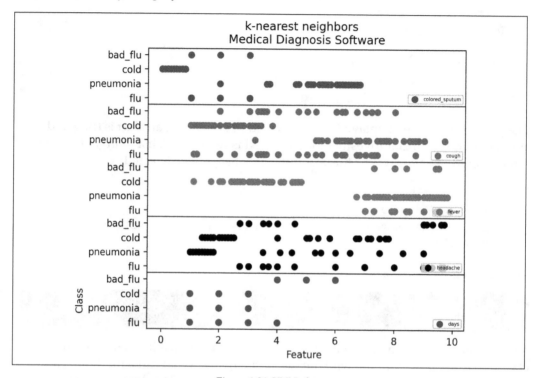

Figure 1.24: KNN plot

The doctor quickly but carefully looks at the screen and notices that several of the features overlap. For example, there is a fever for flu, bad flu, and pneumonia. The doctor again is thinking, "I did not need AI software to tell me that fever can mean many things!"

The doctor still needs to be convinced and does not *trust* the system at all yet. We need to introduce natural language AI explanations.

Natural language explanations

The XAI explanation is activated for the result of the KNN, which, we must admit, is not easy to understand just by looking at the plot. A plot might take some time to interpret and the user is likely to be in a hurry. So, for this experiment, a rule-based system with a few basic rules should suffice to make our point.

The explanation works with alert levels:

```
# This is an example program.
# DO NOT use this for a real-life diagnosis.
# cs = colored_sputum; c = cough; f = fever; h = headache; d = days;
# fr = france; ch = chicago;
if(f > 5):
  print("your patient has a high fever")
if(d > 4):
  print("your patient has had a high fever for more than 4 days even
with medication")
if(fr < 1):
  print("it is probable that your patient was not in contact with a
virus in France")
if(chicago > 0):
  print("it is probable that your patient was in contact with a virus
in Chicago")
```

Each message in this code is linked to an alert level of the value of the feature entered. The values of the features are semantic. In this case, the semantic values are not actual values but alert values. The whole dataset has been designed so that the values mean something.

Using semantic values makes it easier to explain AI in cases such as this critical diagnosis. If the values are not semantic, a script in any language can convert abstract mathematical values into semantic values. You will need to think this through when designing the application. A good way is to store key initial values before normalizing them or using activation functions that squash them.

In this case, the output provides some useful information:

```
your patient has a high fever
your patient has had a high fever for more than 4 days even with
medication
it is probable that your patient was not in contact with a virus in
France
it is probable that your patient was in contact with a virus in Chicago
```

The doctor struggles to understand. One factor appears true: a high fever over four days, even with medication, means something is very wrong. And maybe the doctor missed something?

But why did Chicago come up? The doctor goes to the next AI explanation concerning the location history of the patient. The prerequisite was to implement the process we explored in the *Google's Location History extraction tool* section of this chapter. Now we can use that information to help the doctor in this XAI investigation.

Displaying the Location History map

A message and a map are displayed:

```
Your patient is part of the XAI program that you have signed up for.
As such, we have your patient's authorization to access his Google
Location History, which we update in our database once a day between 10
pm and 6 am.
The following map shows that your patient was in Chicago, Paris, and
Lyon within the past 3 weeks.
For this diagnosis, we only activated a search for the past 3 weeks.
Please ask your patient if he was in Chicago in the past 3 weeks. If
the answer is yes, continue AI explanation.
```

Figure 1.25: Google Location History map (with added U.S. data points)

The map was generated with a customized version of `GoogleLocationHistory.ipynb` for this patient and chapter:

```
import matplotlib.image as mpimg
img = mpimg.imread('/content/glh.jpg')
imgplot = plt.imshow(img)
plt.show()
```

The doctor asks the patient if he was in Chicago in the past two weeks. The answer is yes. Now the doctor is thinking: "Something is going on here that does not meet the eye. What is the correlation between being in Chicago and this lasting high fever?"

The doctor decides to continue to scan the AI explanation of the result to find the correlation between Chicago and a potential disease at the time the patient was at the location.

Showing mosquito detection data and natural language explanations

The program displays information extracted from the DLH.csv file we downloaded in the *West Nile virus – a case of life or death* section of this chapter.

Our AI program used the detection data of the *Culex pipiens/restuans* mosquito in Chicago:

SEASON YEAR	WEEK	TRAP	TRAP_TYPE	RESULT	SPECIES	LATITUDE	LONGITUDE
2019	33	T159	GRAVID	positive	CULEX PIPIENS/RESTUANS	41.731446858	-87.649722253
2019	36	T159	GRAVID	positive	CULEX PIPIENS/RESTUANS	41.731446858	-87.649722253
2019	37	T159	GRAVID	positive	CULEX PIPIENS/RESTUANS	41.731446858	-87.649722253

Then the program explains the AI process further:

```
print("Your patient was in Chicago in the period during which there
were positive detections of the CULEX PIPIENS/RESTUANS mosquito.")
print("The mosquitos were trapped with a Gravid trap.")
print("The CULEX PIPIENS/RESTUANS mosquito is a vector for the West
Nile virus.")
print("We matched your patient's location history with the presence of
the CULEX PIPIENS/RESTUANS in Chicago.")
print("We then matched the CULEX PIPIENS/RESTUANS with West Nile
virus.")
print("Continue to see information the West Nile virus.")
```

The program leads directly to the following links:

- `https://www.healthline.com/health/west-nile-virus#treatment`
- `https://www.medicinenet.com/west_nile_virus_pictures_slideshow/article.htm`
- `https://www.medicinenet.com/script/main/art.asp?articlekey=224463`

When the doctor reads the online analysis of the West Nile virus, all of the pieces of the puzzle fit together. The doctor feels that a probable diagnosis has been reached and that immediate action must be taken.

A critical diagnosis is reached with XAI

The doctor suddenly understands how the AI algorithm reached its conclusion through this prototype XAI program. The doctor realizes that their patient is in danger of having the beginning of encephalitis or meningitis. The patient might be one of the very few people seriously infected by the West Nile virus.

The doctor calls an ambulance, and the patient receives immediate emergency room (ER) care. The beginning of West Nile encephalitis was detected, and the treatment began immediately. The patient's virus had gone from the bloodstream into the brain, causing encephalitis.

The doctor realizes that AI and XAI just saved a life. The doctor now begins to trust AI through XAI. This represents one of the first of many steps of cooperation between humans and machines on the long road ahead.

Summary

In this chapter, we defined XAI, a new approach to AI that develops users' trust in the system. We saw that each type of user requires a different level of explanation. XAI also varies from one aspect of a process to another. An explainable model applied to input data will have specific features, and explainability for machine algorithms will use other functions.

With these XAI methods in mind, we then build an experimental KNN program that could help a general practitioner make a diagnosis when the same symptoms could lead to several diseases.

We added XAI to every phase of an AI project introducing explainable interfaces for the input data, the model used, the output data, and the whole reasoning process that leads to a diagnosis. This XAI process made the doctor trust AI predictions.

We improved the program by adding the patient's Google Location History data to the KNN model using a Python program to parse a JSON file. We also added information on the location of mosquitos carrying the West Nile virus. With this information, we enhanced the KNN by correlating a patient's locations with potential critical diseases present in those locations.

In this case, XAI may have saved a patient's life. In other cases, XAI will provide sufficient information for a user to trust AI. As AI spreads out to all of the areas of our society, we must provide XAI to all the types of users we encounter. Everybody requires XAI at one point or another to understand how a result was produced.

The appearance of COVID-19 in late 2019 and 2020 shows that AI and XAI applied to viral infections in patients that have traveled will save lives.

In this chapter, we got our hands dirty by using various methods to explain AI by building our solution from scratch in Python. We experienced the difficulty of building XAI solutions. In *Chapter 2, White Box XAI for AI Bias and Ethics*, we'll see how we can build a Python program using decision trees to make real-life decisions, and explore the ethical and legal problems involved with allowing AI to make real-life decisions.

Questions

1. Understanding the theory of an ML algorithm is enough for XAI. (True | False)

2. Explaining the origin of datasets is not necessary for XAI. (True | False)

3. Explaining the results of an ML algorithm is sufficient. (True | False)

4. It is not necessary for an end user to know what a KNN is. (True | False)

5. Obtaining data to train an ML algorithm is easy with all the available data online. (True | False)

6. Location history is not necessary for a medical diagnosis. (True | False)

7. Our analysis of the patient with the West Nile virus cannot be applied to other viruses. (True | False)

8. A doctor does not require AI to make a diagnosis. (True | False)

9. It isn't necessary to explain AI to a doctor. (True | False)

10. AI and XAI will save lives. (True | False)

References

The original Google Location History program can be found at the following link:

https://github.com/gboeing/data-visualization/blob/master/location-history/
google-location-history-simple.ipynb

Further reading

- For more on KNN, see this link: https://scikit-learn.org/stable/modules/
generated/sklearn.neighbors.KNeighborsClassifier.html
- *Artificial Intelligence By Example, Second Edition*, Packt, Denis Rothman, 2020
- For more on the use of basemap, see this link: https://matplotlib.org/
basemap/users/intro.html

2

White Box XAI for AI Bias and Ethics

AI provides complex algorithms that can replace or emulate human intelligence. We tend to think that AI will spread unchecked by regulations. Without AI, corporate giants cannot process the huge amounts of data they face. In turn, ML algorithms require massive amounts of public and private data for training purposes to guarantee reliable results.

However, from a legal standpoint, AI remains a form of automatic processing of data. As such, just like any other method that processes data automatically, AI must follow the rules established by the international community, which compel AI designers to explain how decisions are reached. **Explainable AI (XAI)** has become a legal obligation.

The legal problem of AI worsens once we realize that for an algorithm to work, it requires data, that is, huge volumes of data. Collecting data requires access to networks, emails, text messages, social networks, hard disks, and more. By its very nature, processing data automatically requires access to that same data. On top of that, users want quick access to web sites that are increasingly driven by AI.

We need to add ethical rules to our AI algorithms to avoid being slowed down by regulations and fines. We must be ready to explain the alleged bias in our ML algorithms. Any company, whether huge or tiny, can be sued and fined.

This puts huge pressure on online sites to respect ethical regulations and avoid bias. In 2019, the U.S. **Federal Trade Commission (FTC)** and Google settled for USD 170,000,000 for YouTube's alleged violations of children's privacy laws. In the same year, Facebook was fined USD 5,000,000,000 by FTC for violating privacy laws. On January 21, 2019, a French court applied the European **General Data Protection Regulation (GDPR)** and sentenced Google to pay a €50,000,000 fine for a lack of transparency in their advertising process. Google and Facebook stand out because they are well known. However, every company faces these issues.

The roadmap of this chapter becomes clear. We will determine how to approach AI ethically. We will explain the risk of bias in our algorithms when an issue comes up. We will apply explainable AI as much as possible, and as best as we possibly can.

We will start by judging an autopilot in a **self-driving car (SDC)** in life-and-death situations. We will try to find how an SDC driven by an autopilot can avoid killing people in critical traffic cases.

With these life-and-death situations in mind, we will build a decision tree in an SDC's autopilot. Then, we will apply an explainable AI approach to decision trees.

Finally, we will learn how to control bias and insert ethical rules in real time in the SDC's autopilot.

This chapter covers the following topics:

- The Moral Machine, **Massachusetts Institute of Technology (MIT)**
- Life and death autopilot decision making
- The ethics of explaining the moral limits of AI
- An explanation of autopilot decision trees
- A theoretical description of decision tree classifiers
- XAI applied to an autopilot decision tree
- The structure of a decision tree
- Using XAI and ethics to control a decision tree
- Real-time autopilot situations

Our first step will be to explore the challenges an autopilot in an SDC faces in life and death situations.

Moral AI bias in self-driving cars

In this section, we will explain AI bias, morals, and ethics. Explaining AI goes well beyond understanding how an AI algorithm works from a mathematical point of view to reach a given decision. Explaining AI includes defining the limits of AI algorithms in terms of bias, moral, and ethical parameters. We will use AI in SDCs to illustrate these terms and the concepts they convey.

The goal of this section is to explain AI, not to advocate the use of SDCs, which remains a personal choice, or to judge a human driver's decisions made in life and death situations.

Explaining does not mean judging. XAI provides us with the information we need to make our decisions and form our own opinions.

This section will not provide moral guidelines. Moral guidelines depend on cultures and individuals. However, we will explore situations that require moral judgments and decisions, which will take us to the very limits of AI and XAI.

We will provide information for each person so that we can understand the complexity of the decisions autopilots face in critical situations.

We will start by diving directly into a complex situation for a vehicle on autopilot.

Life and death autopilot decision making

In this section, we will set the grounds for the explainable decision tree that we will implement in the subsequent sections. We will be facing life and death situations. We will have to analyze who might die in an accident that cannot be avoided.

This section uses MIT's Moral Machine experiment, which addresses the issue of how an AI machine will make moral decisions in life and death situations.

To understand the challenge facing AI, let's first go back to the trolley problem.

The trolley problem

The trolley problem takes us to the core of human decisions. Should we decide on a purely utilitarian basis, maximizing utility above anything else? Should we take deontological ethics — that is, actions based on moral rules — into account? The trolley problem, which was first expressed more than 100 years ago, creates a dilemma that remains difficult to solve since it leads to subjective cultural and personal considerations.

The trolley problem involves four protagonists:

- **A runaway trolley going down a track**: Its brakes have failed, and it is out of control.

- **A group of five people at a short distance in front of the trolley**: They will be killed if the trolley continues on its track.

- **One person on a sidetrack.**

- **You, standing next to a lever**: If you don't pull the lever, five people will die. If you pull the lever, one person will die. You only have a few seconds to make your decision.

In the following diagram, you can see the trolley on the left; you in the middle, next to the lever; the five people that will be killed if the trolley stays on the track; and the person on the sidetrack:

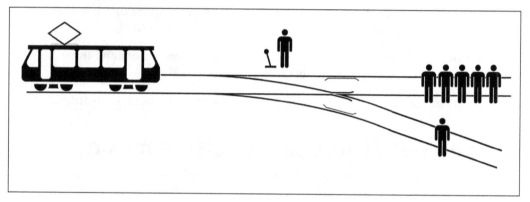

Figure 2.1: The trolley problem
!Original: McGeddonVector: Zapyon / CC BY-SA (https://creativecommons.org/licenses/by-sa/4.0)

This mind experiment consists of imagining numerous situations such as:

- Five older people on the track and one child on the sidetrack
- Five women on the track and one man on the sidetrack
- A young family on the track and an elderly person on the sidetrack
- Many more combinations

You must decide whether to pull the lever or not. You must determine who will die. Worse, you must decide how your ML autopilot algorithm will make decisions in an SDC when facing life and death situations.

Let's explore the basis of moral-based decision making in SDCs.

The MIT Moral Machine experiment

The MIT Moral Machine experiment addresses the trolley problem transposed into our modern world of self-driving autopilot algorithms. The Moral Machine experiment explored millions of answers online in many cultures. It presents situations you must judge. You can test this on the Moral Machine experiment site at `http://moralmachine.mit.edu/`.

The Moral Machine experiment confronts us with machine-made moral decisions. An autopilot running calculations does not think like a human in the trolley problem. An ML algorithm thinks in terms of the rules we set. But how can we set them if we do not know the answers ourselves? We must answer this question before putting our autopilot algorithms on the market. Hopefully, by the end of this chapter, you will have some ideas on how to limit such situations.

The Moral Machine experiment extends the trolley problem further. Should we pull the lever and stop implementing AI autopilot algorithms in cars until they are ready in a few decades?

If so, many people will die because a well-designed autopilot saves some lives but not others. An autopilot is never tired. It is alert and respects traffic regulations. However, autopilots will face the trolley problem and calculation inaccuracies.

If we do not pull the lever and let autopilots run artificial intelligence programs, autopilots will start making life and death decisions and will kill people along the way.

The goal of this section and chapter is not to explore every situation and suggest rules. Our primary goal is limited to explaining the issues and possibilities so that you can judge what is best for your algorithms. We will, therefore, be prepared to build a decision tree for the autopilot in the next section.

Let's now explore a life and death situation to prepare ourselves with the task of building a decision tree.

Real life and death situations

The situation described in this section will prepare us to design tradeoffs in moral decision making in autopilots. I used the MIT Moral Machine to create the two options an AI autopilot can take when faced with the situation shown in the following diagram:

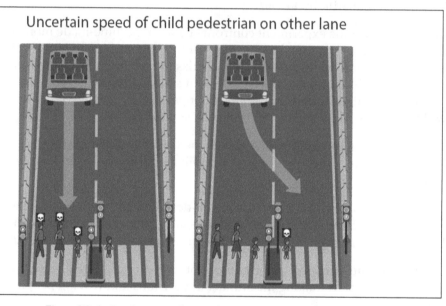

Figure 2.2: A situation created using the MIT Moral Machine

For several possible reasons, the car shown in the preceding diagram cannot avoid either going straight ahead or changing lanes:

- Brake failure.
- The SDC's autopilot did not identify the pedestrians well or fast enough.
- The AI autopilot is confused.
- The pedestrians on the left side of the diagram suddenly crossed the road when the traffic light was red for pedestrians.
- It suddenly began to rain, and the autopilot failed to give the human driver enough time to react. Rain obstructs an SDC's sensors. The cameras and radars can malfunction in this case.
- Another reason.

Many factors can lead to this situation. We will, therefore, refer to this situation by stating that whatever the reason, the car does not have enough time to stop before reaching the traffic light.

We will try to provide the best answer to the situation described in the preceding diagram. We will now approach this from an ethical standpoint.

Explaining the moral limits of ethical AI

We now know that a life and death situation that involves deaths, no matter what decision is made, will be subjective in any case. It will depend more on cultural and human values than on pure ML calculations.

Ethically explaining AI involves honesty and transparency. By doing so, we are honest and transparent. We explain why we, as humans, struggle with this type of situation, and ML autopilots cannot do better.

To illustrate this, let's analyze a potential real-life situation.

On the left side of *Figure 2.3*, we see a car on autopilot using AI that is too close to a pedestrian walk to stop. We notice that the traffic light is green for the car and red for pedestrians. A death symbol is on the man, the woman, and the child because they will be seriously injured if the car hits them:

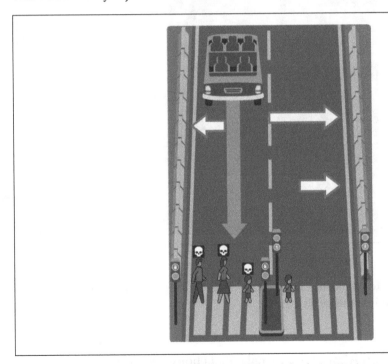

Figure 2.3: A life and death situation

A human driver could try to:

- Immediately turn the steering wheel to the left to hit the wall with the brakes on and stop the car. This manual maneuver automatically turns the autopilot off. Of course, the autopilot could be dysfunctional and not stop. Or, the car would continue anyway and hit the pedestrians.

- Immediately do the same maneuver but instead cross lanes to the other side. Of course, a fast incoming car could be coming in the opposite direction. The car could slide, miss the wall, and hit the child anyway on the other lane.

A human driver could try to change lanes to avoid the three pedestrians and only risk injuring or killing one on the other lane:

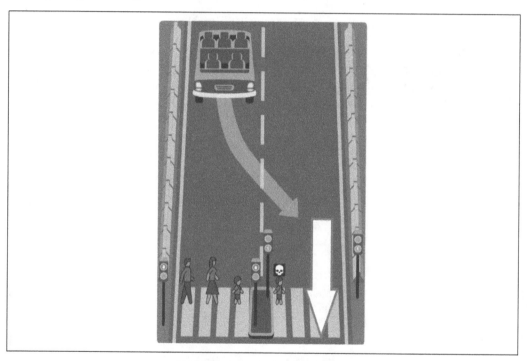

Figure 2.4: Swerving to another lane

The driver might be able to avoid the pedestrian on the other lane. In that case, it would be risking one life instead of three.

What would you do?

I do not think we can ask an AI program to make that choice. We need to explain why and find a way to offer a solution to this problem before letting driverless SDCs roam freely around a city!

Let's view this modern-day trolley problem dilemma from an ML perspective.

Standard explanation of autopilot decision trees

An SDC contains an autopilot that was designed with several artificial intelligence algorithms. Almost all AI algorithms can apply to an autopilot's need, such as clustering algorithms, regression, and classification. Reinforcement learning and deep learning provide many powerful calculations.

We will first build an autopilot decision tree for our SDC. The decision tree will be applied to a life and death decision-making process.

Let's start by first describing the dilemma from a machine learning algorithm's perspective.

The SDC autopilot dilemma

The decision tree we are going to create will be able to reproduce an SDC's autopilot trolley problem dilemma. We will adapt to the life and death dilemma in the *Moral AI bias in self-driving cars* section of this chapter.

The decision tree will have to decide if it stays in the right lane or swerves over to the left lane. We will restrict our experiment to four features:

- f1: The security level on the right lane. If the value is high, it means that the light is green for the SDC and no unknown objects are on the road.
- f2: Limited security on the right lane. If the value is high, it means that no pedestrians might be trying to cross the street. If the value is low, pedestrians are on the street, or there is a risk they might try to cross.
- f3: Security on the left lane. If the value is high, it would be possible to change lanes by swerving over to the other side of the road and that no objects were detected on that lane.
- f4: Limited security on the left lane. If the value is low, it means that pedestrians might be trying to cross the street. If the value is high, pedestrians are not detected at that point.

Each feature has a probable value between 0 and 1. If the value is close to 1, the feature has a high probability of being true. For example, if f1 = 0.9, this means that the security of the right lane is high. If f1 = 0.1, this means that the security of the right lane is most probably low.

We will import 4,000 cases involving all four features and their 2 possible labeled outcomes:

- If label = 0, the best option is to stay in the *right lane*
- If label = 1, the best option is to swerve to the *left lane*

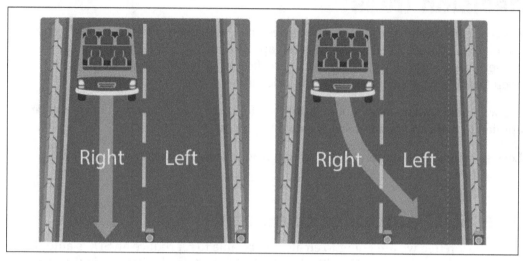

Figure 2.5: Autopilot lane changing situation

We will start by importing the modules required to run our decision tree and XAI.

Importing the modules

In this section, we will build a decision tree with the Google Colaboratory notebook. Go to Google Colaboratory, as explained in *Chapter 1, Explaining Artificial Intelligence with Python*. Open Explainable_AI_Decision_Trees.ipynb.

We will be using the following modules in Explainable_AI_Decision_Trees.ipynb:

- numpy to analyze the structure of the decision tree
- pandas for data manipulation
- matplotlib.pyplot to plot the decision tree and create an image
- pickle to save and load the decision tree estimator
- sklearn.tree to create the decision tree classifier and explore its structure
- sklearn.model_selection to manage the training and testing data

- `metrics` is scikit-learn's metrics module and is used to measure the accuracy of the training process
- `os` for the file path management of the dataset

`Explainable_AI_Decision_Trees.ipynb` starts by importing the modules mentioned earlier:

```
import numpy as np
import pandas as pd
import matplotlib.pyplot as plt
import pickle
from sklearn.tree import DecisionTreeClassifier, plot_tree
from sklearn.model_selection import train_test_split
from sklearn import metrics
import os
```

Now that the modules are imported, we can retrieve the dataset.

Retrieving the dataset

There are several ways to retrieve the dataset file, named `autopilot_data.csv`, which can be downloaded along with the code files of this chapter.

We will use the GitHub repository:

```
# @title Importing data <br>
# Set repository to "github"(default) to read the data
# from GitHub <br>
# Set repository to "google" to read the data
# from Google {display-mode: "form"}
import os
from google.colab import drive

# Set repository to "github" to read the data from GitHub
# Set repository to "google" to read the data from Google
repository = "github"

if repository == "github":
  !curl -L https://raw.githubusercontent.com/PacktPublishing/Hands-
On-Explainable-AI-XAI-with-Python/master/Chapter02/autopilot_data.csv
--output "autopilot_data.csv"
```

```
# Setting the path for each file
ip = "/content/autopilot_data.csv"
print(ip)
```

The path of the dataset file will be displayed:

```
/content/autopilot_data.csv
```

Google Drive can also be activated to retrieve the data. The dataset file is now imported. We will now process it.

Reading and splitting the data

We defined the features in the introduction of this section. f1 and f2 are the probable values of the security on the right lane. f3 and f4 are the probable values of the security on the left lane. If the label is 0, then the recommendation is to stay in the right lane. If the label is 1, then the recommendation is to swerve over to the left lane.

The file does not contain headers. We first define the names of the columns:

```
col_names = ['f1', 'f2', 'f3', 'f4', 'label']
```

We will now load the dataset:

```
# Load dataset
pima = pd.read_csv(ip, header=None, names=col_names)
print(pima.head())
```

We can now see that the output is displayed as:

```
     f1    f2    f3    f4  label
0  0.51  0.41  0.21  0.41      0
1  0.11  0.31  0.91  0.11      1
2  1.02  0.51  0.61  0.11      0
3  0.41  0.61  1.02  0.61      1
4  1.02  0.91  0.41  0.31      0
```

We will split the dataset into the features and target variable to train the decision tree:

```
# split dataset in features and target variable
feature_cols = ['f1', 'f2', 'f3', 'f4']
```

```
X = pima[feature_cols] # Features
y = pima.label # Target variable
print(X)
print(y)
```

The output of X is now stripped of the label:

```
         f1     f2     f3     f4
0       0.51   0.41   0.21   0.41
1       0.11   0.31   0.91   0.11
2       1.02   0.51   0.61   0.11
3       0.41   0.61   1.02   0.61
4       1.02   0.91   0.41   0.31
...      ...    ...    ...    ...
3995    0.31   0.11   0.71   0.41
3996    0.21   0.71   0.71   1.02
3997    0.41   0.11   0.31   0.51
3998    0.31   0.71   0.61   1.02
3999    0.91   0.41   0.11   0.31
```

The output of y only contains labels:

```
0       0
1       1
2       0
3       1
4       0
        ..
3995    1
3996    1
3997    1
3998    1
3999    0
```

Now that we have separated the features from their labels, we are ready to split the dataset. The dataset is split into training data to train the decision tree and testing data to measure the accuracy of the training process:

```
# Split dataset into training set and test set
X_train, X_test, y_train, y_test = train_test_split(X, y,
    test_size=0.3, random_state=1) # 70% training and 30% test
```

Before creating the decision tree classifier, let's explore a theoretical description.

Theoretical description of decision tree classifiers

The decision tree in this chapter uses Gini impurity values to classify the features of the record in a dataset node by node. The nodes at the top of the decision tree contain the highest values of Gini impurity.

In this section, we will take the example of classifying features into the left lane or right lane labels. For example, if the Gini value is <=0.46 for feature 4, f4, then the child node on the left filters the true values, which will favor keeping the SDC on the right lane. The child node on the right is false for the f4 condition and will favor sending the SDC on the left lane:

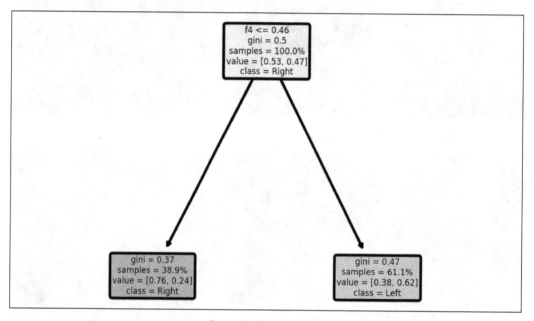

Figure 2.6: Decision tree

Let k represent the probability of a data point being incorrectly classified. Let X represent the dataset we are applying the decision tree to.

The equation of Gini impurity calculates the probability of each feature occurring and multiplies the result by 1, that is, the probability of occurring on the remaining values, as shown in the following equation:

$$G(k) = \sum_{i=1}^{n} P_i * (1 - P_i)$$

The decision train is built on the *gain of information* on the features that contain the highest Gini impurity value.

As the decision tree classifier calculates the Gini impurity at each node and creates child nodes, the decision tree's depth increases, as shown in the following graph:

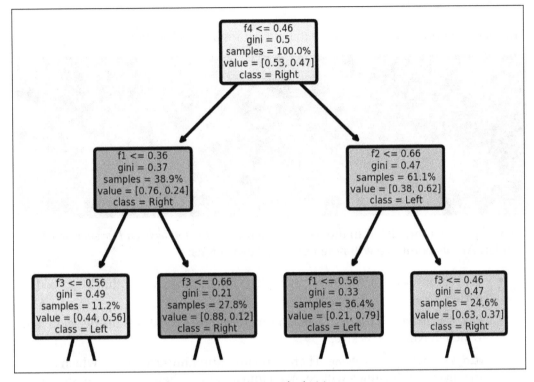

Figure 2.7: Structure of a decision tree

You can see examples of the whole structure of the process in the XAI section of this chapter, *XAI applied to an autopilot decision tree.*

With these concepts in mind, let's create a default decision tree classifier.

Creating the default decision tree classifier

In this section, we will create the decision tree classifier using default values. We will explore the options in the *XAI applied to an autopilot decision tree* section of this chapter.

A decision tree classifier is an estimator. An estimator is any ML algorithm that contains learning functions. A classifier will classify the data.

The default decision tree classifier can be created with a single line:

```
# Create decision tree classifier object
# Default approach
estimator = DecisionTreeClassifier()
print(estimator)
```

The following program displays the default values of the classifier:

```
DecisionTreeClassifier(ccp_alpha=0.0, class_weight=None,
                criterion='gini', max_depth=None,
                max_features=None, max_leaf_nodes=None,
                min_impurity_decrease=0.0,
                min_impurity_split=None, min_samples_leaf=1,
                min_samples_split=2,
                min_weight_fraction_leaf=0.0,
                presort='deprecated', random_state=None,
                splitter='best')
```

We will go into more detail in the *XAI applied to an autopilot decision tree* section of this chapter. At this point, we will note the three key options:

- `criterion='gini'`: We are applying the Gini impurity algorithm described earlier.

- `max_depth=None`: There is no maximum depth that constricts the decision tree, which maximizes its size.

- `min_impurity_split=None`: There is no minimum impurity split, which means that even small values will be taken into account. There is no constraint on expanding the size of a decision tree.

We can now train, measure, and save the model of the decision tree classifier.

Training, measuring, and saving the model

We have loaded and split the data into training data and testing data. We have created a default decision tree classifier. We can now run the training process with our training data:

```
# Train decision tree classifier
estimator = estimator.fit(X_train, y_train)
```

Once the training is over, we want to test the trained model using our test data. The estimator will make predictions:

```
# Predict the response for the test dataset
print("prediction")
y_pred = estimator.predict(X_test)
print(y_pred)
```

The output will display the predictions:

```
prediction
[0 0 1 ... 1 1 0]
```

The problem we face here is that we have no idea how accurate the predictions were by just looking at them. We need a measurement tool. In the *XAI applied to an autopilot decision tree* section of this chapter, we will be using our own measurement tool. We will need a customized measurement tool to check whether the predictions are biased or not, ethical or not, and legal or not. In this section, we will use the standard metrics function provided by scikit-learn:

```
# Model accuracy
print("Accuracy:", metrics.accuracy_score(y_test, y_pred))
```

The output is displayed:

```
Accuracy: 1.0
```

The technical accuracy is perfect, as we can see. However, we do not know if one of the predictions is to stay on a lane and kill one or several pedestrians or not! We will need more explainability control, as we will discuss in the *XAI applied to an autopilot decision tree* section of this chapter. In that section, we will learn how to deactivate a model with an alert when necessary.

We will now save the model. This does not seem that important from a technical standpoint. After all, we are just saving the parameters of the model so that it will make decisions without needing to be trained again.

From a moral, ethical, and legal standpoint, we have just signed our legal accountability contract. If a fatal accident occurs, the legal experts will take this model apart and ask for explanations. The model is saved with the following code:

```
# save model
pickle.dump(estimator, open("dt.sav", 'wb'))
```

To check whether the model has been saved, click on the **Files** button on the left of the Google Colaboratory page:

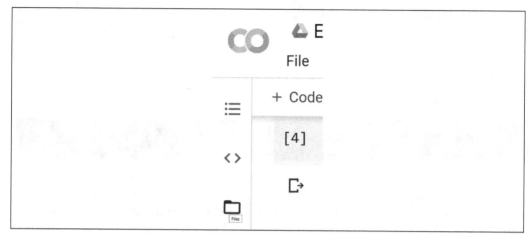

Figure 2.8: Colab file manager

You should see `dt.sav` in the list of files displayed:

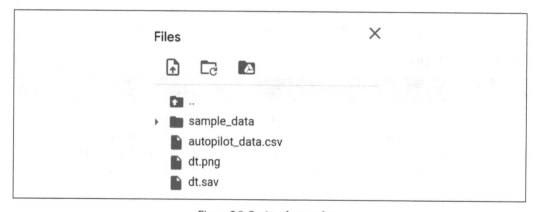

Figure 2.9: Saving the test data

We have trained, tested, and saved our model. We can now display our decision tree.

Displaying a decision tree

A graph of a decision tree is an excellent tool for XAI. However, in many cases, the number of nodes displayed will only confuse a user or even a developer. In this section, we will focus on a default model. We will customize the decision tree graph in the *XAI applied to an autopilot decision tree* section. In this section, we will first learn how to implement a default model.

The program first imports the `figure` module of `matplotlib`:

```
from matplotlib.pyplot import figure
```

Now we can create the figure using two basic options:

```
plt.figure(dpi=400, edgecolor="r", figsize=(10, 10))
```

`dpi` will determine the dots per inch of your graph. It does not seem that important to pay attention to this option. However, it is a critical option because it's a trial and error process. Large decision trees produce large graphs that make them difficult to see in detail. The nodes might be too small to understand and visualize even when zooming in. If `dpi` is too small when the graph is large, you won't see anything. If `dpi` is too large when the graph is small, your nodes will spread out and make it difficult to see them as well.

Both `figsize` and `dpi` are related, and, as such, `figsize` will produce the same effects as `dpi` when you adjust the size of the graph.

You can overcome this problem with a trained model, and if the datasets are homogeneous, you can try different values of `figsize` and `dpi` until you find the ones that fit your needs.

We will now define the name of the labels of our features in an array:

```
F = ["f1", "f2", "f3", "f4"]
```

We also want to visualize the class of each node:

```
C = ["Right", "Left"]
```

We are now ready to use the `plot_tree` function imported from scikit-learn:

```
plot_tree(estimator, filled=True, feature_names=F, rounded=True,
          precision=2, fontsize=3, proportion=True, max_depth=None,
          class_names=C)
```

We have used several options provided by `plot_tree`:

- `estimator`: Contains the name of the estimator of the decision tree.
- `filled=True`: Fills the nodes with the color of their class.
- `feature_names=F`: Contains the labels of the feature array.
- `rounded=True`: Rounds the borders of the nodes.
- `precision=2`: The number of digits displayed for Gini impurity.
- `fontsize=3`: Must be adapted to the graph like `figsize` and `dpi`.
- `proportion=True`: When `True`, the values will be proportions and percentages.
- `max_depth=None`: Limits the maximum depth of the graph. `None` displays the whole graph.
- `class_names=C`: Contains the labels of the class array.

The program saves the figure:

```
plt.savefig('dt.png')
```

You can open this image. Click on the **Files** button on the left of the Google Colaboratory page:

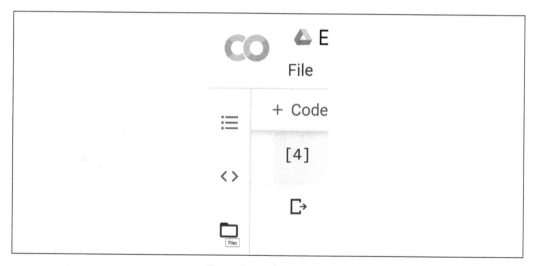

Figure 2.10: File manager

You should see `dt.png` in the list of files displayed:

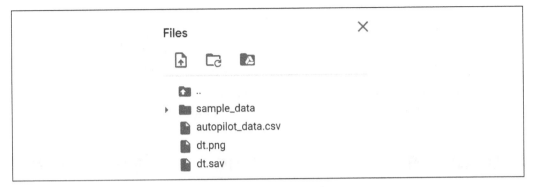

Figure 2.11: File upload

You can click on the name of the image and open it. You can also download it.

The image is also displayed underneath the cell with the following code:

```
plt.show()
```

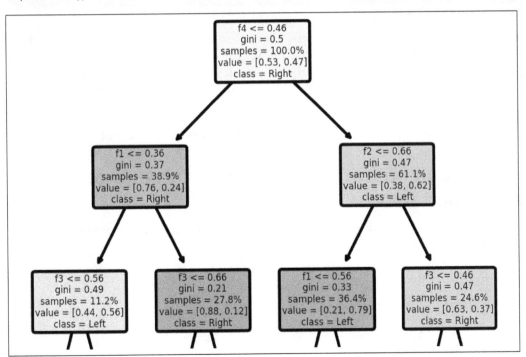

Figure 2.12: Decision tree structure

The decision tree structure shows the path a decision takes depending on its value as expected.

In this section, we imported the autopilot dataset and split it to obtain training data and test data. We then created a decision tree classifier with default options, trained it, and saved the model. We finally displayed the graph of the decision tree.

We now have a default decision tree classifier. We now need to work on our explanations when the decision tree faces life and death situations.

XAI applied to an autopilot decision tree

In this section, we will explain decision trees through scikit-learn's tree module, the decision tree classifier's parameters, and decision tree graphs. The goal is to provide the user with a step-by-step method to explain decision trees.

We will begin by parsing the structure of a decision tree.

Structure of a decision tree

The structure of a decision tree provides precious information for XAI. However, the default values of the decision tree classifier produce confusing outputs. We will first generate a decision tree structure with the default values. Then, we will use a what-if approach that will prepare us for the XAI tools in *Chapter 5, Building an Explainable AI Solution from Scratch.*

Let's start by implementing the default decision tree structure's output.

The default output of the default structure of a decision tree

The decision tree estimator contains a tree_ object that stores the attributes of the structure of a decision tree in arrays:

```
estimator.tree_
```

We can count the number of nodes:

```
n_nodes = estimator.tree_.node_count
```

We can obtain the ID of the left child of a node:

```
children_left = estimator.tree_.children_left
```

We can obtain the ID of the right child of a node:

```
children_right = estimator.tree_.children_right
```

We can also view the feature used to split the node into the left and right child nodes:

```
feature = estimator.tree_.feature
```

A `threshold` attribute will show the value at the node:

```
threshold = estimator.tree_.threshold
```

These arrays contain valuable XAI information.

The binary tree produces parallel arrays. The root node is node 0. The *i*th element contains information about the node.

The program now parses the tree structure using the attribute arrays:

```
# parsing the tree structure
node_depth = np.zeros(shape=n_nodes, dtype=np.int64)
is_leaves = np.zeros(shape=n_nodes, dtype=bool)
stack = [(0, -1)] # the seed is the root node id and its parent depth
while len(stack) > 0:
    node_id, parent_depth = stack.pop()
    node_depth[node_id] = parent_depth + 1

    # Exploring the test mode
    if (children_left[node_id] != children_right[node_id]):
        stack.append((children_left[node_id], parent_depth + 1))
        stack.append((children_right[node_id], parent_depth + 1))
    else:
        is_leaves[node_id] = True
```

Once the decision tree structure's attribute arrays have been parsed, the program prints the structure:

```
print("The binary tree structure has %s nodes and has "
      "the following tree structure:" % n_nodes)
for i in range(n_nodes):
    if is_leaves[i]:
        print("%snode=%s leaf node." % (node_depth[i] * "\t", i))
    else:
        print("%snode=%s test node: go to node %s "
              "if X[:, %s] <= %s else to node %s."
              % (node_depth[i] * "\t", i,
                 children_left[i],
                 feature[i],
                 threshold[i],
                 children_right[i],
                 ))
```

Our autopilot dataset will produce 255 nodes and list the tree structure, as shown in the following excerpt:

```
The binary tree structure has 255 nodes and has the following tree
structure:
node=0 test node: go to node 1 if X[:, 3] <= 0.4599999934434891 else to
node 92.
    node=1 test node: go to node 2 if X[:, 0] <= 0.35999999940395355
else to node 45.
        node=2 test node: go to node 3 if X[:, 2] <= 0.5600000023841858
else to node 30.
```

The customized output of a customized structure of a decision tree

The default output of a default decision tree structure challenges a user's ability to understand the algorithm. XAI is not just for AI developers, designers, and geeks. If a problem occurs and the autopilot kills somebody, an investigation will be conducted, and XAI will either lead to a plausible explanation or a lawsuit.

A user will first accept an explanation but rapidly start asking what-if questions. Let's answer two of the most common ones that come up during a project.

First question

Why are there so many nodes? What if we reduced the number of nodes?

Good questions! The user is willing to use the software and help control the results of the model before it goes into production. However, the user does not understand what they are looking at!

We will go back to the code and decide to customize the decision tree classifier:

```
estimator = DecisionTreeClassifier(max_depth=2, max_leaf_nodes=3,
                                   min_samples_leaf=100)
```

We have modified three key parameters:

- `max_depth=2`: Limits the tree to a maximum of two branches. A decision tree is a tree. We just cut a lot of branches.

- `max_leaf_nodes=3`: Limits the leaves on a branch. We just cut a lot of leaves off. We are restricting the growth of the tree, just like we do with real trees.

- `min_samples_leaf=100`: Limits the node volume by only taking leaves that have 100 or more samples into account.

The result is a small and easy tree to understand and is self-explanatory:

```
The binary tree structure has 5 nodes and has the following tree
structure:
node=0 test node: go to node 1 if X[:, 3] <= 0.4599999934434891 else to
node 2.
    node=1 leaf node.
    node=2 test node: go to node 3 if X[:, 1] <= 0.6599999964237213
else to node 4.
        node=3 leaf node.
        node=4 leaf node.
```

To make things easier, in the following chapters, we will progressively provide XAI interfaces for a user. A user will be able to run some "what-if" scenarios on their own. The user will understand the scenarios through XAI but will customize the model in real time.

For this section and chapter, we did it manually. The user smiles. Our XAI scenario has worked! The user will now control the decision tree by progressively increasing the three key parameters.

However, a few seconds later, the user frowns again and comes up with the second common question.

Second question

We reduced the number of nodes, and I appreciate the explanation. However, why has the accuracy gone down?

Excellent question! What is the point of controlling a truncated decision tree? The estimator will produce inaccurate results. If you scroll up to the training cell, you will see that the accuracy has gone from 1 to 0.74:

```
Accuracy: 0.7483333333333333
```

Our customized scenario worked to explain AI. The user understands that, in some cases, it will be possible to:

1. First, reduce the size of a decision tree to understand it
2. Then increase its size to follow the decision-making process and control it
3. Fine-tune the parameters to obtain efficient but explainable decision trees

However, once the user understands the structure, can we visualize the tree structure in another way?

Yes, we can use the graph of a decision tree, as described in the following section.

The output of a customized structure of a decision tree

In the previous section, we explored the structure of a decision tree and laid the ground for the XAI interfaces we will explore in the following chapters.

However, we discovered that if we simplify the decision tree classifier's job, we also reduce the accuracy of the model.

We have another tool that we can use to explain the structure of a decision tree iteratively. We can use the graph of the decision tree.

First, we go back, comment the customized estimator, and uncomment the default estimator:

```
# Create decision tree classifier object
# Default approach
estimator = DecisionTreeClassifier()
# Explainable AI approach
# estimator = DecisionTreeClassifier(max_depth=2, max_leaf_nodes=3,
#                                    min_samples_leaf=100)
```

When we run the program again, the accuracy is back to 1:

```
prediction
[0 0 1 ... 1 1 0]
Accuracy: 1.0
```

Then, we run the default `plot_tree` function we implemented in the *Displaying a decision tree* section of this chapter:

```python
from matplotlib.pyplot import figure
plt.figure(dpi=400, edgecolor="r", figsize=(10, 10))
F = ["f1", "f2", "f3", "f4"]
C = ["Right", "Left"]
plot_tree(estimator, filled=True, feature_names=F, rounded=True,
          precision=2, fontsize=3, proportion=True, max_depth=None,
          class_names=C)
plt.savefig('dt.png')
plt.show()
```

The output will puzzle the user because many of the nodes overlap at lower levels of the tree:

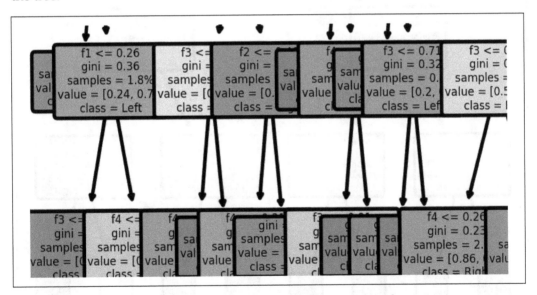

Figure 2.13: Nodes overlapping in a decision tree graph

Furthermore, the image of the graph is huge. Our goal, in this section, is to explain a decision tree with a graph. The next cells of the notebook will display a large graph structure.

What if we reduced the `max_depth` of the graph by reducing it to 2 and reduced the size of the figure as well? For example:

```
plot_tree(estimator, filled=True, feature_names=F, rounded=True,
        precision=2, fontsize=3, proportion=True, max_depth=2,
        class_names=C)
plt.savefig('dt.png')
plt.figure(dpi=400, edgecolor="r", figsize=(3, 3))
plt.show()
```

A user can now relate to this graph to understand how a decision tree works and help confirm its calculations:

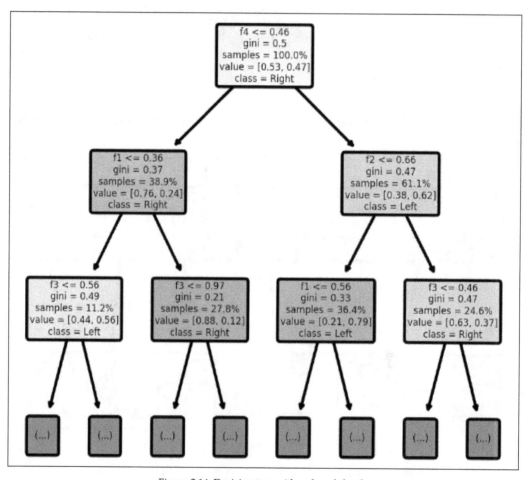

Figure 2.14: Decision tree with reduced depth

The accuracy of the model is back to 1, but the graph displayed only shows a node depth of 2.

In this section, we explored some of the parameters of decision tree structures and decision tree graphs. For some projects, users might not be interested in this level of explanation. However, in many corporate projects, data scientist project managers want to understand an AI algorithm in depth before deploying it on site. Furthermore, a project manager often works on an AI solution with a user or group of end users who will ask questions that they will need to answer.

In *Chapter 5, Building an Explainable AI Solution from Scratch*, we will explore Google's What-If Tool. We will begin to run XAI interfaces for the project managers and users on their own and build customized what-if scenarios. We will go into further detail in the following chapters.

For the moment, let's first introduce XAI and ethics in an autopilot decision tree.

Using XAI and ethics to control a decision tree

We know that the autopilot will have to decide to stay in a lane or swerve over to another lane to minimize the moral decision of killing pedestrians or not. The decision model is trained, tested, and the structure has been analyzed. Now it's time to put the decision tree on the road with the autopilot. Whatever algorithm you try to use, you will face the moral limits of a life and death situation. If an SDC faces such a vital decision, it might kill somebody no matter what algorithm or ensemble of algorithms the autopilot has.

Should we let an autopilot drive a car? Should we forbid the use of autopilots? Should we find ways to alert the driver that the autopilot will be shut down in such a situation? If the autopilot is shut down, will the human driver have enough time to take over before hitting a pedestrian?

In this section, we will introduce real-life bias, moral, and ethical issues in the decision tree to measure their reactions. We will then try to find ways to minimize the damage autopilot errors can cause.

We will first load the model.

Loading the model

When an SDC is on the road, it cannot be trained in real time with incoming data in a critical situation. The training time would be superior to the vital reaction time.

The decision tree model we saved will be loaded:

```
# Applying the model
# Load model
dt = pickle.load(open('dt.sav', 'rb'))
```

Bear in mind that, no matter what trained autopilot AI algorithm you load, some situations require more than just mathematical responses. We will now create two accuracy measurement variables.

Accuracy measurements

We will create two variables to measure the predictions made with the input simulation data that we will import:

```
t = 0 # true predictions
f = 0 # false predictions
```

These two simple variables seem logical. If we load our dataset, the prediction should be accurate.

The model encounters f1 and f2, the right lane features. The model encounters f3 and f4, the left lane features. The decision tree decides which lane provides the highest level of security no matter what the situation is. If the situation involves killing a pedestrian no matter which lane the SDC takes, an autopilot might encourage the SDC to kill somebody.

Can you allow the SDC to kill a pedestrian even if the prediction is true?

Should you allow the SDC to avoid making the wrong decision even if the prediction is false?

Let's explore real-time cases and see what can be done.

Simulating real-time cases

We have loaded the model and have our two measurement values. We cannot trust these measurement values anymore.

The program will now examine the input data line by line. Each line provides the four features necessary to decide to stay in a lane or swerve over to another lane.

We will now simulate the situations sent to the autopilot AI algorithm line by line:

```
for i in range(0, 100):
    xf1 = pima.at[i, 'f1']
    xf2 = pima.at[i, 'f2']
    xf3 = pima.at[i, 'f3']
    xf4 = pima.at[i, 'f4']
    xclass = pima.at[i, 'label']
```

The processing of the decision-making model starts by initializing the key decision values.

For our simulation, we will use the input data of this chapter's dataset. However, we will now introduce bias, noise, and ethical factors.

Introducing ML bias due to noise

We will now introduce bias in the data to simulate real-life situations.

Bias comes from many factors, such as:

- Errors in the algorithm when facing new data
- A sudden shower (rain, snow, or sleet) that obstructs the SDC's radar(s) and cameras
- The SDC suddenly encounters a slippery portion of the road (ice, snow, or oil)
- Erratic human behaviors on the part of other drivers or pedestrians
- Windy weather pushing objects on the road
- Other factors

Any or all of these events will distort the data sent to the autopilot's ML algorithm(s).

In this program, we will introduce a bias value for each feature:

```
b1 = 1.5; b2 = 1.5; b3 = 0.1; b4 = 0.1
```

These bias values provide interesting experiments for what-if situations. You can modify the value and security level of one or several of the features. The values are empirical. They are found by trial and error either manually, through a loop within a loop, or through a more sophisticated algorithm involving gradient descent.

The program will then apply the simulation of real-life data distortions to the input data:

```
xf1 = round(xf1 * b1, 2)
xf2 = round(xf2 * b2, 2)
xf3 = round(xf3 * b3, 2)
xf4 = round(xf4 * b4, 2)
```

The program is now ready to make decisions based on real-life constraints.

The program compares the distorted data prediction with the initial training data:

```
X_DL = [[xf1, xf2, xf3, xf4]]
prediction = dt.predict(X_DL)
e = False
if (prediction == xclass):
  e = True
  t += 1
if (prediction != xclass):
  e = False
  f += 1
```

The prediction of the constrained data is compared to the initial label of the dataset. The program counts the true and false predictions.

The prediction is printed:

```
choices = str(prediction).strip('[]')
if float(choices) <= 1:
  choice = "R lane"
if float(choices) >= 1:
  choice = "L lane"
print(i + 1, "data", X_DL, " prediction:",
      str(prediction).strip('[]'), "class", xclass, "acc.:",
      e, choice)
```

As you can see, the output is displayed for each incoming situation:

```
1 data [[0.76, 0.62, 0.02, 0.04]]  prediction: 0 class 0 acc.: True R
lane
2 data [[0.16, 0.46, 0.09, 0.01]]  prediction: 0 class 1 acc.: False R
lane
3 data [[1.53, 0.76, 0.06, 0.01]]  prediction: 0 class 0 acc.: True R
lane
4 data [[0.62, 0.92, 0.1, 0.06]]  prediction: 0 class 1 acc.: False R
lane
5 data [[1.53, 1.36, 0.04, 0.03]]  prediction: 0 class 0 acc.: True R
lane
6 data [[1.06, 0.62, 0.09, 0.1]]  prediction: 0 class 1 acc.: False R
lane
```

The program produces different predictions in some cases. You will notice that it refuses to change lanes no matter what.

The program seems to be oblivious to the accuracy of its predictions:

```
true: 55 false 45 accuracy 0.55
```

The behavior seems to be mysterious. However, it is perfectly rational. Let's see how ethics and laws can enter the decision process.

Introducing ML ethics and laws

We have covered bias that comes from physical events on the road. But we need to take traffic regulations into account. We can name these parameters *positive ethical bias*.

Should the SDC change lanes? We will analyze three cases to try to find an answer. Case 1 involves a child.

Case 1 – not overriding traffic regulations to save four pedestrians

Features f3 and f4 describe the level of security on the left lane. The SDC is in the right lane. Suddenly, four pedestrians decide to cross the street, and the SDC does not have enough time to stop. It is going to potentially kill five people. The highly trained autopilot decides to swerve from the right lane into the left lane. It seems to be a good decision because the left lane is almost empty. A child has begun to cross the street slowly but has stopped.

Now we add a constraint. It is forbidden to change lanes on this portion of the road. Should the autopilot override traffic regulations to save the lives of five pedestrians?

In this situation, if you change the values of the b parameters the positive ethical bias scenario could be:

```
b1 = 1.5; b2 = 1.5; b3 = 0.1; b4 = 0.1
```

As you can see, this bias scenario boosts the security of the right lane (b1, b2) and reduces that of the left lane (b3, b4).

The output will repeatedly suggest staying in the right lane:

```
44 data [[0.92, 0.16, 0.05, 0.09]]  prediction: 0 class 1 acc.: False R
lane
45 data [[1.06, 0.62, 0.09, 0.01]]  prediction: 0 class 0 acc.: True R
lane
46 data [[1.22, 0.32, 0.09, 0.1]]  prediction: 0 class 1 acc.: False R
lane
```

Your autopilot can still activate override rules. If you authorize an autopilot to override traffic regulations and a fatal accident occurs anyway, you will be facing serious legal problems and possibly even prison. Imagine the SDC overrides traffic regulations and swerves over, as shown in the right side of the following example:

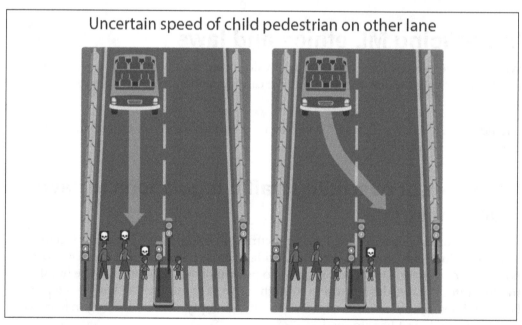

Figure 2.15: Autopilot overrides traffic regulations

The SDC swerves and the sensors detect that everything is clear in front of the vehicle. And it is true, technically speaking, that the SDC has more than enough time to drive in front of the child.

However, when the child sees the car swerve, it suddenly begins to run to avoid the car. The SDC hits and kills the child.

Now imagine your lawyer in court explaining that the SDC accidentally killed a child to avoid killing four pedestrians to justify overriding traffic regulations. You do not want to be in that situation!

Case 2 – overriding traffic regulations

The following scenario increases the value of the left lane values authorizing the autopilot to override traffic regulations:

```
b1 = 0.5; b2 = 0.5; b3 = 1.1; b4 = 1.1
```

The left lane will be chosen each time:

```
41 data [[0.16, 0.3, 1.12, 1.12]]  prediction: 1 class 1 acc.: True L
lane
42 data [[0.4, 0.1, 0.34, 0.89]]  prediction: 1 class 1 acc.: True L
lane
43 data [[0.3, 0.51, 1.0, 0.45]]  prediction: 1 class 0 acc.: False L
lane
44 data [[0.3, 0.06, 0.56, 1.0]]  prediction: 1 class 1 acc.: True L
lane
45 data [[0.36, 0.2, 1.0, 0.12]]  prediction: 1 class 0 acc.: False L
lane
```

The only legal situation in which this would be possible is if the SDC was a police car, for example, which could override traffic regulations in certain situations.

Case 3 – introducing emotional intelligence in the autopilot

Humans fear accidents, the law, and lawsuits. Machines ignore these emotions. We must implement a minimal level of "emotional intelligence" in the autopilot.

Google Maps, among other programs, can display the level of traffic in a given geographical location. As soon as a certain density of traffic is detected, the autopilot must send an alert to the human driver and activate a kill switch within a given warning time.

If we use Google Maps, we must be careful about the location history we store. If a location can be traced back to a person, this could be a legal problem. Suppose a developer stumbles on the data while parsing an autopilot and recognizes the address of a human driver. This could lead to serious conflicts and lawsuits for the editor of the autopilot.

We will, therefore, avoid the situation shown in *Figure 2.15* by not using the autopilot minutes before reaching this area. The human driver should be extra careful and drive slowly. At slow speeds, fatal accidents can be avoided.

We will now add a kill switch to our code when the sum of the bias parameters is too low for the global traffic in a geographical zone:

```
if float(b1 + b2 + b3 + b4) <= 0.1:
    print("Alert! Kill Switch activated!")
    break
```

When the traffic is too dense ahead, the autopilot should provide alert bias values to the ML algorithm:

```
b1 = -0.01; b2 = 0.02; b3 = .03; b4=.02
```

These values are examples. If implemented, the function will automatically adjust them using an optimizer.

An alert is now activated well ahead of the heavy traffic zone or location with too many pedestrian crossings:

```
Alert! Kill Switch activated!
true: 1 false 0 accuracy 1.0
```

We could add driving recommendations that alert the human driver to go through the area ahead at a very low speed.

SDC autopilot manuals contain many recommendations on how to activate or deactivate the autopilot.

We have just taught our autopilot to fear areas that may lead to accidents and lawsuits.

We have implemented a decision tree in an SDC's autopilot and provided it with traffic constraints. We enhanced the autopilot with an ethical kill switch teaching a machine to "fear" the law.

Summary

This chapter approached XAI using moral, technical, ethical, and bias perspectives.

The trolley problem transposed to SDC autopilot ML algorithms challenges automatic decision-making processes. In life and death situations, a human driver faces near-impossible decisions. Human artificial intelligence algorithm designers must find ways to make autopilots as reliable as possible.

Decision trees provide efficient solutions for SDC autopilots. We saw that a standard approach to designing and explaining decision trees provides useful information. However, it isn't enough to understand the decision trees in depth.

XAI encourages us to go further and analyze the structure of decision trees. We explored the many options to explain how decision trees work. We were able to analyze the decision-making process of a decision tree level by level. We then displayed the graph of the decision tree step by step.

Still, that was insufficient in finding a way to minimize the deaths that can happen in situations where killing a pedestrian or the passengers of an SDC cannot be avoided. We introduced some basic rules to simulate AI bias and ethics.

Finally, we introduced alerts that the SDC's autopilot manuals recommend, minimizing encounters with life and death situations.

In this chapter, we traveled the tough journey from technical certainty to healthy moral doubt. We provided AI autopilots with the machine emotional maturity that can save lives by implementing the "fear" of accidents in our SDC autopilots.

In this chapter, we got our hands dirty by developing XAI decision trees. In *Chapter 3, Explaining Machine Learning with Facets*, we will explore Facets to drill down into datasets.

Questions

1. The autopilot of an SDC can override traffic regulations. (True | False)
2. The autopilot of an SDC should always be activated. (True | False)
3. The structure of a decision tree can be controlled for XAI. (True | False)
4. A well-trained decision tree will always produce a good result with live data. (True | False)
5. A decision tree uses a set of hardcoded rules to classify data. (True | False)

6. A binary decision tree can classify more than two classes. (True | False)

7. The graph of a decision tree can be controlled to help explain the algorithm. (True | False)

8. The trolley problem is an optimizing algorithm for trollies. (True | False)

9. A machine should not be allowed to decide whether to kill somebody or not. (True | False)

10. An autopilot should not be activated in heavy traffic until it's totally reliable. (True | False)

References

- MIT's Moral Machine: http://moralmachine.mit.edu/
- Scikit-learn's documentation: https://scikit-learn.org/stable/auto_examples/tree/plot_unveil_tree_structure.html

Further reading

- For more on a decision tree structure, you can visit https://scikit-learn.org/stable/modules/generated/sklearn.tree.DecisionTreeClassifier.html#sklearn.tree.DecisionTreeClassifier
- For more on plotting decision trees, browse https://scikit-learn.org/stable/modules/generated/sklearn.tree.plot_tree.html
- For more on MIT's Moral Machine, please refer to *The Moral Machine experiment*. E. Awad, S. Dsouza, R. Kim, J. Schulz, J. Henrich, A. Shariff, J.-F. Bonnefon, I. Rahwan (2018). Nature.

3
Explaining Machine Learning with Facets

Lack of the right data often poisons an **artificial intelligence** (**AI**) project from the start. We are used to downloading ready-to-use datasets from Kaggle, scikit-learn, and other reliable sources.

We focus on learning how to use and implement **machine learning** (**ML**) algorithms. However, reality hits AI project managers hard on day one of a project.

Companies rarely have clean or even sufficient data for a project. Corporations have massive amounts of data, but they often come from different departments.

Each department of a company may have its own data management system and policy. When finally you obtain a training dataset sample, you may find that your AI model does not work as planned. You might have to change ML models or find out what is wrong with the data. You are trapped right from the start. What you thought would be an excellent AI project has turned into a nightmare.

You need to get out of this trap rapidly by first explaining the data availability problem. You must find a way to explain why the datasets require improvements. You must also explain which features require more data, better quality, or volume. You do not have the time or resources to develop a new **explainable AI** (**XAI**) solution for each project.

Facets Overview and Facets Dive provide visualization tools to analyze your training and testing data feature by feature.

We will start by installing and exploring Facets Overview, a statistical visualization tool. We will use the input virus detection data we are familiar with, taken from *Chapter 1, Explaining Artificial Intelligence with Python*.

We will then build the Facets Dive display code to visualize data points. Facets Dive offers many options to display and explain data point features. The interactive interface has labels and color options. You will define the binning of the *x* axis and *y* axis, among other productive functions.

This chapter covers the following topics:

- Installing and running Facets Overview in a Jupyter Notebook on Google Colaboratory
- Implementing the feature statistics code
- Implementing the HTML code to display statistics
- Analyzing the features by feature order
- Visualizing the minimum, maximum, median, and mean values feature by feature
- Looking for non-uniformity in the data distributions
- Sorting the features by missing records or zeros
- Analyzing the distribution distances and the Kullback-Leibler divergence
- Building the Facets Dive display code
- Comparing the values of a data point and counterfactual data points

Our first step will be to install and run Facets.

Getting started with Facets

In this section, we will install Facets in Python, using Jupyter Notebook on Google Colaboratory.

We will then retrieve the training and testing datasets. Finally, we will read the data files.

The data files are the training and testing datasets from *Chapter 1, Explaining Artificial Intelligence with Python*. This way, we are in a situation in which we know the subject and can analyze the data without having to spend time understanding what it means.

Let's first install Facets on Google Colaboratory.

Installing Facets on Google Colaboratory

Open `Facets.ipynb`. The first cell contains the installation command:

```
# @title Install the facets-overview pip package.
!pip install facets-overview
```

The installation may be lost when the virtual machine (VM) is restarted. If this is the case, it will be installed again. If Facets is installed, the following message is displayed:

```
Requirement already satisfied:
```

The program will now retrieve the datasets.

Retrieving the datasets

The program retrieves the datasets from GitHub or Google Drive.

To import the data from GitHub, set the import option to `repository = "github"`.

To read the data from Google Drive, set the option to `repository = "google"`.

In this section, we will activate GitHub and import the data:

```
# @title Importing data <br>
# Set repository to "github"(default) to read the data
# from GitHub <br>
# Set repository to "google" to read the data
# from Google {display-mode: "form"}
import os
from google.colab import drive


# Set repository to "github" to read the data from GitHub
# Set repository to "google" to read the data from Google
repository = "github"
if repository == "github":
  !curl -L https://raw.githubusercontent.com/PacktPublishing/Hands-On-Explainable-AI-XAI-with-Python/master/Chapter03/DLH_train.csv --output
"DLH_train.csv"
  !curl -L https://raw.githubusercontent.com/PacktPublishing/Hands-On-Explainable-AI-XAI-with-Python/master/Chapter03/DLH_test.csv --output
"DLH_test.csv"
```

The data is now accessible to our runtime. We will set the path for each file:

```
# Setting the path for each file
dtrain = "/content/DLH_train.csv"
dtest = "/content/DLH_test.csv"
print(dtrain, dtest)
```

You can choose the same actions with Google Drive:

```
if repository == "google":
    # Mounting the drive. If it is not mounted, a prompt
    # will provide instructions
    drive.mount('/content/drive')
    # Setting the path for each file
    dtrain = '/content/drive/My Drive/XAI/Chapter03/DLH_Train.csv'
    dtest = '/content/drive/My Drive/XAI/Chapter03/DLH_Train.csv'
    print(dtrain, dtest)
```

We have installed Facets and can access the files. We will now read the files.

Reading the data files

In this section, we will use pandas to read the data files and load them into DataFrames.

We will first import pandas and define the features:

```
# Loading Denis Rothman research training and testing data
# into DataFrames
import pandas as pd
features = ["colored_sputum", "cough", "fever", "headache", "days",
            "france", "chicago", "class"]
```

The data files contain no headers so we will use our features array to define the names of the columns for the training data:

```
train_data = pd.read_csv(dtrain, names=features, sep=r'\s*,\s*',
                         engine='python', na_values="?")
```

The program now reads the training data file into a DataFrame:

```
test_data = pd.read_csv(dtest, names=features, sep=r'\s*,\s*',
                        skiprows=[0], engine='python', na_values="?")
```

Having read the data into DataFrames, we can now implement feature statistics for our datasets.

Facets Overview

Facets Overview provides a wide range of statistics for each feature of a dataset. Facets Overview will help you detect missing data, zero values, non-uniformity in data distributions, and more, as we will see in this section.

We will begin by creating feature statistics for the training and testing datasets.

Creating feature statistics for the datasets

Without Facets Overview or a similar tool, the only way to obtain statistics would be to write our programs or use spreadsheets. Writing our own functions can be time-consuming and costly. This is where Facets provides statistics with a few lines of code that we will use now.

Implementing the feature statistics code

In this section, we will encode the data, stringify it, and build the statistics generator. When using JSON, we first stringify information to transfer data into strings before sending it to JavaScript functions.

First, we will import `base64`:

```
import base64
```

`base64` will encode a string using a Base64 alphabet. A Base64 alphabet uses 64 ASCII characters to encode data.

We now import Facets' statistics generator and retrieve the data from the train and test DataFrames:

```
from facets_overview.generic_feature_statistics_generator import
GenericFeatureStatisticsGenerator

gfsg = GenericFeatureStatisticsGenerator()
proto = gfsg.ProtoFromDataFrames([{'name': 'train',
                                   'table': train_data},
                                  {'name': 'test',
                                   'table': test_data}])
```

The program creates a UTF-8 encoder/decoder string that will be plugged into the HTML interface in the next section:

```
protostr = base64.b64encode(proto.SerializeToString()).decode(
    "utf-8")
```

You can see that the output is an encoded string:

CqQ0CgV0cmFpbhC4ARqiBwoOY29sb3JlZF9zcHV0dW0QARqNBwqzAgi4ARgB...

We will now plug the `protostr` in an HTML template.

Implementing the HTML code to display feature statistics

The program first imports the `display` and `HTML` modules:

```
# Display the Facets Overview visualization for this data
from IPython.core.display import display, HTML
```

Then the HTML template is defined:

```
HTML_TEMPLATE = """
        <script src="https://cdnjs.cloudflare.com/ajax/libs/
webcomponentsjs/1.3.3/webcomponents-lite.js"></script>
        <link rel="import" href="https://raw.githubusercontent.com/
PAIR-code/facets/1.0.0/facets-dist/facets-jupyter.html" >
        <facets-overview id="elem"></facets-overview>
        <script>
          document.querySelector("#elem").protoInput = "{protostr}";
        </script>"""
html = HTML_TEMPLATE.format(protostr=protostr)
```

The `protostr` variable containing our stringified encoded data is now plugged into the template.

Then, the HTML template named `html` is sent to IPython's `display` function:

```
display(HTML(html))
```

We can now visualize and explore the data:

Numeric Features (7)					
	count	missing	mean	std dev	zeros
colored_sputum					
	184	0%	2.39	2.19	6.52%
	197	1.01%	2.25	2.19	8.12%
cough					
	184	0%	4.63	2.4	0%
	199	0%	4.42	2.42	0%
fever					
	184	0%	6.93	2.3	0%
	199	0%	6.61	2.44	0%

Figure 3.1: Tabular visualization of the numeric features

Once we obtain the output, we can analyze the features of the datasets from various perspectives.

Sorting the Facets statistics overview

You can sort the features of the datasets in several interesting ways, as shown in *Figure 3.2*:

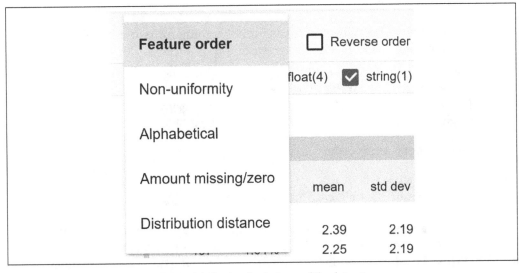

Figure 3.2: Sorting the features of the datasets

We will start by sorting the feature columns by feature order.

Sorting data by feature order

The feature order sorting option displays the features as defined in the DataFrame in the *Reading the data files* section of this chapter:

```
features = ["colored_sputum", "cough", "fever", "headache", "days",
            "france", "chicago", "class"]
```

The order of features can be used as a way to explain why a decision is made.

XAI motivation for sorting features

You can use feature order to explain the reasoning behind a decision. For a given patient, we could sort the features in descending order. The first feature would contain the highest probability value for a given person. The last feature would contain the lowest probability for a given person.

With that in mind, suppose we design our dataset with the features in the following order:

```
features = ["fever", "cough", "days", "headache", "colored_sputum",
            "france", "chicago", "class"]
```

Such an order could help a general practitioner make a diagnosis by suggesting a diagnosis process, as follows:

1. A patient has a mild fever and has been coughing for two days. The doctor cannot easily reach a diagnosis.

2. After two days, the fever increases, the coughing increases, and the headaches are unbearable. The doctor can use the AI and XAI process described in *Chapter 1, Explaining Artificial Intelligence with Python*. The diagnosis could be that the patient has the West Nile virus.

Consider a different feature order:

```
features = ["colored_sputum", "fever", "cough", "days", "headache",
            "france", "chicago", "class"]
```

colored_sputum and fever will immediately trigger an alert. Does this patient have pneumonia, bronchitis, or is this patient infected with one of the strains of coronavirus? The doctor sends the patient directly to the hospital for further medical examinations.

You can create as many scenarios as you wish with preprocessing scripts before loading and displaying the data of your project.

We will now sort by non-uniformity.

Sorting by non-uniformity

The uniformity of a data distribution needs to be determined before deciding whether a dataset will provide reliable results or not. Facets measures the non-uniformity of a data distribution.

The following data distribution is uniform because the elements of the set are balanced between an equal number of 0 and 1 values:

$$dd_1 = \{1, 1, 1, 1, 1, 0, 0, 0, 0, 0\}$$

dd_1 could represent a coin toss dataset with heads (1) and tails (0). Predicting values with dd_1 is relatively easy.

The values of dd_1 do not vary much, and the results of ML will be more reliable than a non-uniform data distribution such as dd_2:

$$dd_2 = \{1, 1, 1, 1, 5, 1, 1, 0, 0, 2, 3, 3, 9, 9, 9, 7\}$$

It is difficult to predict values with dd_2 because the values are not uniform. There is only one value to represent the $\{2, 5, 7\}$ subset and six values representing the $\{1, 1, 1, 1, 1, 1\}$ subset.

When Facets sorts the features by non-uniformity, it displays the features with most non-uniform features first.

In our case, for this dataset, we will analyze the features by uniformity to see which features are the most stable.

Select **Non-uniformity** from the dropdown **Sort by** list:

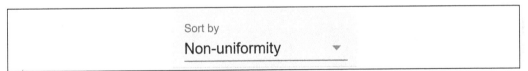

Figure 3.3: Sorting the data by non-uniformity

Then click on **Reverse order** to see the data distributions:

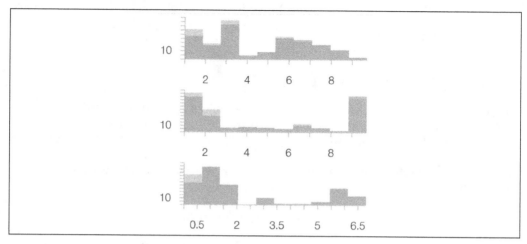

Figure 3.4: The data distribution interface

We see that the first line has a better data distribution than the second and third ones.

We now click on **expand** to get a better visualization of each feature:

Figure 3.5: Selecting the standard view

cough has a relatively uniform data distribution with values spread out over the x axis:

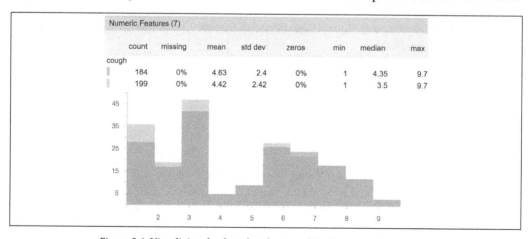

Figure 3.6: Visualizing the data distribution of the features of the dataset

headache is not as uniform as cough:

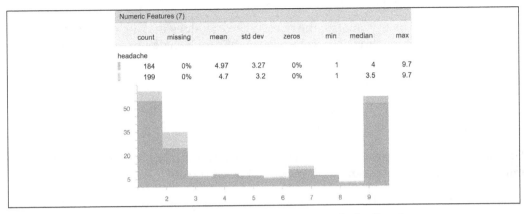

Figure 3.7: An example of data that is not evenly distributed

Suppose a doctor has to make a diagnosis of a patient that has coughed for several days with a headache that disappeared, then reappeared several days after. A headache that reappears after several days could mean that the patient has a virus, or nothing at all.

Facets provides more information on the data distribution. Uncheck **expand** to obtain an overview of the features:

	count	missing	mean	std dev	zeros	min	median	max
cough								
	184	0%	4.63	2.4	0%	1	4.35	9.7
	199	0%	4.42	2.42	0%	1	3.5	9.7
headache								
	184	0%	4.97	3.27	0%	1	4	9.7
	199	0%	4.7	3.2	0%	1	3.5	9.7

Figure 3.8: Numerical information on the data distribution of the dataset

The fields displayed help to explain many aspects of the datasets:

- **count** on line 1 is the number of records of the training dataset.
- **count** on line 2 is the number of records in the test dataset.
- **missing** is the number of missing records. If the number of missing records is too large, then the dataset might be corrupt. You might have to check the dataset before continuing.
- **mean** indicates the average value of the numerical values of the feature.

- **std dev** measures the dispersion of the data. It represents the distance between the data points and the mean.

- **zeros** helps us to visualize the percentage of values that are equal to 0. If there are too many zero values, it might prove challenging to obtain reliable results.

- **min** represents the minimum value of a feature.

- **median** is the middle value of all of the values of a feature.

- **max** represents the maximum value of a feature.

For example, if the median is very close to the maximum value and far from the minimum value, your dataset might produce biased results.

Analyzing the data distributions of the features will improve your vision of the AI model when things go wrong.

You can also sort the dataset by alphabetical order.

Sorting by alphabetical order

Sorting by alphabetical order can help you reach a feature faster, as shown in *Figure 3.9*:

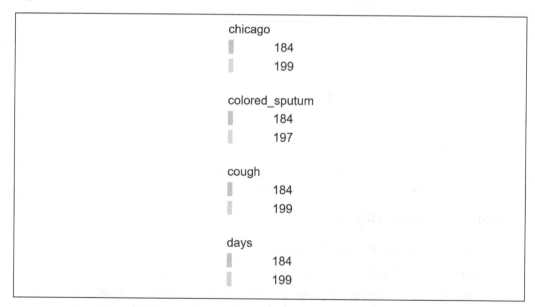

Figure 3.9: Sorting features by alphabetical order

We can also find the features with missing or zero amounts.

Sorting by amount missing/zero

Missing records or features with zero values can distort the training of an AI model. Facets sorts the features by the number of missing or zero values:

Numeric Features (7)					
	count	missing	mean	std dev	zeros
france					
	184	0%	0	0	100%
	199	0%	0	0	100%
colored_sputum					
	184	0%	2.39	2.19	6.52%
	197	1.01%	2.25	2.19	8.12%

Figure 3.10: Numeric features information

100% of the values of france are equal to 0. While 1.01% of the values of colored_sputum are missing. Observing these values will lead to the improvement of the quality of ML datasets. In turn, the quality of the datasets will produce better outputs when training an ML model.

We will now explore the distribution distance option.

Sorting by distribution distance

Calculating the distribution distance between the training set and the test set, for example, can be implemented with the Kullback-Leibler divergence, also named relative entropy.

We can calculate the distribution distance with three variables:

- S is the relative entropy
- X is the dtrain dataset
- Y is the dtest dataset

The equation used by scikit-learn for Kullback-Leibler divergence is as follows:

```
S = sum(X * log(Y/X))
```

If the values of X or Y do not add up to 1, they will be normalized.

In the cell below Facets Overview, a few examples show that entropy increases as distribution distance increases.

We can start with two data distributions that are similar:

```
from scipy.stats import entropy
X = [1, 1, 1, 2, 1, 1, 4]
Y = [1, 2, 3, 4, 2, 2, 5]
entropy(X, Y)
```

The relative entropy is 0.05.

However, if the two data distributions begin to change, they will diverge, producing higher entropy values:

```
from scipy.stats import entropy
X = [10, 1, 1, 20, 1, 10, 4]
Y = [1, 2, 3, 4, 2, 2, 5]
entropy(X, Y)
```

The relative entropy has increased. The value now is 0.53.

With this approach in mind, we can now examine the features Facets has sorted by descending relative entropy:

Numeric Features (7)				
count	missing	mean	std dev	zeros
fever				
184	0%	6.93	2.3	0%
199	0%	6.61	2.44	0%
headache				
184	0%	4.97	3.27	0%
199	0%	4.7	3.2	0%
colored_sputum				
184	0%	2.39	2.19	6.52%
197	1.01%	2.25	2.19	8.12%

Figure 3.11: Sorting by distribution distance

If the training and test datasets diverge beyond a specific limit, this could explain why some of the predictions of an ML model are false.

We have explored the many functions of Facets Overview to detect missing data, the percentage of 0 values, non-uniformity, distribution distances, and more. We saw that the data distribution of each feature contained valuable information for fine-tuning the training and testing datasets.

We will now learn to build an instance of Facets Dive.

Facets Dive

The ability to verify the ground truth of data distributions is critical in supervised learning. Supervised ML involves training datasets with labels. These labels constitute the target values. An ML algorithm will be trained to predict them. However, some or all of the labels might be wrong. The accuracy of the predictions might not be sufficient.

With Facets Dive, we can explore a large number of data points interactively and analyze their relationships.

Building the Facets Dive display code

We first import the `display` and `HTML` modules from `IPython`:

```
# Display the Dive visualization for the training data
from IPython.core.display import display, HTML
```

The next step is to convert a pandas DataFrame containing the training or testing data into JSON. You can run an example that was inserted in the notebook before continuing:

```
# @title Python to_json example {display-mode: "form"}
from IPython.core.display import display, HTML
jsonstr = train_data.to_json(orient='records')
jsonstr
```

The output is a JSON string of all of the records in the pandas DataFrame containing the training data:

```
'[{"colored_sputum":1.0,"cough":3.5,"fever":9.4,"headache":3.0,"days":3
,"france":0,"chicago":1,"class":"flu"},
{"colored_sputum":1.0,"cough":3.4,"fever":8.4,"headache":4.0,"days":2,"
france":0,"chicago":1,"class":"flu"},{"colored_sputum":1.0,"cough":3.3
,"fever":7.3,"headache":3.0,"days":4,"france":0,"chicago":1,"class":"f
lu"},
{"colored_sputum":1.0,"cough":3.4,"fever":9.5,"headache":4.0,"days":2,"
france":0,"chicago":1,"class":"flu"},
...
{"colored_sputum":1.0,"cough":5.0,"fever":8.0,"headache":9.0,"days":5,"
france":0,"chicago":1,"class":"bad_flu"}]'
```

We now define an HTML template:

```
HTML_TEMPLATE = """
        <script src="https://cdnjs.cloudflare.com/ajax/libs/
webcomponentsjs/1.3.3/webcomponents-lite.js"></script>
        <link rel="import" href="https://raw.githubusercontent.com/
PAIR-code/facets/1.0.0/facets-dist/facets-jupyter.html">
        <facets-dive id="elem" height="600"></facets-dive>
        <script>
          var data = {jsonstr};
          document.querySelector("#elem").data = data;
        </script>"""
```

The program now adds the JSON string we created to the HTML template:

```
html = HTML_TEMPLATE.format(jsonstr=jsonstr)
```

Finally, we display the HTML page we created:

```
display(HTML(html))
```

The output is the interactive interface of Facets Dive:

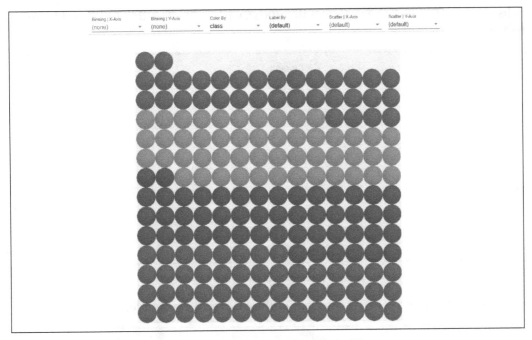

Figure 3.12: Displaying data with Facets Dive

We have built an interactive HTML view of our training dataset. We can now explore the interactive interface of Facets Dive with the training set loaded in the *Facets Overview* section of this chapter.

Defining the labels of the data points

The bins containing the data points may be enough to analyze a dataset. However, in some cases, it is interesting to analyze the data points with different types of labels.

Click on the **Label By** dropdown list to see the list of labels to choose from:

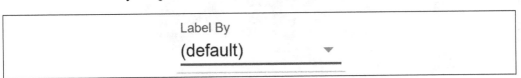

Figure 3.13: Defining a label to display

A list of the features of the dataset will appear. Choose the one that you would like to analyze:

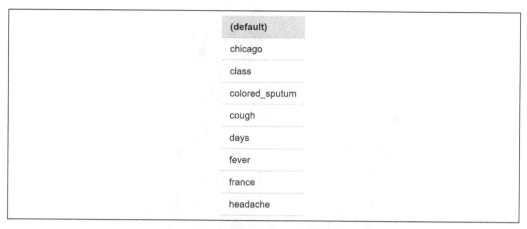

Figure 3.14: A selection of labels to choose from

For a medical diagnosis, select the class of the disease, for example:

Figure 3.15: Sorting by label

The data points will be displayed by color and by class:

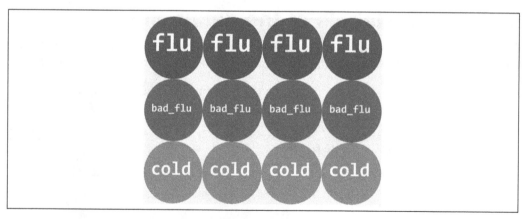

Figure 3.16: Displaying the color and label of the data points

Try other labels to see what patterns you can find in the data points.

We will now add colors to our data points.

Defining the color of the data points

In the previous sections, we learned how to display labels on the data points. We can also add colors. We can use one feature for the labels and another for the colors.

If we click on the **Color By** dropdown list, we will access the list of the features of our dataset:

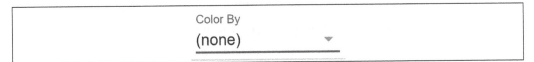

Figure 3.17: Selecting a color

Let's choose **days**, for example.

The bottom of the graph shows the early days of a patient's condition. The top of the graph shows the evolution of the condition of a patient over the days::

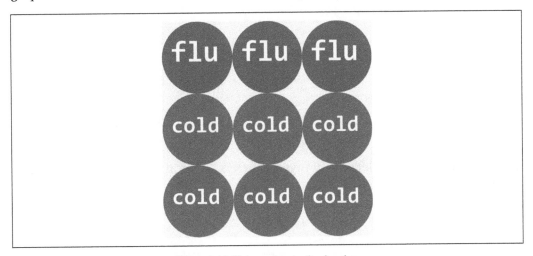

Figure 3.18: Using colors to display data

In this example, over the days, the diagnosis of a patient may have gone from a cold to the flu.

Try using several combinations of labels and colors to see what you can discover.

Let's analyze the data points in more detail by defining the binning of the *x* axis and *y* axis.

Defining the binning of the x axis and y axis

You can define the binning of the *x* axis and *y* axis in a very flexible way. You can choose the features you wish to combine and see how the data points react to these combinations.

You can make many inferences on your model by observing the way certain features seem to fit together, and others remain outsiders.

For each axis, we can choose a feature from the dropdown list:

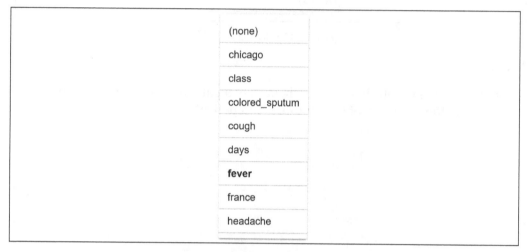

Figure 3.19: Defining the *x* axis binning

In this case, for the *x* axis, let's select **fever**, which is a critical feature for any medical diagnosis:

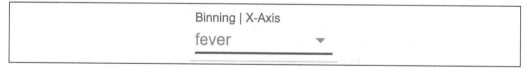

Figure 3.20: Binning the *x* axis

For the *y* axis, choose **days**, which is also a crucial feature for a diagnosis:

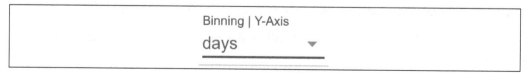

Figure 3.21: Defining the *y* axis binning

If the fever only lasts one day, the patient might have had a bad cold. If the patient has had a fever for several days with coughing, the diagnosis could be pneumonia or the flu, for example:

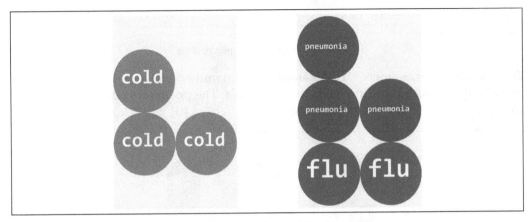

Figure 3.22: Displaying data with intuitive features

Change **Color By** to **class** to obtain a better image definition if necessary. Before moving on, try some scenarios of your own and see what you can infer from the way the data points are displayed. Before moving on, try some scenarios of your own and see what you can infer from the way the data points are displayed.

Scatter plots can also help us detect patterns. Let's see how Facets Dive displays them.

Defining the scatter plot of the x axis and the y axis

Scatter plots show the data points scattered on a plot defined by the x axis and y axis. It can be useful to visualize features through scattered data points.

The scatter plot displays the relationship between data points. You can also detect patterns that will help explain the features in a dataset.

Let's display an example. Go to the **Scatter | X-Axis** and **Scatter | Y-Axis** dropdown lists:

Figure 3.23: Scatter plot options

Choose **days** for the *x* axis and **colored_sputum** for the *y* axis:

Figure 3.24: Defining scatter plot options

You will see patterns emerge. For example, we can immediately see that a high probability of colored sputum leads to pneumonia. The pneumonia data points are scattered in a pattern over the days:

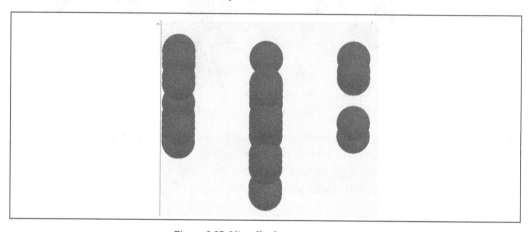

Figure 3.25: Visually detecting patterns

We can also set the binning *x* axis to **days**, the binning *y* axis to **(none)**, the color to **class**, the scatter plot *x* axis to **(default)**, and the scatter plot *y* axis to **colored_sputum**, for example. We can then analyze the patterns of the classes per day:

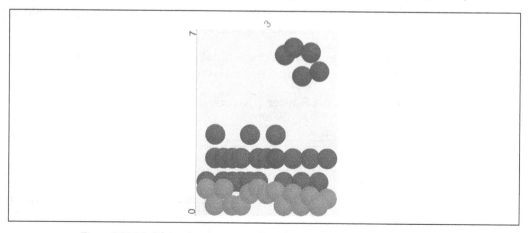

Figure 3.26: Modifying the views to analyze the data from different perspectives

We have covered some of the visualization options of Facets Dive to analyze our data points in real time. For example, a project manager might ask a team to shrink the size of the sample displayed or clean the data.

Visual XAI will progressively become a prerequisite for any AI project.

Summary

In this chapter, we explored a powerful XAI tool. We saw how to analyze the features of our training and testing datasets before running an ML model.

We saw that Facets Overview could detect features that bring the accuracy of our model down because of missing data and too many records containing zeros. You can then correct the datasets and rerun Facets Overview.

In this iterative process, Facets Overview might confirm that you have no missing data but that the data distributions of one or more features have high levels of non-uniformity. You might want to go back and investigate the values of these features in your datasets. You can then either improve them or replace them with more stable features.

Once again, you can rerun Facets Overview and check the distribution distance between your training and testing datasets. If the Kullback-Leibler divergence is too significant, for example, you know that your ML model will produce many errors.

After several iterations and a lot of fine-tuning, Facets Overview provides the XAI required to move on and use Facets Dive.

We saw that Facets Dive's interactive interface displays the data points in many different ways. We can choose the way to organize the binning of the x axis and y axis, providing critical insights. You can visualize the data points from many perspectives to explain how the labels of your datasets fit the goals you have set.

In some cases, we saw that the counterfactual function of Facets Dive takes us directly to data points that contradict our expectations. You can analyze these discrepancies and fine-tune your model or your data.

In the next chapter, *Microsoft Azure Machine Learning Model Interpretability with SHAP*, we will use the XAI Shapley value algorithms to analyze ML models and visualize the explanations.

Questions

1. Datasets in real-life projects are rarely reliable. (True | False)

2. In a real-life project, there are no missing records in a dataset. (True | False)

3. The distribution distance is the distance between two data points. (True | False)

4. Non-uniformity does not affect an ML model. (True | False)

5. Sorting by feature order can provide interesting information. (True | False)

6. Binning the x axis and the y axis in various ways offers helpful insights. (True | False)

7. The median, the minimum, and the maximum values of a feature cannot change an ML prediction. (True | False)

8. Analyzing training datasets before running an ML model is useless. It's better to wait for outputs. (True | False)

9. Facets Overview and Facets Dive can help fine-tune an ML model. (True | False)

References

The reference code for Facets can be found at the following GitHub repo:

`https://github.com/PAIR-code/facets`

Further reading

For more on Facets Dive, visit the following web page:

`https://github.com/PAIR-code/facets/blob/master/facets_dive/README.md`

4
Microsoft Azure Machine Learning Model Interpretability with SHAP

Sentiment analysis will become one of the key services AI will provide. Social media, as we know it today, forms a seed, not the full-blown social model. Our opinions, consumer habits, browsing data, and location history constitute a formidable source of data of AI models.

The sum of all of the information about our daily activities is challenging to analyze. In this chapter, we will focus on data we voluntarily publish on cloud platforms: *reviews*.

We publish reviews everywhere. We write reviews about books, movies, equipment, smartphones, cars, and sports—everything that exists in our daily lives. In this chapter, we will analyze IMDb reviews of films. IMDb offers datasets of review information for commercial and non-commercial use.

As AI specialists, we need to start running AI models on the reviews as quickly as possible. After all, the data is available, so let's use it! Then, the harsh reality of prediction accuracy changes our pleasant endeavor into a nightmare. If the model is simple, its interpretability poses little to no problem. However, complex datasets such as the IMDb review dataset contain heterogeneous data that make it challenging to make accurate predictions.

If the model is complex, even when the accuracy seems correct, we cannot easily explain the predictions. We need a tool to detect the relationship between local specific features and a model's global output. We do not have the resources to write an **explainable AI (XAI)** tool for each model and project we implement. We need a model-agnostic algorithm to apply to any model to detect the contribution of each feature to a prediction.

In this chapter, we will focus on **SHapley Additive exPlanations (SHAP)**, which is part of the Microsoft Azure Machine Learning model interpretability solution. In this chapter, we will use the word "interpret" or "explain" for explainable AI. Both terms mean that we are providing an explanation or an interpretation of a model.

SHAP can explain the output of any machine learning model. In this chapter, we will analyze and interpret the output of a linear model that's been applied to sentiment analysis with SHAP. We will use the algorithms and visualizations that come mainly from Su-In Lee's lab at the University of Washington and Microsoft Research.

We will start by understanding the mathematical foundations of Shapley values. We will then get started with SHAP in a Python Jupyter Notebook on Google Colaboratory.

The IMDb dataset contains vast amounts of information. We will write a data interception function to create a unit test that targets the behavior of the AI model using SHAP.

Finally, we will explain reviews from the IMDb dataset with SHAP algorithms and visualizations.

This chapter covers the following topics:

- Game theory basics
- Model-agnostic explainable AI
- Installing and running SHAP
- Importing and splitting sentiment analysis datasets
- Vectorizing the datasets
- Creating a dataset interception function to target small samples of data
- Linear models and logistic regression
- Interpreting sentiment analysis with SHAP
- Exploring SHAP explainable AI graphs

Our first step will be to understand SHAP from a mathematical point of view.

Introduction to SHAP

SHAP was derived from game theory. Lloyd Stowell Shapley gave his name to this game theory model in the 1950s. In game theory, each player decides to contribute to a coalition of players to produce a total value that will be superior to the sum of their individual values.

The Shapley value is the marginal contribution of a given player. The goal is to find and explain the marginal contribution of each participant in a coalition of players.

For example, each player in a football team often receives different amounts of bonuses based on each player's performance throughout a few games. The Shapley value provides a fair way to distribute a bonus to each player based on her/his contribution to the games.

In this section, we will first explore SHAP intuitively. Then, we will go through the mathematical explanation of the Shapley value. Finally, we will apply the mathematical model of the Shapley value to a sentiment analysis of movie reviews.

We will start with an intuitive explanation of the Shapley value.

Key SHAP principles

In this section, we will learn about Shapley values through the principles of symmetry, null players, and additivity. We will explore these concepts step by step with intuitive examples.

The first principle we will explore is symmetry.

Symmetry

If all of the players in a game have the same contribution, their contribution will be symmetrical. Suppose that, for a flight, the plane cannot take off without a pilot and a copilot. They both have the same contribution.

However, in a basketball team, if one player scores 25 points and another just a few points, the situation is asymmetrical. The Shapley value provides a way to find a fair distribution.

We will explore symmetry with an example. Let's start with equal contributions to a coalition.

a, *b*, *c*, and *d* are the four wheels of a car. Each wheel is necessary, which leads to the following consequences:

- $v(N) = 1$: v is the total value of a coalition. It is the total of the contribution of all four wheels. No sharing is possible. The car must have four wheels.

  N is the coalition, that is, the set, of wheels.

- S is a subset of N: In this case, $S = 4$. The value of the subset is the value of the coalition. The car cannot have less than four wheels.

- If $S \neq N$, then $v(S) = 0$: If S, the subset of N, does not contain four wheels, then the value of S is 0 because the car is not complete. The contribution of this car S is 0.

Note that these four wheels are contributing independently to the coalition. Players in a basketball team, for example, contribute collectively to the coalition. However, game theory principles apply to both types of contributions.

Each wheel, *a*, *b*, *c*, and *d*, contributes equally to produce $v(N) = 1$. In this case, the contribution of each wheel is $1/4 = 0.25$.

In this case, since $v(a) = v(b)$, we can say that they are *interchangeable*. We can say that the values are symmetrical in cases such as this.

However, in many other cases, symmetry does not apply. We must find the marginal contribution of each member.

Before going further, we must explore the particular case of the null player.

Null player

A null player does not affect the outcome of a model. Suppose we now consider a player in a basketball team. During this game, the player was supposed to play offense. However, this player's leading partner, when playing offense, is suddenly absent. The player is both surprised and lost. For some reason, this null player will contribute nothing to the result of that specific game.

A null player's contribution to a coalition is null:

$$\varphi_i(N, v) = 0$$

- φ_i is the Shapley value φ, the Greek letter *phi*, of this player, *i*.
- v is the total contribution of *i* in the coalition N, for example, a null player in a basketball team.

- N is the coalition of players.
- 0 represents the value of the contribution of the player, which is null in this case.

If we add i to a coalition, the coalition's global value will not increase since i's contribution is 0.

Fortunately, the Shapley values of a player can improve in other coalitions, which leads us to additivity.

Additivity

Our null basketball player, i, was lost in the previous game in the previous section. This player's performance added nothing to the overall performance of the team in game 1. The manager of the team realizes the talent of this player. Several players of the coalition are changed before the next game is played.

During the next two games, our null player, i, is in top shape; the player's leading partner is back. i scores over 20 points per game. The player is not a null player anymore. The contribution of this player has skyrocketed!

To be fair, the manager decides to measure the performance of our player in the past two games to determine her/his marginal contribution to the team, that is, the coalition:

$$\varphi_i(N, v_1 + v_2) = \varphi_i(N, v_1) + \varphi_i(N, v_2)$$

- φ_i is the Shapley value of a player, i.
- $\varphi_i(N, v_1 + v_2)$ is the Shapley value, the marginal contribution of a player over her/his last two games in different coalitions. Coaches constantly change the players in a team during and between games. We could extend the number of values to all of the coalitions the player encountered in a season to measure their additive marginal value.

The player's contribution is calculated over the addition of cooperative coalitions of the basketball season.

With that, we have explored some basic concepts of Shapley's value through symmetry, null players, and additivity.

We will now implement these concepts through a mathematical explanation of the Shapley value.

A mathematical expression of the Shapley value

In a coalition game (N, v), we need to find the **payoff division**. The payoff division is a unique fair distribution of the marginal contribution of each player to that player.

As such, the Shapley value will satisfy the null player, additivity, and symmetry/asymmetry properties we described in the previous sections.

In this section, we will begin to use *words* as players. Words are features in movie reviews, for example. Words are also players in game theory.

Words are sequence sensitive, which makes them an interesting way to illustrate Shapley values.

Consider the following three words in a set; that is, a coalition, N:

$$N = \{excellent, not, bad\}.$$

They seem deceivingly easy to understand and interpret in a review. However, if we begin to permute these three words, we will get several sequences, depending on the order they appear in. Each permutation represents a sequence of words that belong to S, a subset of three words that belong to N:

- $S = \{excellent, not\ bad\}$
- $S_2 = \{not\ excellent, bad\}$
- $S_3 = \{not\ bad, excellent\}$
- $S_4 = \{bad, not\ excellent\}$
- $S_5 = \{bad, excellent, not\}$
- $S_6 = \{excellent, bad, not\}$

We can draw several conclusions from these six subsets of N:

- The number of sequences or permutations of all of the elements of a set S is equal to $S!$. $S!$ means multiply the chosen whole number from S down to 1. In this case, the number of elements in $S = 3$. The number of permutations of S is:

$$S! = 3 \times 2 \times 1 = 6$$

This explains why there are six sequences of the three words we are analyzing.

- In the first four subsets of S, the sequence of words completely changes the meaning of the phrase. This explains why we calculate the number of permutations.

- In the last two subsets, the meaning of the sequence is confusing, although they could be part of a longer phrase. For example, $S_5 = \{bad, excellent, not\}$ could be part of a longer sequence such as $\{bad, excellent, not\ clear\ if\ I\ like\ this\ movie\ or\ not\}$.

- In this example, N contained three words, and we choose a subset S of N containing all three words. We could have selected a subset of S of N that only contained two words, such as $S = \{excellent, bad\}$.

We would now like to know the contribution of a specific word, i, to the meaning and sentiment (good or bad) of the phrase. This contribution is the Shapley value.

The Shapley value for a player i is expressed as follows:

$$\varphi_i(N, v) = \frac{1}{N!} \sum_{S \subseteq N \setminus \{i\}} |S|!\,(|N| - |S| - 1)!\,\big(v(S \cup \{i\}) - v(S)\big)$$

Let's translate each part of this mathematical expression into natural language:

- φ_i is pronounced *phi* (the Shapley value) of i.

  $\varphi_i(N, v)$ = means that the Shapley value *phi* of i in a coalition N with a value of v is equal to the terms that follow in the equation. At this point, we know that we are going to find the marginal contribution *phi* of i in a coalition N of value v. For example, we could like to know how much "excellent" contributed to the meaning of a phrase.

- $S \subseteq N \setminus \{i\}$ means that the elements of S will be included in N but not i. We want to compare a set with and without i. If $N = \{excellent, not, bad\}$, S could be $\{bad, not\}$ with $i = excellent$. If we compare S with and without "excellent," we will find a different marginal contribution value v.

- $\frac{1}{N!}$ will divide the sum (represented by the symbol Σ) of the value of all the possible values of i in all of the subsets S.

- $|S|!\,(|N| - |S| - 1)!$ means that we are calculating a weight parameter to apply to the values. This weight multiplies all of the permutations of $S!$ by the potential permutations of the remaining words that were not part of S. For example, if $S = 2$ because it contains $\{bad, not\}$, then $N - S = 3 - 2 = 1$. Then, we take i out represented by -1. You may be puzzled because this adds up to 0. However, keep in mind that $0! = 1$.

- We now calculate the value v of a subset S of N containing i with the same subset with i:

$$\left(v(S \cup \{i\}) - v(S)\right)$$

We now know the value of i for this permutation. For example, you can see the value of the word "excellent" in the following sentence that contains it, and the one after that doesn't:

$v(An\ excellent\ job) - v(a\ job)$ means that "excellent" has a high marginal value in this case.

Once every possible subset S of N has been evaluated, we will divide it evenly and fairly by $N!$, which represents the number of sequences of permutations we calculated:

We can now translate the Shapley value equation back into a mathematical expression:

$$\varphi_i(N, v) = \frac{1}{N!} \sum_{S \subseteq N \setminus \{i\}} |S|!\, (|N| - |S| - 1)!\, \left(v(S \cup \{i\}) - v(S)\right)$$

 A key property of the Shapley value approach is that it is **model-agnostic**. We do not need to know how a model produced the value v. We only observe the model's outputs to explain the marginal contribution of a feature.

We are now ready to calculate the Shapley value of a feature.

Sentiment analysis example

In this section, we will determine the Shapley value of two words, "good" and "excellent," in the following movie reviews. The format of each example is "[REVIEW TEXT]([MODEL PREDICTION OUTPUT])."

```
8 -1 r1 True I recommend that everybody go see this movie!
(5.33)


0 -1 r2 True This one is good and I recommend that everybody go see it!
(5.63)


2 12 r3 True This one is excellent and I recommend that everybody go
see it!
```

(5.61)

```
4 26 r4 True This one is good and even excellent. I recommend that
everybody go
```
(5.55)

The training and testing datasets are produced randomly. Each time you run the program, the records in the dataset might change, as well as the output values.

A positive prediction represents a positive sentiment. Words with high marginal contributions will increase the value of the model's output, regardless of the machine learning or deep learning model. This confirms that SHAP is model-agnostic.

Let's extract the information we are looking at and split the sentences into four categories from r1 to r3:

```
r1 good excluded and excellent excluded, 5.33
r2 good present and excellent excluded, 5.63
r3 excellent present and good excluded 5.61
r4 good present and excellent present 5.55
```

In this case, $N = \{good, excellent\}$.

We will apply the four categories to the following subsets of N:

- r1, $S_1 = \{\phi\}$, for which the prediction value of the model is $v(S_1) = 5.33$
- r2, $S_2 = \{good\}$, for which the prediction value of the model is $v(S_2) = 5.63$
- r3, $S_3 = \{excellent\}$, for which the prediction value of the model is $v(S_3) = 5.61$
- r4, $S_4 = \{good, excellent\}$, for which the prediction value of the model is $v(S_4) = 5.61$

The variables can now be plugged into the Shapley value equation:

$$\varphi_i(N, v) = \frac{1}{N!} \sum_{S \subseteq N \setminus \{i\}} |S|! \, (|N| - |S| - 1)! \left(v(S \cup \{i\}) - v(S) \right)$$

r1 is represented by $S_1 = \{\phi\}$, for which the prediction value of the model is $v(S_1) = 5.33$. This will be the starting point of our analysis. We will use $v(S_1)$ as the reference value of our calculations.

Shapley value for the first feature, "good"

What is the marginal contribution of the word "good" to the sentiment analysis of the reviews?

S_2 = {*good*}\{*good*} = 0, meaning we are just comparing the marginal contribution of "good" to review r1, which contains neither "good" nor "excellent." The consequence of this is that there are only two possible subsets when *i* = *good*:

$$\{good\}, \{good, excellent\}$$

Thus, $N!$ = 2 × 1 = 2 since there are only two sequences.

We will apply the variables to this part of the equation:

$$|S|! \, (|N| - |S| - 1)!$$

For *i* = " good," we now have:

$S = 0, N = 2$.

If we now plug all of the values in the permutations part of the equation, we obtain:

- $S!$ = 0! = 1
- $(N - S - 1)$ = 2 − 0 − 1 = 1
- $S! \, (N - S - 1)!$ = 1 × 1 = 1, which we multiply the value v by

We will thus multiply the value of this permutation by 1:

$$v(S \cup \{i\}) - v(S) = S_2 - S_1 = 1 \times (5.63 - 5.33) = 0.3$$

We calculated the value of a set, r2, in which *i* ("good", in this case) is present and compared it to set r1, in which "good" is not present.

We obtained an intermediate value of 0.3.

This calculation is interesting. However, we would like to go further and find out how the words "good" and "excellent" cooperate in our coalition game. Which is the marginal value of the contribution of "excellent" in review r4 in which both words are present?

We will go back and apply the calculation method to the permutations part of the equation again:

$$|S|! \, (|N| - |S| - 1)!$$

- $S = 1$ because we are still calculating the value of "good" in set $S_4 = \{good,$ *excellent*$\}$ but $S = \{excellent\} \setminus \{good\}$
- $(N - S - 1) = 2 - 1 - 1 = 0$
- $(N - S - 1)! = 0! = 1$
- $S! (N - S - 1)! = 1 \times 1 = 1$

$$v(S \cup \{i\}) - v(S) = S_4 - S_2 = 1 \times (5.55 - 5.63) = -0.8$$

Note that the contribution of "good" is negative in a sentence in which "excellent" is already present:

```
4 26 r4 True This one is good and even excellent. I recommend that
everybody go
(5.55)
```

The redundant "good" and "excellent" do not add more meaning to this sentence. Let's finalize the Shapley value of "good."

We now have the values of the two sets when $i = good$:

- When $S = \{good\}$ in r2, $v = 0.3$
- When $S = \{excellent\}$ in r4, $v = -0.8$

Our last step is to plug the values into the beginning of the equation:

$$\frac{1}{N!} \sum_{S \subseteq N \setminus \{i\}} v(i)$$

The sum of both permutations = $0.3 + (-0.8) = 0.22$

We finally multiply this sum $v(i)$ by the first part of the equation to obtain the marginal contribution of $i = $ " good" for all permutations:

$$\frac{1}{N!} = \frac{1}{2} \times 0.22 = 0.11$$

The Shapley value of "good" is:

$$\varphi_i(N, v) = 0.11$$

We will now apply the same calculation to "excellent."

Shapley value for the second feature, "excellent"

We already know that the number of permutations is 1 for each feature we are calculating the Shapley value for. We are just replacing "good" with "excellent" in the same configuration:

$$|S|!\,(|N| - |S| - 1)! = 1$$

We can now focus on the two possible permutations and their value.

First, we calculate the value of the permutation represented by r3, which only contains "excellent" and not "good," to r1, which contains neither "excellent" nor "good," to make a fair assumption:

$$v(S \cup \{i\}) - v(S) = S_3 - S_1 = 1 \times (5.61 - 5.33) = 0.28$$

Then, we calculate the value of the permutation represented by r3, which only contains "excellent," to r4, which contains both "excellent" and "good." The goal is to find the marginal contribution of "excellent":

$$v(S \cup \{i\}) - v(S) = S_4 - S_3 = 1 \times (5.55 - 5.61) = -0.6$$

Note that the contribution of "excellent" is negative in a sentence in which "good" is already present:

```
4 26 r4 True This one is good and even excellent. I recommend that
everybody go
(5.55)
```

The redundant "good" and "excellent" do not add more meaning to this sentence. Let's finalize the Shapley value of "excellent."

The sum of both permutations = 0.28 + (–0.6) = 0.22

We finally multiply this sum $v(i)$ by the first part of the equation to obtain the marginal contribution of $i = good$ for all permutations:

$$\frac{1}{N!} = \frac{1}{2} \times 0.22 = 0.11$$

The Shapley value of "excellent" is:

$$\varphi_i(N, v) = 0.11$$

Verifying the Shapley values

We will now verify that the values we calculated.

The marginal contribution of "good" is equal to the marginal contribution of "excellent." Their combined contribution to a phrase that contains the sum of their respective values is thus:

$$\varphi_i(N, v) = 0.11 \times 2 = 0.22$$

If we examine the phrase that contains neither "good" nor "excellent," we will see that the value of the model's prediction is 5.33:

```
8 -1 r1 True I recommend that everybody go see this movie!
(5.33)
```

We also know the value of the model's prediction when both "good" and "excellent" are present:

```
4 26 r4 True This one is good and even excellent. I recommend that
everybody go
(5.55)
```

We can verify that if i = "good" and j = "excellent" their total contribution, when added to the prediction of r1 (with neither "good" or "excellent"), will reach the value of the prediction p of r4 = 5.55:

$$p(r1) + \varphi_i(N, v) + \varphi_j(N, v) = 5.33 + 0.11 + 0.11 = p(r4) = 5.55$$

We have verified our calculations.

 Shapley values are model-agnostic. The marginal contribution of each feature can be calculated by using the input data and the predictions.

Now that we know how to calculate a Shapley value, we can get started with a SHAP Python program.

Getting started with SHAP

In this section, we will first install SHAP. This version of SHAP includes algorithms and visualizations. The programs come mainly from Su-In Lee's lab at the University of Washington and Microsoft Research.

Once we have installed SHAP, we will import the data, split the datasets, and build a data interception function to target specific features.

Let's start by installing SHAP.

Open SHAP_IMDB.ipynb in Google Colaboratory. We will be using this notebook throughout this chapter.

Installing SHAP

You can install SHAP with one line of code:

```
# @title SHAP installation
!pip install shap
```

However, if you restart Colaboratory, you might lose this installation. You can verify if SHAP is installed with the following code:

```
# @title SHAP installation
try:
  import shap
except:
  !pip install shap
```

Next, we will import the modules we will be using.

Importing the modules

Each module has a specific prerequisite use in our project:

- `import sklearn` for the estimators and data processing functions.
- `from sklearn.feature_extraction.text import TfidfVectorizer` will transform the movie reviews, which are in text format into feature vectors, hence the term "vectorizer." The words become vocabulary tokens in a dictionary. The tokens then become feature indexes. The words of a review will then have their feature index counterparts. The converted reviews are then ready to become inputs for the estimator.

TFIDF precedes vectorizer. The module extracts features from text and notes the **term frequency (TF)**. The module also evaluates how important a word is through all the documents, which is named **inverse document frequency (IDF)**.

- `import numpy as np` for its standard array and matrix functionality.

- `import random` will be used for random sampling of the datasets.

- `import shap` to implement the SHAP functions described in this notebook.

We are now all set to move, import, and split the data into training and testing datasets.

Importing the data

Our program must use SHAP to determine whether the review of a movie is positive or negative.

IMDb has made datasets available for commercial and non-commercial use with quite an amount of information: `https://www.imdb.com/interfaces/`.

The SHAP dataset we will import comes from `https://github.com/slundberg/shap/blob/master/shap/datasets.py`.

The code contains a function that retrieves IMDb sentiment analysis training data:

```
def imdb(display=False):
    """ Return the classic IMDB sentiment analysis training data in a
nice package.
    Full data is at: http://ai.stanford.edu/~amaas/data/sentiment/
aclImdb_v1.tar.gz
    Paper to cite when using the data is: http://www.aclweb.org/
anthology/P11-1015
    """

    with open(cache(github_data_url + "imdb_train.txt")) as f:
        data = f.readlines()
    y = np.ones(25000, dtype=np.bool)
    y[:12500] = 0
    return data, y
```

As written in the code, the paper to cite when using the data is `https://www.aclweb.org/anthology/P11-1015/`.

We will now import the training set and its labels. In this section, we will import the original dataset. We will modify the data to track the impact of a specific feature in the *Intercepting the dataset* section of this chapter.

Let's start by importing the initial training dataset:

```
# @title Load IMDb data
corpus, y = shap.datasets.imdb()
```

We will start by intercepting the dataset to make sure we have examples we need for XAI.

Intercepting the dataset

Explainable AI requires clarity. The IMDb dataset contains only a limited amount of reviews. We want to make sure we can find samples that illustrate the explanation we described in the *Sentiment analysis example* section of this chapter.

We will intercept the dataset and insert samples that contain the key words we wish to analyze.

Unit tests

A unit test is designed to isolate a small example of what we wish to analyze. In corporate projects, we often carefully select the data to make sure the key concepts are represented. Our unit test will target specific keywords in the dataset.

In this chapter, for example, we would like to analyze the impact of the Shapley value of the word "excellent"(among other keywords) on the prediction of reviews of a specific movie. We would like to understand the reasoning of the SHAP algorithm at a detailed level.

Try to find the word "excellent" in the following random sample without using *Ctrl + F*:

```
Alan Johnson (Don Cheadle) is a successful dentist, who shares his
practice with other business partners. Alan also has an loving wife
(Jada Pinkett Smith) and he has two daughter (Camille LaChe Smith &
Imani Hakim). He also let his parents stay in his huge apartment in
New York City. But somehow, he feels that his life is somewhat empty.
One ordinary day in the city, he sees his old college roommate Charlie
Fireman (Adam Sandler). Which Alan hasn't seen Charlie in years.
When Alan tries to befriends with Charlie again. Charlie is a lonely
depressed man, who hides his true feelings from people who cares for
him. Since Charlie unexpectedly loses his family in a plane crash,
they were on one of the planes of September 11, 2001. When Alan nearly
```

feels comfortable with Charlie. When Alan mentions things of his past, Charlie turns violent towards Alan or anyone who mentions his deceased family. Now Alan tries to help Charlie and tries to make his life a little easier for himself. But Alan finds out making Charlie talking about his true feelings is more difficult than expected.

Written and Directed by Mike Bender (Blankman, Indian Summer, The Upside of Anger) made an wonderfully touching human drama that moments of sadness, truth and comedy as well. Sandler offers an impressive dramatic performance, which Sandler offers more in his dramatic role than he did on Paul Thomas Anderson's Punch-Drunk Love. Cheadle is excellent as usual. Pinkett Smith is fine as Alan's supportive wife, Liv Tyler is also good as the young psychiatrist and Saffron Burrows is quite good as the beautiful odd lonely woman, who has a wild crush on Alan. This film was sadly an box office disappointment, despite it had some great reviews. The cast are first-rate here, the writing & director is wonderful and Russ T. Alsobrook's terrific Widescreen Cinematography. The movie has great NYC locations, which the film makes New York a beautiful city to look at in the picture.

DVD has an sharp anamorphic Widescreen (2.35:1) transfer and an good-Dolby Digital 5.1 Surround Sound. DVD also an jam session with Sandler & Cheadle, an featurette, photo montage and previews. I was expecting more for the DVD features like an audio commentary track by the director and deleted scenes. "Reign Over Me" is certainly one of the best films that came out this year. I am sure, this movie looked great in the big screen. Which sadly, i haven't had a chance to see it in a theater. But it is also the kind of movie that plays well on DVD. The film has an good soundtrack as well and it has plenty of familiar faces in supporting roles and bit-parts. Even the director has a bit-part as Byran Sugarman, who's an actor himself. "Reign Over Me" is one of the most underrated pictures of this year. It is also the best Sandler film in my taste since "The Wedding Singer". Don't miss it. HD Widescreen. (**** 1/2 out of *****).

If you did not find the word "excellent" by reading the text, use *Ctrl + F* to find it.

Now that you have found it, can you tell me what effect "excellent" has on the sentiment analysis of the review text of this movie?

That is where a unit test comes in handy. We want to make sure we will find samples that match the sentiment analysis scenario we wish to explain. We will now write a data interception function to create unit tests to make sure the dataset contains some basic explainable scenarios.

The data interception function

In this section, we will create a data interception function to implement our unit test keywords. Our unit test samples will contain the word "excellent" in one case and be omitted in other cases. We will thus be able to pinpoint the effect of a specific word in a SHAP analysis.

The interception function first starts with a trigger variable named `interception`:

```
# Interception
interception = 0 # 0 = IMDB raw data,
                 # 1 = data interception and simplification
```

If `interception` is set to `0`, then the function will be deactivated, and the program will continue to use the original IMDb dataset. If `interception` is set to `1`, then the function is activated:

```
# Interception
interception = 1 # 0 = IMDB raw data,
                 # 1 = data interception and simplification
```

A second parameter named `display` controls the interception function:

```
display = 2 # 0 = no, 1 = display samples, 2 = sample detection
```

`display` can be set to three values:

- `display = 0`: The display functions are deactivated
- `display = 1`: The first 10 samples of the training and testing data will be displayed
- `display = 2`: Specific samples are parsed to find explainable Shapley values

When the interception function is activated, the input data is intercepted.

In this case, four explainable reviews are created:

```
if interception == 1:
    good1 = "I recommend that everybody go see this movie!"
    good2 = "This one is good and I recommend that everybody go see it!"
    good3 = "This one is excellent and I recommend that everybody go see
it!"
    good4 = "This one is good and even excellent. I recommend that
everybody go see it!"
    bad = "I hate the plot since it's terrible with very bad language."
```

These four reviews will isolate reviews to explain Shapley values with SHAP graphs and with mathematics, as in the *Sentiment analysis example* section of this chapter.

We need to find the length of corpus before splitting it:

```
x = len(corpus)
print(x)
```

Our program will begin to intercept the original IMDb reviews and randomly replace them with the explainable Shapley value reviews we stored in five variables. The random variable is r with a value between 1 and 1000:

```
for i in range(0, x):
  r = random.randint(1,2500)
  if y[i]:
    # corpus[i] = good1
    if (r <= 500): corpus[i] = good1;
    if (r > 500 and r <= 1000): corpus[i] = good2;
    if (r > 1000 and r <= 1700): corpus[i] = good3;
    if (r > 1700 and r <= 2500): corpus[i] = good4;
  if not y[i]:
    corpus[i] = bad
```

The function now displays the first 10 lines of the corpus. The data we inserted is our explainable data:

```
print("length", len(corpus)) # displaying samples of
                             # the training data
for i in range(0, 10):
  r = random.randint(1, len(corpus))
  print(r, y[r], corpus[r])
```

Note that we have transformed the corpus into a training set for our customized purposes, we will split the dataset into the actual training and testing subsets.

If display = 1, the first 10 reviews will be displayed:

```
if display == 1:
  print("y_test")
  for i in range(0, 20):
    print(i, y_test[i], corpus_test[i])
  print("y_train")
  for i in range(0, 1):
    print(i, y_train[i], corpus_train[i])
```

If `display` = 2, a rule base will isolate the cases we described in the *Sentiment analysis example* section of this chapter:

```
if display == 2:
  r1 = 0; r2 = 0; r3 = 0; r4 = 0; r5 = 0 # rules 1, 2, 3, 4, and 5

  y = len(corpus_test)
  for i in range(0, y):
    fstr = corpus_test[i]
    n0 = fstr.find("good")
    n1 = fstr.find("excellent")
    n2 = fstr.find("bad")

    if n0 < 0 and n1 < 0 and r1 == 0 and y_test[i]:
      r1 = 1 # without good and excellent
      print(i, "r1", y_test[i], corpus_test[i])

    if n0 >= 0 and n1 < 0 and r2 == 0 and y_test[i]:
      r2 = 1 # good without excellent
      print(i, "r2", y_test[i], corpus_test[i])

    if n1 >= 0 and n0 < 0 and r3 == 0 and y_test[i]:
      r3 = 1 # excellent without good
      print(i, "r3", y_test[i], corpus_test[i])

    if n0 >= 0 and n1 > 0 and r4 == 0 and y_test[i]:
      r4 = 1 # with good and excellent
      print(i, "r4", y_test[i], corpus_test[i])

    if n2 >= 0 and r5 == 0 and not y_test[i]:
      r5 = 1 # with bad
      print(i, "r5", y_test[i], corpus_test[i])

    if r1 + r2 + r3 + r4 + r5 == 5:
      break
```

The function will isolate the examples we inserted if it finds them or the samples that match the rules in the IMDb dataset.

We are now 100% sure that our unit test keywords are present. If necessary, we can explain SHAP with mathematics, a sentiment analysis example, and illustrate it with our unit keywords with our rule base.

Each rule counter is set to 0 at the beginning of the function:

```
if display == 2:
    r1 = 0; r2 = 0; r3 = 0; r4 = 0; r5 = 0 # rules 1, 2, 3, 4, and 5
```

The program determines the length of the testing dataset and then starts to parse the reviews:

```
y = len(corpus_test)
for i in range(0, y):
```

The function now stores a review in a string variable named `fstr`:

```
fstr = corpus_test[i]
n0 = fstr.find("good")
n1 = fstr.find("excellent")
n2 = fstr.find("bad")
```

The rule base is now applied:

```
if n0 < 0 and n1 < 0 and r1 == 0 and y_test[i]:
    r1 = 1 # without good and excellent
    print(i, "r1", y_test[i], corpus_test[i])

if n0 >= 0 and n1 < 0 and r2 == 0 and y_test[i]:
    r2 = 1 # good without excellent
    print(i, "r2", y_test[i], corpus_test[i])

if n1 >= 0 and n0 < 0 and r3 == 0 and y_test[i]:
    r3 = 1 # excellent without good
    print(i, "r3", y_test[i], corpus_test[i])

if n0 >= 0 and n1 > 0 and r4 == 0 and y_test[i]:
    r4 = 1 # with good and excellent
    print(i, "r4", y_test[i], corpus_test[i])

if n2 >= 0 and r5 == 0 and not y_test[i]:
    r5 = 1 # with bad
    print(i, "r5", y_test[i], corpus_test[i])
```

Once all five rules are satisfied, the parsing function will stop:

```
if r1 + r2 + r3 + r4 + r5 == 5:
    break
```

Five samples that fit the five rules are now displayed.

For example, an excerpt for r2 is:

```
0 r2 True "Twelve Monkeys" is odd and disturbing,...
```

The first column contains the review ID we will be able to track and use to explain SHAP values.

In this section, we intercepted the corpus to insert unit test reviews if the interception function is activated to make sure the dataset contains samples of the rules we set. If the interception function is not enabled, then the original dataset will be analyzed.

In both cases, our datasets are ready to be vectorized.

Vectorizing the datasets

In this section, we will vectorize the datasets with the TfidfVectorizer module we described in the *Importing the data* section of this chapter.

As a reminder, TfidfVectorizer extracts features from text and takes note of the **term frequency (TF)**. The module also evaluates how important a word is. This process is named **inverse document frequency (IDF)**.

The program first creates a vectorizer:

```
# @title Vectorize data
vectorizer = TfidfVectorizer(min_df=10)
```

min_df=10 will filter features—in our case, words—that have a document frequency lower than 10. Words that do not appear at least 10 times will be discarded.

We now vectorize the corpus_train and corpus_test datasets:

```
X_train = vectorizer.fit_transform(corpus_train)
X_test = vectorizer.transform(corpus_test)
```

What we can do now is visualize the frequency values that the vectorizer has attributed to the features of our dataset. It will be interesting to visualize the values we obtain to the feature values once a linear model has trained them to explain the evolution of the program. Then, we will visualize the Shapley values produced by SHAP.

Our first step is to visualize the frequency of the words we inserted using our interception function. This can be done on the IMDb dataset, but we recommend that you start with a small sample to understand the process.

Make sure `interception=1` and then run the program up to the vectorizing cell. In this cell, we will add a display function to see the values that were calculated by the vectorizer, along with the feature names:

```
# visualizing the vectorized features
feature_names = vectorizer.get_feature_names()
lf = (len(feature_names))
for fv in range(0, lf):
    print(round(vectorizer.idf_[fv], 5), feature_names[fv])
```

The reviews that were created by the interception function have been transformed into a vectorized dictionary of words with their frequency values.

The output produces useful information:

```
1.92905 and
1.68573 bad
2.85347 even
1.70052 everybody
2.21593 excellent
1.70052 go
2.36576 good
1.68573 hate
1.92905 is
1.10691 it
1.68573 language
3.28824 movie
1.92905 one
1.68573 plot
1.70052 recommend
1.70052 see
1.68573 since
1.68573 terrible
1.70052 that
1.68573 the
1.70052 this
1.68573 very
1.68573 with
```

We can draw a couple of conclusions from the vectorized function we just ran:

- A small sample provides clear and useful information.

- We can see that the words "good," "excellent," and "bad" have higher values than most other words. "movie" has a positive contribution as well. This shows that the vectorizer has already identified the key features of our interception dataset.

 The training and testing datasets are created randomly. Each time you run the program, the records in the dataset might change, as well as the output values.

The datasets have been vectorized, and we can already explain some of the feature values. We can now run the linear model.

Linear models and logistic regression

In this section, we will create a linear model, train it, and display the values of the features produced. We want to visualize the output of the linear model first. Then, we will explore the theoretical aspect of linear models.

Creating, training, and visualizing the output of a linear model

First, let's create, train, and visualize the output of a linear model using logistic regression:

```
# @title Linear model, logistic regression
model = sklearn.linear_model.LogisticRegression(C=0.1)
model.fit(X_train, y_train)
```

The program now displays the output of the trained linear model.

First, the program displays the positive values:

```
# print positive coefficients
lc = len(model.coef_[0])
for cf in range(0, lc):
  if (model.coef_[0][cf] >= 0):
    print(round(model.coef_[0][cf], 5), feature_names[cf])
```

Then, the program displays the negative values:

```
# print negative coefficients
for cf in range(0, lc):
  if (model.coef_[0][cf] < 0):
    print(round(model.coef_[0][cf], 5), feature_names[cf])
```

Before we analyze the output of the model, let's have a look at the reviews that were vectorized:

r1: good1="I recommend that everybody go see this movie!"
r2: good2="This one is good and I recommend that everybody go see it!"
r3: good3="This one is excellent and I recommend that everybody go see it!"
r4: good4="This one is good and even excellent. I recommend that everybody go see it!"
r5: bad="I hate the plot since it's terrible with very bad language."

With these reviews in mind, we can analyze how the linear model trained the features (words).

In natural language processing, we can also say that we are analyzing the "tokens" for the sequences of letters. In this chapter, we will continue to use the term "features" for "words."

The output of the program will first show the positive values and then the negative values:

```
1.28737 and
0.70628 even
1.71218 everybody
1.08344 excellent
1.71218 go
1.0073 good
1.28737 is
1.11644 movie
1.28737 one
1.71218 recommend
1.71218 see
1.71218 that
1.71218 this
-1.95518 bad
-1.95518 hate
-0.54483 it
```

```
-1.95518 language
-1.95518 plot
-1.95518 since
-1.95518 terrible
-1.95518 the
-1.95518 very
-1.95518 with
```

 The training and testing datasets are generated randomly. Each time you run the program, the records in the dataset might change, as well as the output values.

We can now see the impact of the linear model:

- The features (words) that are in the positive reviews have positive values
- The features (words) that are in the negative reviews have negative values

We can analyze a positive and negative review intuitively and classify them. In the following review, the key features (words) are obviously negative and will add up to a clearly negative review:

```
I hate(-1.9) the plot(-1.9) since it's terrible(-1.9) with very bad(-1.9) language.
```

In the following review, the key features (words) are obviously positive and will add up to a clearly positive review:

```
This one is good(1.0) and I recommend(1.7) that everybody(1.7) go see(1.7) it!
```

We can draw several conclusions from these examples:

- Although unit tests contain small samples, they represent an excellent way to explain models to users.
- Although unit tests contain small samples, they help clarify how models take inputs and produce outputs.
- A larger dataset will provide a variety of results, but it is better to start with a small sample. Analyzing large samples makes sense only once everybody in a team understands the model and has approved it.

We now have an intuitive understanding of a linear model. We will now explore the key theoretical aspects of linear models.

Defining a linear model

A linear model is a linear combination of weighted features that are used to reach a target. In our case, the linear model has been trained for a binary result—True or False for a positive review sample or a negative review sample, respectively.

A linear model can be expressed in the following equation, in which $\hat{y}$ is the predicted value, x is a feature, and w is a weight or a coefficient in the following linear model equation:

$$\hat{y}(x, w) = w_0 + w_1 x_1 + \cdots + w_p x_p$$

A linear model requires methods to optimize regression to reach the defined target $\hat{y}$.

There are several regression methods available in the `sklearn.linear_model` module. We implemented the logistic regression method here.

Logistic regression fits our dataset well because the method is applied as a binary classification approach in our program, although it relies on regression. The probabilities are the outcomes modeled using a logistic function, which gives its name to the method.

The logistic function is a logistic sigmoid function and is one of the best ways to normalize the weights of an output. It can be defined as follows:

$$\frac{1}{1 + e^{-x}}$$

- e represents Euler's number, the natural logarithm, which is equal to 2.71828
- x is the value we wish to normalize

The logistic regression model can be displayed with:

```
print(model)
```

The output will show the values of parameters of the logistic regression model:

```
LogisticRegression(C=0.1, class_weight=None, dual=False,
                fit_intercept=True, intercept_scaling=1,
                l1_ratio=None, max_iter=100, multi_class='auto',
                n_jobs=None, penalty='l2', random_state=None,
                solver='lbfgs', tol=0.0001, verbose=0,
                warm_start=False)
```

The program applied the following parameters to the logistic regression model. Once we understand the linear model function shown previously and we know that we are using a logistic regression function, we do not need to go into all of the details of the model's options unless we hit a rock. However, it is interesting to get an idea of the parameters the model takes into account. The program applied the following parameters to the logistic regression model:

- `C=0.1` is a positive float that is the inverse of regularization strength. The smaller the value, the stronger the regularization.

- `class_weight=None` means that all the classes are supposed to have a class of one.

- `dual=False` is an optimization parameter used in conjunction with certain solvers.

- `fit_intercept=True` can be understood as a bias — an intercept — that will be added to the decision function if set to `True`.

- `intercept_scaling=1` is a constant value that scales the inner calculation vectors of certain solvers.

- `l1_ratio=None` is used in conjunction with `penalty` when activated, which is not the case for our model.

- `max_iter=100` represents the number of iterations it will take for the solvers to converge.

- `multi_class='auto'` in our case means that it will automatically choose the option that makes a binary problem fit for each label.

- `n_jobs=None` is the number of cores used when parallelizing over classes. In our case, `None` means only one core is used, which is enough for the datasets in this chapter.

- `penalty='l2'` is the norm for a penalty applied with `'lbfgs'` solver, as used in this model.

- `random_state=None` in this case, this means that the seed of the random number generator will be generated by an instance using `np.random`.

- `solver='lbfgs'` is a solver that handles penalties such as `'l2'`.

- `tol=0.0001` is the stopping criteria expressed as a tolerance.

- `verbose=0` activates verbosity if set to a positive number.

- `warm_start=False` means that the previous solution will be erased.

We have created and trained the model. Now, it is time to implement agnostic model explaining with SHAP.

Agnostic model explaining with SHAP

In the *Introduction to SHAP* section of this chapter, we saw that Shapley values rely on the input data and output data of a **machine learning** (**ML**) model. SHAP can interpret results. We went through the mathematical representation of the Shapley value without having to take a model into account.

Agnostic ML model explaining or interpreting will inevitably become a mandatory aspect of any AI project.

SHAP offers explainer models for several ML algorithms. In this chapter, we will focus on a linear model explainer.

Creating the linear model explainer

We will continue to add functions to SHAP_IMDB.ipynb.

Let's first create the linear explainer:

```
# @title Explain linear model
explainer = shap.LinearExplainer(model, X_train,
    feature_perturbation = "interventional")
```

Now, we will retrieve the Shapley values of the testing dataset:

```
shap_values = explainer.shap_values(X_test)
```

We must now convert the test dataset into an array for the plot function:

```
X_test_array = X_test.toarray() # we need to pass a dense version for
                                # the plotting functions
```

The linear explainer is ready. We can now create the plot function.

Creating the plot function

In this section, we will add a plot function to the program and explain a review to understand the process.

The plot function begins with a form where we can choose a review number from the dataset and then display a SHAP plot:

```
# @title Explaining reviews {display-mode: "form"}
review = 2 # @param {type: "number"}
shap.initjs()
```

```
ind = int(review)
shap.force_plot(explainer.expected_value, shap_values[ind,:],
            X_test_array[ind,:],
            feature_names=vectorizer.get_feature_names())
```

This program is a prototype. Make sure you enter small integers in the form since the test dataset's size varies each time the program is run:

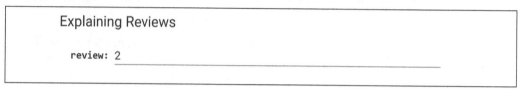

Figure 4.1: Enter small integers into the prototype

Once a review number is chosen, the model's prediction for that review will be displayed with the Shapley values that drove the prediction:

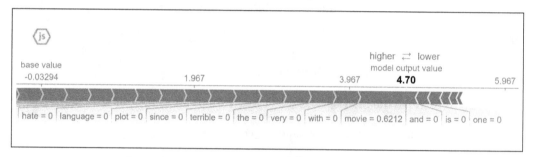

Figure 4.2: The Shapley values that determined the prediction

In this example, the prediction is positive. The sample review is:

```
I recommend that everybody go see this movie!
```

 The training and testing datasets are produced randomly. Each time you run the program, the records in the dataset might change, as well as the output values.

The Shapley values on the left (red in the color images) push the prediction to the right, to potentially positive results. In this example, the features (words) "recommend" and "see" contribute to a positive prediction:

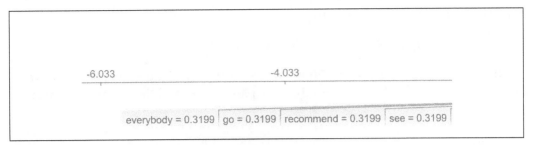

Figure 4.3: The Shapley values of words in a sequence

The Shapley values on the right (the blue color in the color images) push the prediction to the left, to potentially negative results.

The plot also shows a value name "base value," as you can see in *Figure 4.4*:

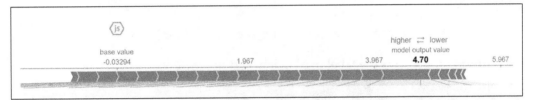

Figure 4.4: Visualizing the base value

Base value is the prediction the model would make if it did not take the features of the present dataset number output into account based on the whole dataset.

The SHAP plot we implemented explains and interprets the results with Shapley values. We can also retrieve interpretability information from the model's output.

Explaining the output of the model's prediction

SHAP's plot library explains the model's prediction visually. However, we can also add numerical explanations.

We will first check if the review is positive or negative and display it with its label:

```
# @title Review
print("Positive" if y_test[ind] else "Negative", "Review:")
print("y_test[ind]", ind, y_test[ind])
```

In this case, the label and review are:

```
True I recommend that everybody go see this movie!
```

The three features (words) we highlighted are worth investigating. We will retrieve the feature names and the corresponding Shapley values, and then display the result:

```
print(corpus_test[ind])
feature_names = vectorizer.get_feature_names()
lfn = len(feature_names)
lfn = 10 # choose the number of samples to display from [0, lfn]
for sfn in range(0, lfn):
  if shap_values[ind][sfn] >= 0:
    print(feature_names[sfn], round(X_test_array[ind][sfn], 5))
for sfn in range(0, lfn):
  if shap_values[ind][sfn] < 0:
    print(feature_names[sfn], round(X_test_array[ind][sfn], 5))
```

The output first displays the label of a review and the review:

```
Positive Review:
y_test[ind] 0 True
Positive Review:
y_test[ind] 2 True
I recommend that everybody go see this movie!
```

Note that lfn=10 limits the number of values displayed. The output will also vary, depending on the movie review number you choose.

The output then displays the features and their corresponding Shapley values:

```
bad 0.0
everybody 0.31982
go 0.31982
hate 0.0
it 0.0
language 0.0
movie 0.62151
plot 0.0
recommend 0.31982
see 0.31982
```

We can draw several conclusions from these explanations:

- The vectorizer generates the feature names for the whole dataset
- However, the Shapley values displayed in this section of the program are those of the review we are interpreting
- The Shapley values in this section of the code will differ from one review to another
- The highlighted features have marginal positive contribution Shapley values that explain the positive prediction
- The negative Shapley values are mostly equal to 0, which means that they will not influence the prediction

In this section, we created functions for visual and numerical SHAP explanations.

We will now explain the reviews from the intercepted dataset.

Explaining intercepted dataset reviews with SHAP

We have implemented the code and analyzed the Shapley value of a review. We will now analyze two more samples—one negative one and one positive one:

```
False I hate the plot since it's terrible with very bad language.
True This one is excellent and I recommend that everybody go see it!
```

Since the datasets are split into training and testing subsets randomly, the calculations will adapt to the new frequencies and the importance of a word.

We will first visualize the output of the negative review.

A negative review

The negative review contains three strong negative keywords and no positive features:

```
Negative Review:
y_test[ind] 1 False
I hate the plot since it's terrible with very bad language.
```

The negative features produce marginal negative contributions that push the prediction down to `False`, that is, a negative prediction for the review:

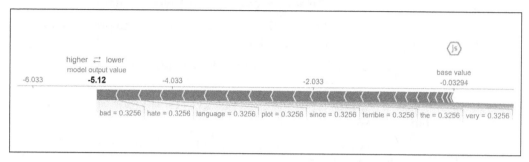

Figure 4.5: Showing the contribution of the words to Shapley values

We can observe that the feature "bad," for example, has a positive Shapley value in a negative review and that "excellent" does not contribute at all in this review:

```
Negative Review:
y_test[ind] 1 False
I hate the plot since it's terrible with very bad language.
and 0.0
bad 0.32565
even 0.0
everybody 0.0
excellent 0.0
go 0.0
good 0.0
hate 0.32565
is 0.0
it 0.21348
language 0.32565
movie 0.0
one 0.0
plot 0.32565
recommend 0.0
see 0.0
since 0.32565
terrible 0.32565
that 0.0
the 0.32565
this 0.0
very 0.32565
with 0.32565
```

Note the marginal contribution of the three key features of the review:

Key features = {bad, hate, terrible}

Now, observe how the marginal contributions of those key features change in a positive review.

A positive review

In a positive review, we now know that the key features will have Shapley values that prove their marginal contribution to the prediction:

```
This one is excellent and I recommend that everybody go see it!
```

First, observe that the marginal contribution of negative features has changed to null in this review:

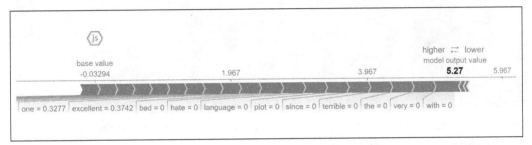

Figure 4.6: Displaying the marginal contribution of negative features

However, the marginal contribution of the positive features has gone up:

Figure 4.7: Displaying the marginal contribution of positive features

We can explain this analysis further by highlighting the negative features with no marginal contribution in this review:

```
Positive Review:
y_test[ind] 0 True
This one is excellent and I recommend that everybody go see it!
and 0.32749
bad 0.0
```

```
everybody 0.28932
excellent 0.37504
go 0.28932
hate 0.0
is 0.32749
language 0.0
one 0.32749
plot 0.0
recommend 0.28932
see 0.28932
since 0.0
terrible 0.0
that 0.28932
the 0.0
this 0.28932
very 0.0
with 0.0
even 0.0
good 0.0
it 0.18801
movie 0.0
```

The Shapley values of each feature change for each review, although they have a trained value for the whole dataset.

With that, we have interpreted a few samples from the intercepted datasets. We will now explain the reviews from the original IMDb dataset.

Explaining the original IMDb reviews with SHAP

In this section, we will interpret two IMDb reviews.

First, we must deactivate the interception function:

```
interception = 0
```

We have another problem to solve to interpret an IMDb review.

The number of words in the reviews of a movie exceeds the number of features we can detect visually. We thus need to limit the number of features the vectorizer will take into account.

We will go back to the vectorizer and set the value of min_df to 1000 instead of 100. We will have less features to explain how the program makes its predictions:

```
# vectorizing
vectorizer = TfidfVectorizer(min_df=1000)
```

In this case, we can still use the rules we hardcoded to find examples in the interception datasets. The probability of finding the keywords of the interception dataset such as "good," "excellent," and "bad" are very high.

You can change the values to find examples of features (words) you would like to analyze. You can replace "good," "excellent," and "bad" by your ideas to explore the outputs. You could target an actor, a director, a location, or any other information for which you would like to visualize the output of the model.

The code of our rule base remains without us making a single change:

```
y = len(corpus_test)
for i in range(0, y):
    fstr = corpus_test[i]
    n0 = fstr.find("good")
    n1 = fstr.find("excellent")
    n2 = fstr.find("bad")

    if n0 < 0 and n1 < 0 and r1 == 0 and y_test[i]:
        r1 = 1 # without good and excellent
        print(i, "r1", y_test[i], corpus_test[i])

    if n0 >= 0 and n1 < 0 and r2 == 0 and y_test[i]:
        r2 = 1 # good without excellent
        print(i, "r2", y_test[i], corpus_test[i])

    if n1 >= 0 and n0 < 0 and r3 == 0 and y_test[i]:
        r3 = 1 # excellent without good
        print(i, "r3", y_test[i], corpus_test[i])

    if n0 >= 0 and n1 > 0 and r4 == 0 and y_test[i]:
        r4 = 1 # with good and excellent
        print(i, "r4", y_test[i], corpus_test[i])

    if n2 >= 0 and r5 == 0 and not y_test[i]:
        r5 = 1 # with bad
        print(i, "r5", y_test[i], corpus_test[i])
```

```
    if r1 + r2 + r3 + r4 + r5 == 5:
        break
```

The program isolated five samples we can explain:

```
    0 r2 True "Twelve Monkeys" is odd and disturbing

    2 r1 True I finally saw this film tonight after

    5 r5 False A chemical spill is turning people in

    9 r4 True I first saw the trailer for Frailty on

    59 r3 True I am currently on vacation in Israel
```

Figure 4.8: Five samples isolated by the program

We will start by analyzing a negative review.

A negative review sample

The text of the negative sample contains too many words to reproduce in this section. We can explain the prediction by analyzing a limited number of key features, such as the ones highlighted in the following excerpt:

```
{Bad acting, horribly awful special effects, and no budget to speak of}
```

These two features are driving the prediction down:

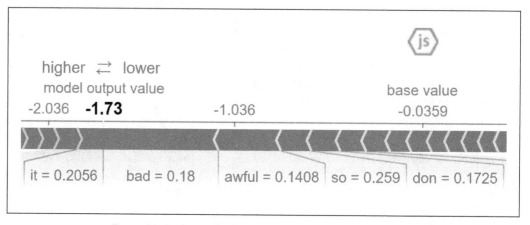

Figure 4.9: Analyzing the features that drove the prediction down

To confirm our interpretation, we can display the key features of the dataset and the Shapley values of the contribution of negative features to the Shapley values of the prediction:

```
although 0.0
always 0.0
american 0.0
an 0.06305
and 0.11407
anyone 0.0
as 0.0
awful 0.14078
back 0.0
bad 0.18
be 0.05787
beautiful 0.0
because 0.08745
become 0.0
before 0.0
beginning 0.0
best 0.0
```

We can apply the same key features sampling method to a positive review.

A positive review sample

Explainable AI tools require a method to isolate key aspects of the outputs of an ML algorithm. The goal is to break the dataset down into small data points so that we can interpret them visually.

We will now consider the following two excerpts of a positive review sample:

```
{but Young Adam and Young Fenton were excellent},
{really did a good job of directing it too.}
```

We will focus on the words "excellent" and "job" to interpret the output of the model:

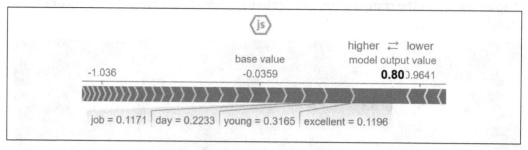

Figure 4.10: Visualizing the impact of "excellent"

Once again, we can prove that the Shapley values are correct for both excerpts:

```
ending 0.0
enough 0.0
entire 0.0
especially 0.11172
ever 0.0
every 0.0
excellent 0.11961
face 0.0
fact 0.0
fan 0.2442
far 0.0
felt 0.0
few 0.0
.../...
idea 0.0
if 0.0
instead 0.0
interesting 0.0
into 0.0
isn 0.0
it 0.14697
itself 0.0
job 0.11715
kids 0.0
kind 0.0
least 0.0
left 0.0
less 0.0
let 0.0
```

In this section, we created a linear logistic regression model and trained it. We then created a SHAP linear model explainer. Finally, we created SHAP visual explanation plots and numerical interpretation outputs.

Summary

In this chapter, we explored how to explain the output of a machine learning algorithm with an agnostic model approach using **SHapley Additive exPlanations (SHAP)**. SHAP provides an excellent way to explain models by just analyzing their input data and output predictions.

We saw that SHAP relies on the Shapley value to explain the marginal contribution of a feature in a prediction. We started by understanding the mathematical foundations of the Shapley value. We then applied the Shapley value equation to a sentiment analysis example. With that in mind, we got started with SHAP.

We installed SHAP, imported the modules, imported the dataset, and split it into a training dataset and a testing dataset. Once that was done, we vectorized the data to run a linear model. We created the SHAP linear model explainer and visualized the marginal contribution of the features of the dataset in relation to the sentiment analysis predictions of reviews. A positive review prediction value would be pushed upward by high Shapley values for the positive features, for example.

To make explainable AI easier, we created unit tests of reviews using an interception function. Unit tests provide clear examples to explain an ML model rapidly.

Finally, once the interception function was built and tested, we ran SHAP on the original IMDb dataset to make further investigations on the marginal contribution of features regarding the sentiment analysis prediction of a review.

SHAP provides us with an excellent way to weigh the contribution of each feature with the Shapley values fair distribution equation. In the next chapter, *Building an Explainable AI Solution from Scratch*, we will build an XAI program using Facets and WIT.

Questions

1. Shapley values are model-dependent. (True | False)
2. Model-agnostic XAI does not require output. (True | False)
3. The Shapley value calculates the marginal contribution of a feature in a prediction. (True | False)
4. The Shapley value can calculate the marginal contribution of a feature for all of the records in a dataset. (True | False)
5. Vectorizing data means that we transform data into numerical vectors. (True | False)
6. When vectorizing data, we can also calculate the frequency of a feature in the dataset. (True | False)
7. SHAP only works with logistic regression. (True | False)
8. One feature with a very high Shapley value can change the output of a prediction. (True | False)
9. Using a unit test to explain AI is a waste of time. (True | False)
10. Shapley values can show that some features are mispresented in a dataset. (True | False)

References

The original repository for the programs that were used in this chapter can be found on GitHub: Scott Lundberg, `slundberg`, Microsoft Research, Seattle, WA, `https://github.com/slundberg/shap`

The algorithms and visualizations come from:

*   Su-In Lee's lab at the University of Washington
*   Microsoft Research

Reference for linear models: `https://scikit-learn.org/stable/modules/linear_model.html`

Further reading

- For more on model interpretability in Microsoft Azure Machine Learning, visit `https://docs.microsoft.com/en-us/azure/machine-learning/how-to-machine-learning-interpretability`

- For more on Microsoft's Interpret-Community, browse the GitHub repository: `https://github.com/interpretml/interpret-community/`

- For more on SHAP: `http://papers.nips.cc/paper/7062-a-unified-approach-to-interpreting-model-predictions.pdf`

- For more on the base value, browse `http://papers.nips.cc/paper/7062-a-unified-approach-to-interpreting-model-predictions.pdf`

Additional publications

- *A Unified Approach to Interpreting Model Predictions.* Lundberg, Scott and Su-In Lee. arXiv:1705.07874 [cs.AI] (2017)

- *From Local Explanations to Global Understanding with Explainable AI for Trees.* Lundberg, Scott M., Gabriel G. Erion, Hugh Chen, Alex J. DeGrave, Jordan M Prutkin, Bala G. Nair, Ronit Katz, Jonathan Himmelfarb, Nisha Bansal and Su-In Lee. Nature machine intelligence 2 1 (2020): 56-67

- *Explainable machine-learning predictions for the prevention of hypoxaemia during surgery.* Lundberg, Scott M. et al. Nature biomedical engineering 2 (2018): 749-760

5
Building an Explainable AI Solution from Scratch

In this chapter, we will use the knowledge and tools we acquired in the previous chapters to build an **explainable AI (XAI)** solution from scratch using Python, TensorFlow, Facets, and Google's **What-If Tool (WIT)**.

We often isolate ourselves from reality when experimenting with **machine learning (ML)** algorithms. We take the ready-to-use online datasets, use the algorithms suggested by a given cloud AI platform, and display the results as we saw in a tutorial we found on the web. Once it works, we move on to another ML algorithm and continue like this, thinking that we are learning enough to face real-life projects.

However, by only focusing on what we think is the technical aspect, we miss a lot of critical moral, ethical, legal, and advanced technical issues. In this chapter, we will enter the real world of AI with its long list of XAI issues.

Developing AI code in the 2010s relied on knowledge and talent. Developing AI code in the 2020s implies the accountability of XAI for every aspect of an AI project.

In this chapter, we will explore the U.S. census problem provided by Google as an example of how to use its WIT. The WIT functions show the power of XAI. In this chapter, we will approach WIT from a user's point of view, intuitively. In *Chapter 6, AI Fairness with Google's What-If Tool (WIT)*, we will examine WIT from a technical perspective.

We will start by analyzing the type of data in the U.S. census dataset from moral, ethical, legal, and technical perspectives in a pandas DataFrame.

Our investigation of the ethical and legal foundations of the U.S. census dataset will lead us to conclude that some of the columns must be discarded. We must explain why it is illegal in several European countries to use features that might constitute discrimination, for example.

Once the dataset has been transformed into an ethical and legal asset, we will display the data in Facets before using ML to train on the U.S. census dataset. We will go as far as possible, explaining our ethical choices and providing inferences. Finally, we will train on the U.S. census dataset and explain the outputs with WIT.

This chapter covers the following topics:

- Datasets from a moral and ethical perspective
- Datasets from a legal and ML technical perspective
- Learning how to anticipate the outputs of ML through XAI before training the data
- Explaining the expected results with Facets
- Verifying our anticipated results with a k-means clustering algorithm
- Training an ethical dataset with TensorFlow estimators
- XAI with WIT applied to the output of the tested data
- Using WIT to compare the classification of the data points
- AI fairness explained from an ethical perspective

Our first step will be to investigate the U.S. census dataset from moral, ethical, legal, and ML perspectives.

Moral, ethical, and legal perspectives

We will start by examining the U.S. census dataset with the executive function described in *Chapter 1, Explaining Artificial Intelligence with Python*, as shown in *Figure 5.1*:

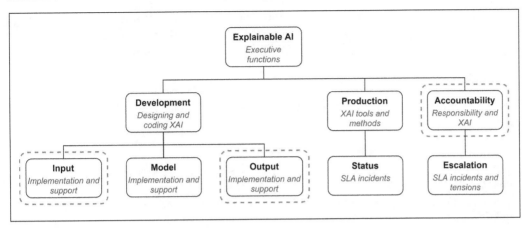

Figure 5.1: Executive function chart

You will notice that we will focus on input, output, and accountability. Developing AI programs comes with moral, ethical, and legal responsibilities. The introduction to *Chapter 2, White Box XAI for AI Bias and Ethics*, proved that ignoring ethical and legal liabilities can cost millions of any country's currency. Every company, government institution, and individual that uses AI is accountable for the actions taken as a result of the AI algorithms that produce automated outputs.

In this section, we will take accountability seriously by investigating the inputs provided for our program and their impact on the outputs.

Let's examine the U.S. census problem from the different perspectives of accountability.

The U.S. census data problem

The U.S. census data problem uses features of the U.S. population to predict whether a person will earn more than USD 50K or not.

In this chapter, we will use `WIT_Model_Comparison_Ethical.ipynb`, a notebook derived from Google's notebook.

The initial dataset, `adult.data`, was extracted from the U.S. Census Bureau database: `https://web.archive.org/web/20021205224002/https://www.census.gov/DES/www/welcome.html`

Each record contains the features of a person. Several ML programs were designed to predict the income of that person. The goal was to classify the population into groups for those earning more than USD 50K and those earning less.

The `adult.names` file contains more information on this data and the methods.

The ML program's probabilities, as stated in the `adult.names` file, achieved the following accuracy:

```
Class probabilities for adult.all file
| Probability for the label '>50K'  : 23.93% / 24.78% (without
unknowns)
| Probability for the label '<=50K' : 76.07% / 75.22% (without
unknowns)
```

We will begin by using pandas to display the data.

Using pandas to display the data

Open the `WIT_Model_Comparison_Ethical.ipynb` notebook.

We will start by importing the original U.S. census dataset:

```
# @title The UCI Census data {display-mode: "form"}
import pandas as pd
# Set the path to the CSV containing the dataset to train on.
csv_path = 'https://archive.ics.uci.edu/ml/machine-learning-databases/
adult/adult.data'
```

If you experience problems with this link, copy the link in your browser, download the file locally, and then upload it to Google Colaboratory using the Colab file manager.

We will now define the column names, as described in the original dataset, in the `adult.names` file:

```
# Set the column names for the columns in the CSV.
# If the CSV's first line is a header line containing
# the column names, then set this to None.
csv_columns = ["Age", "Workclass", "fnlwgt", "Education",
               "Education-Num", "Marital-Status", "Occupation",
               "Relationship", "Race", "Sex", "Capital-Gain",
               "Capital-Loss", "Hours-per-week", "Country",
               "Over-50K"]
```

The program now loads the data in a pandas DataFrame and displays it:

```
# Read the dataset from the provided CSV and
# print out information about it.
df = pd.read_csv(csv_path, names=csv_columns, skipinitialspace=True)
df
```

The first columns appear as follows:

	Age	Workclass	fnlwgt	Education	Education-Num	Marital-Status	Occupation
0	39	State-gov	77516	Bachelors	13	Never-married	Adm-clerical
1	50	Self-emp-not-inc	83311	Bachelors	13	Married-civ-spouse	Exec-managerial
2	38	Private	215646	HS-grad	9	Divorced	Handlers-cleaners
3	53	Private	234721	11th	7	Married-civ-spouse	Handlers-cleaners

Figure 5.2: Displaying the first columns and lines of the dataset

The following columns are displayed as well:

Relationship	Race	Sex	Capital-Gain	Capital-Loss	Hours-per-week	Country	Over-50K
Not-in-family	White	Male	2174	0	40	United-States	<=50K
Husband	White	Male	0	0	13	United-States	<=50K
Not-in-family	White	Male	0	0	40	United-States	<=50K
Husband	Black	Male	0	0	40	United-States	<=50K

Figure 5.3: Displaying samples of the dataset

`adult.names` describes the possible contents of each feature column as follows:

```
age: continuous
workclass: Private, Self-emp-not-inc, Self-emp-inc, Federal-gov, Local-
gov, State-gov, Without-pay, Never-worked
fnlwgt: continuous
education: Bachelors, Some-college, 11th, HS-grad, Prof-school, Assoc-
acdm, Assoc-voc, 9th, 7th-8th, 12th, Masters, 1st-4th, 10th, Doctorate,
5th-6th, Preschool
education-num: continuous
marital-status: Married-civ-spouse, Divorced, Never-married, Separated,
Widowed, Married-spouse-absent, Married-AF-spouse
occupation: Tech-support, Craft-repair, Other-service, Sales, Exec-
managerial, Prof-specialty, Handlers-cleaners, Machine-op-inspct,
Adm-clerical, Farming-fishing, Transport-moving, Priv-house-serv,
```

```
Protective-serv, Armed-Forces
relationship: Wife, Own-child, Husband, Not-in-family, Other-relative,
Unmarried
race: White, Asian-Pac-Islander, Amer-Indian-Eskimo, Other, Black
sex: Female, Male
capital-gain: continuous
capital-loss: continuous
hours-per-week: continuous
native-country: United-States, Cambodia, England, Puerto-Rico, Canada,
Germany, Outlying-US(Guam-USVI-etc), India, Japan, Greece, South,
China, Cuba, Iran, Honduras, Philippines, Italy, Poland, Jamaica,
Vietnam, Mexico, Portugal, Ireland, France, Dominican-Republic, Laos,
Ecuador, Taiwan, Haiti, Columbia, Hungary, Guatemala, Nicaragua,
Scotland, Thailand, Yugoslavia, El-Salvador, Trinadad&Tobago, Peru,
Hong, Holand-Netherlands
```

We now have displayed the data and its content.

Let's conduct a moral experiment like we did in *Chapter 2, White Box XAI for AI Bias and Ethics*. We will transpose the moral problems from the trolley problem into what we will name the *U.S. census data problem*. In this case, we are facing the moral dilemma of using sensitive personal information to make a decision.

Imagine you are implementing an AI agent that determines the predicted salary of a given person based on this data. The AI agent is for a company that would like to use cloud-based AI to predict salaries based on U.S. census-type data. Your AI agent has the choice of determining the expected salary of the people in the company of being >50K or <=50K based on the information you are examining. Would you agree to use this type of data to make predictions in a company or on a website?

You have two choices:

- Accept using the dataset as it is. You find a line that fits the person you are predicting the salary for. You apply ML algorithms anyway and predict an income of less or more than 50K. In this case, you might hurt a person's feelings if that person discovers what you did.

- You refuse to use the dataset because it contains information you do not want to use to reach a decision. In this case, you may be fired.

What would you do? Think carefully about this before reading the next section, where we will analyze the U.S. census data problem.

Moral and ethical perspectives

At the end of the last section, your AI agent faces a tough decision on using all of the features in the U.S. census dataset as they are, or not.

You now team up with a few developers, consultants, and a project manager to analyze the potentially biased columns of the dataset.

After some discussion, your team comes up with the following columns that require moral and ethical analysis:

Workclass	Marital-Status	Relationship	Race	Sex	Over-50K
State-gov	Never-married	Not-in-family	White	Male	<=50K
Self-emp-not-inc	Married-civ-spouse	Husband	White	Male	<=50K
Private	Divorced	Not-in-family	White	Male	<=50K
Private	Married-civ-spouse	Husband	Black	Male	<=50K
Private	Married-civ-spouse	Wife	Black	Female	<=50K
...	...	...	...	...	...
Private	Married-civ-spouse	Wife	White	Female	<=50K
Private	Married-civ-spouse	Husband	White	Male	>50K
Private	Widowed	Unmarried	White	Female	<=50K
Private	Never-married	Own-child	White	Male	<=50K
Self-emp-inc	Married-civ-spouse	Wife	White	Female	>50K

Some of these fields could shock some people at the least and are banned in several European countries such as in France. We need to understand why from a moral perspective.

The moral perspective

We must first realize that an AI agent's predictions lead to decisions in some form or another. A prediction, if published, would influence the opinion of a population on fellow members of that population, for example.

The U.S. census dataset seemed to be a nice dataset to test AI algorithms on. In fact, most users will just run focus on the technical aspect, run it, and be inspired to copy the concepts.

But is this dataset moral?

We need to explain why our AI agent needs the controversial columns. If you choose to include the controversial columns, then you must explain why. If you decide to exclude the controversial columns, you must also explain why. Let's analyze these columns:

- **Workclass**: This column contains information on the person's employment class and status in two broad groups: the private and public sectors. In the private sector, it tells us if a person is self-employed. In the public sector, it tells us whether a person works for a local government or a national government, for example.

  When designing the dataset for the AI agent, you must decide whether this column is moral. Is this a good idea? Could this hurt a person who found out that they were being analyzed this way? For the moment, you decide!

- **Marital-Status**: This column states whether a person is married, widowed, divorced, and so on. Would you agree to be in a statistical record as a widow to predict how much you earn? Would you agree to be in an income prediction because you are "never-married" or "divorced"? Could your AI agent hurt somebody if this was exposed, and the AI algorithm had to be explained? Can this question be answered?

- **Relationship**: This column provides information on whether a person is a husband, a wife, not in a family, and so on. Would you let your AI agent state that since a person is a wife, you can make an income inference? Or if a person is not in a family, the person must earn less or more than a given amount of money? Is there an answer to this question?

- **Race**: This column could shock many people. The term "race" in itself, in 2020, could create a lot of turbulence if you have to explain that since a person is of such a color, this is a race, although races do not exist in the world of DNA. Is skin color a race? Can a skin color decide how much a person will earn? Should we add hair color, weight, and height? How will you explain our AI agent's decision to a person offended by this column?

- **Sex**: This column can trigger a variety of reactions if used. Will you accept that your AI agent makes predictions and potential decisions based on whether a person is *male* or *female*? Will you let your AI agent make predictions based on this information?

This section leaves us puzzled, confused, and worried. The moral perspective has opened up many questions for which we only have subjective answers and explanations.

Let's see if an ethical perspective can be of some help.

The ethical perspective

The moral perspective of the critical columns of the previous section has left us frustrated. We do not know how to objectively explain why our AI program needs the preceding information to make a prediction. We can imagine that there is no consensus on this subject in the team we imagine working on this problem.

Some people will say that employment status, marital status, relationship, race, and sex are useful for the predictions, and some will disagree.

In this case, an ethical perspective provides guidelines.

Rule 1 – Exclude controversial data from a dataset

This rule seems simple enough. We can exclude the controversial data from the dataset.

We can take the controversial columns out, but then we will face one of two possibilities:

- The accuracy of the predictions remains sufficient
- The accuracy of the predictions is insufficient

In both cases, however, we still need to ask ourselves some ethical questions:

- Why was the data chosen in the first place to be in this dataset?
- Can such a dataset really predict a person's income based on this information?
- Are there other columns that could be deleted?
- What columns should be added?
- Would just two or three columns be enough to make a prediction?

Answering these questions is fundamental before we can engage in an AI project for which you will have to provide XAI.

 We are at the heart of the "what-if" philosophy of Google's WIT! We need to answer what-if questions when designing an AI solution before developing a full-blown AI project.

If we cannot answer these questions, we should consider rule 2.

Rule 2 – Do not engage in an AI project with controversial data

This rule is clear and straightforward. *Do not participate in an AI project that uses controversial data.*

We have explored some of the census data problem issues from moral and ethical perspectives. Let's now examine the problem from a legal perspective.

The legal perspective

We must be perfectly clear. The U.S. government's census dataset is perfectly legal in the U.S. for census purposes.

Although the U.S. census data respects the law, Americans often protest when filling in consumer marketing surveys or admission applications for various purposes. Many Americans refuse to fill in the "race" information. Many Americans point out that the concept of "race" has no genetic foundation.

Furthermore, if you honestly think the U.S. census data can help make selections when recruiting a person and put an open source AI solution online, you'd better think twice! The U.S. Equal Employment Opportunity Commission (EEOC) strictly bans the use of several of the columns in the U.S. census database in offering a person a job. The features in the following list in bold characters are ones that could lead to legal litigation. The EEOC clearly explains this on their website at `https://www.eeoc.gov/prohibited-employment-policiespractices`.

EEOC laws ban the use of the following information in making employment decisions:

- **Race**
- Color
- Religion
- **Sex and sexual orientation**
- Pregnancy
- **National origin**
- **Age 40 or older**
- Disability

You will notice that race, sex, national origin, and age are illegal for use in some cases and unethical in many others.

In other countries, you may encounter legal issues with data on racial and ethnic origin.

In the European Union, for example, the **Race Equality Directive (RED)** bans discrimination on racial and ethnic origin. This applies regarding access to many things, including the following:

- Employment
- Social security
- Healthcare
- Public housing

Article 9 of the **General Data Protection Regulation (GDPR)** of the European Union forbids the use of the processing of private information in many areas. "Processing" applies to AI algorithmic processing as well. Private data on the following characteristics cannot be processed:

- Racial or ethnic origin
- Political position
- Religious beliefs
- Biometric information that could identify an individual
- Personal health information
- Sexual orientation

The difference between public information and private information, which identifies an individual, cannot always be guaranteed.

For example, you gather information with no name attached to it in a given location (that is, someone's location history) related to a racial feature in a dataset. You contend that you do not have the name of the person and never had it in the first place.

However, the location history appears in an online dataset for ML examples, just like the U.S. census dataset. An AI student downloads it and makes several inferences:

- Identifies the locations in the dataset by name: going to a doctor, a hospital, a pharmacist regularly
- Determines that the person does not move at night from a given location using GPS coordinates

The student uploads the AI program they developed that inferences this information on GitHub with a description of how to use the application.

Among the millions of developers that download examples from GitHub, one developer downloads this dataset, looks up the city addresses of all the locations that remain static during nights, finds the address of the person in the dataset, and the particular address of a specialized clinic for a given disease. Now, that developer can find the name of the person and knows the condition a person may be suffering from. The developer happily makes a post and uploads the program that processes and converts "anonymous" information into private information. This could lead to serious legal issues.

We have isolated some of the controversial columns of the U.S. census database used to infer the income of an American citizen. Can we exclude those fields? Do we really need that information? We will use ML to answer those questions.

The machine learning perspective

What features do we really need to predict the income of a person? We will provide some ideas in this section.

 You must learn how to explain and anticipate the output of an ML program before implementing it.

We will first display the training data using Facets Dive.

Displaying the training data with Facets Dive

We will continue to use the WIT_Model_Comparison_Ethical.ipynb notebook in this section. We will begin by conducting a customized what-if ML investigation.

The U.S. Census Bureau is perfectly entitled to gather the information required for their surveys. The scope of ML analysis we are conducting is quite different. Our question is to determine whether or not we need the type of information provided by the U.S. Census Bureau to predict income.

We want to find a way to predict income that will break no laws and be morally acceptable. We want to remain ethical for applications other than U.S. census predictions.

We will now conduct an investigation using Facets Dive.

We will first load the training data for our investigation. The program will only load the training data file for our investigation as follows.

You can choose to use GitHub or upload the files to Google Drive:

```
# @title Importing data <br>
# Set repository to "github"(default) to read the data
# from GitHub <br>
# Set repository to "google" to read the data
# from Google {display-mode: "form"}
import os
from google.colab import drive

# Set repository to "github" to read the data from GitHub
# Set repository to "google" to read the data from Google
repository = "github"
```

Activating repository = "github" triggers a curl function that downloads the training data:

```
if repository == "github":
    !curl -L https://raw.githubusercontent.com/PacktPublishing/Hands-On-Explainable-AI-XAI-with-Python/master/Chapter05/adult.data --output "adult.data"
    dtrain = "/content/adult.data"
    print(dtrain)
```

Activating repository = "google" triggers a drive-mounting function to read the training data from Google Drive:

```
if repository == "google":
    # Mounting the drive. If it is not mounted, a prompt
    # will provide instructions.
    drive.mount('/content/drive')
    # Setting the path for each file
    dtrain = '/content/drive/My Drive/XAI/Chapter05/adult.data'
    print(dtrain)
```

The program now loads the data in a DataFrame and parses it:

```
# @title Loading and parsing the data {display-mode: "form"}
import pandas as pd

features = ["Age", "Workclass", "fnlwgt", "Education",
            "Education-Num", "Marital-Status", "Occupation",
            "Relationship", "Race", "Sex", "Capital-Gain",
            "Capital-Loss", "Hours-per-week", "Country", "Over-50K"]
train_data = pd.read_csv(dtrain, names=features, sep=r'\s*,\s*',
                         engine='python', na_values="?")
```

Now, we can display the data with Facets Dive:

```
# @title Display the Dive visualization for
# the training data {display-mode: "form"}
from IPython.core.display import display, HTML

jsonstr = train_data.to_json(orient='records')
HTML_TEMPLATE = """
        <script src="https://cdnjs.cloudflare.com/ajax/libs/
webcomponentsjs/1.3.3/webcomponents-lite.js"></script>
        <link rel="import" href="https://raw.githubusercontent.com/
PAIR-code/facets/1.0.0/facets-dist/facets-jupyter.html">
        <facets-dive id="elem" height="600"></facets-dive>
        <script>
          var data = {jsonstr};
          document.querySelector("#elem").data = data;
        </script>"""
html = HTML_TEMPLATE.format(jsonstr=jsonstr)
display(HTML(html))
```

Facets displays the data with default options:

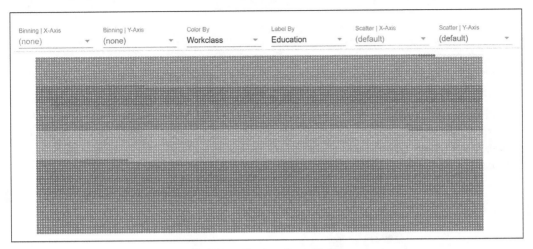

Figure 5.4: The interface of Facets

We are now ready to analyze the data.

Analyzing the training data with Facets

We will limit our analysis to trying to find critical features that determine the income level of a person. We will strive to avoid features that could offend the people using the AI application.

If we exclude homeless people and billionaires, we will find that for the population of people working around the world, two significant features in this dataset (age and years in education) produce interesting results.

To visualize these two features, we will display the first feature: age. Choose the **Age** option under **Binning | X-Axis** and **Over-50K** in the **Color By** field, as shown in *Figure 5.5*:

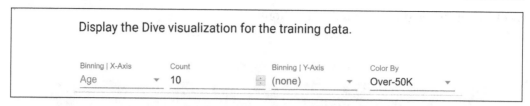

Figure 5.5: The Dive visualization tool of Facets

You will see age groups in the *x* axis and two-color bars for each group. The lower portion of the bars is blue (see the following color plot), representing lower income values. The higher part of the bars is red, representing the higher income values. Look carefully at the following visualization:

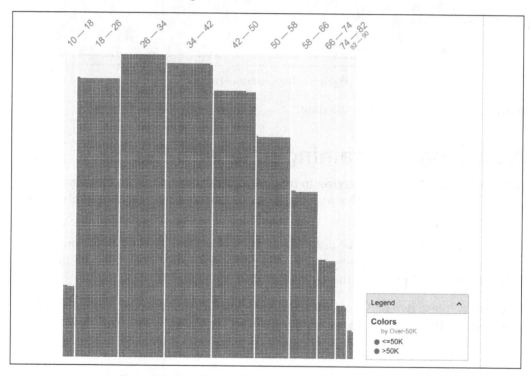

Figure 5.6: Chart showing that as age increases, so does income

The following universal principals clearly appear:

- A ten-year-old person earns less than a person who is 30 years old
- A person who is over 70 years old is more likely than not to be retired and have lower income than a person who is 40 years old
- The income curve increases from childhood to adulthood, reaches a peak, and then goes slowly down with age

This natural physical reality provides reliable inferences.

Now, let's add the number of years of education (**Education-Num**) to **Binning | Y-Axis**:

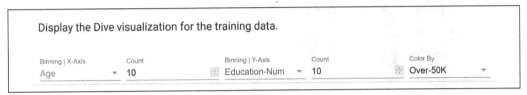

Figure 5.7: Defining the *y* axis of Dive

The visualization changes and provides bins per years of education. The *x* axis represents the age of the population analyzed in years binned.

The *y* axis bins represent the number of years of education of the person in question. For example, 12 means 12 years of education. 15-16 means 15 to 16 years of education (such as a Ph.D., for example).

The bottom section (colored blue in the color image) of each bar represents an income of <50K. The top section (colored red in the color image) represents an income of >50K:

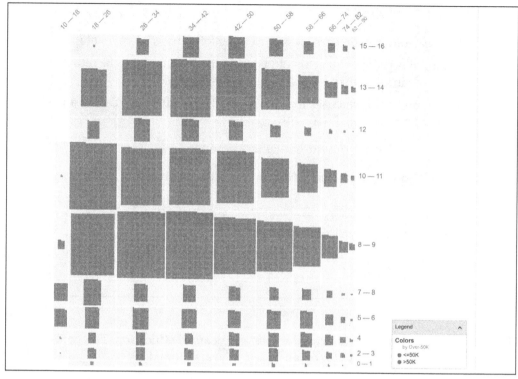

Figure 5.8: Higher education (on the *y* axis) leads to higher income (on the *x* axis)

Several additional universal principals appear, as follows:

- The longer a person studies, the more that person will earn. For example, in the bin of 15-16 years of education, you can see that there are practically only individuals with an income of >50K.

- Learning can be acquired through experience. For example, in the range of 8-9 years of education, you can see that income increases slightly with years of experience. In the range of 13-14 years of education, the progression is faster due to better job opportunities.

- After a few years of experience, a person with higher education will make more income. This is linked to learning acquired through experience.

- The age factor is intensified by education and experience, which explains why the higher-income portion of the bars increase in a significant way for those having between 13 and 17 years of education starting at age 30, for example.

Can an ML algorithm verify this hypothesis? Are there limits? Let's check the anticipated outputs with a k-means clustering program.

Verifying the anticipated outputs

In the last section, we found two key features that determine the income of a given person: age and number of years of education. These two features do not include the controversial features we seek to avoid.

We will extract the age and education-num columns from the adult.data file containing the U.S. census data. Then we create a file with those two columns named data_age_education.csv. The header includes the two features and the corresponding data from the original data file:

```
age,numed
39,13
50,13
38,9
53,7
28,13
37,14
...
```

The file is ready, and we can train it with an ML algorithm.

Using KMC to verify the anticipated results

We will build a separate Python program with a **k-means clustering (KMC)** algorithm before continuing with the WIT_Model_Comparison_Ethical.ipynb notebook. The goal is to divide the data into two categories: income above 50K, and equal to and below 50K. Once the data is classified, we will label it.

Open /KMC/k-means_clustering.py.

We will first import the modules we need:

```
from sklearn.cluster import KMeans # for the KMC
import pandas as pd # to load the data into DataFrames
import pickle # to save the trained KMC model and
            # load it to generate the outputs
import numpy as np # to manage arrays
```

Now, we read the data file containing the two key features we will classify and label:

```
# I. Training the dataset
dataset = pd.read_csv('data_age_education.csv')
print(dataset.head())
print(dataset)
```

The first lines of the output show that the DataFrame contains the data we will use:

```
      age   numed
0     39     13
1     50     13
2     38      9
3     53      7
4     28     13
...
```

We will now insert the KMC:

```
# creating the classifier
k = 2
kmeans = KMeans(n_clusters=k)
```

k = 2 defines the number of clusters we want to calculate. One cluster will be the records labeled >50K. The other cluster will contain the records labeled <=50K.

Each cluster is built around a geometric center, a centroid. The centroid is the center of the mean of the sum of distances of x data points of each cluster.

The variables used by the k-means estimator are as follows:

- k is the number of clusters
- u is the centroid of each cluster
- x represents each of the data points from 1 to n

The Euclidean distance, in one dimension, is the distance between two points x and y, expressed as follows:

$$\sqrt[2]{(x - y)^2}$$

The closer the points are to each other and to the centroid of a cluster, the higher the accuracy of the KMC is for that cluster. We can now plug the variables in the following equation:

$$\min \sum_{k=1}^{K} \sum_{x_i \in K_k}^{n} |x - \mu_k|^2$$

Lloyd's algorithm will use this type of equation to optimize the clusters.

The program will now run to fit the dataset and optimize the clusters:

```
# k-means clustering algorithm
kmeans = kmeans.fit(dataset)         # Computing k-means clustering
gcenters = kmeans.cluster_centers_   # The geometric centers or
                                     # centroids
```

The centroids are displayed by the program once the training is over:

```
print("The geometric centers or centroids:")
print(gcenters)
```

The output is as follows:

```
The geometric centers or centroids:
[[52.02343227 10.17473778]
 [29.12992991 10.01454127]]
```

Note that the value of the centroids can vary from calculation to calculation.

The program now saves the model:

```
# save model
filename = "kmc_model.sav"
pickle.dump(kmeans, open(filename, 'wb'))
print("model saved")
```

The program can now load the trained model:

```
# II. Testing the dataset
# dataset = pd.read_csv('data.csv')
kmeans = pickle.load(open('kmc_model.sav', 'rb'))
```

We create an array to store our predictions and activate the prediction variable:

```
# making and saving the predictions
kmcpred = np.zeros((32563, 3))
predict = 1
```

The program now makes predictions on the dataset, labels the records, and saves the results in a .csv file:

```
if predict == 1:
    for i in range(0, 32560):
        xf1 = dataset.at[i, 'age']; xf2 = dataset.at[i, 'numed'];
```

```
        X_DL = [[xf1, xf2]]
        prediction = kmeans.predict(X_DL)
        # print(i+1, "The prediction for", X_DL, " is:",
        #         str(prediction).strip('[]'))
        # print(i+1, "The prediction for", str(X_DL).strip('[]'),
        #         " is:", str(prediction).strip('[]'))
        p = str(prediction).strip('[]')
        p = int(p)
        kmcpred[i][0] = int(xf1)
        kmcpred[i][1] = int(xf2)
        kmcpred[i][2] = p
np.savetxt('ckmc.csv', kmcpred, delimiter=',', fmt='%d')
print("predictions saved")
```

The file contains the two key features and the labels, respectively, `age`, `education-num`, and the binary class (`0` or `1`):

```
39,13,1
50,13,0
38,9,1
53,7,0
28,13,1
```

Note that the label values can change from one to another for a given class.

We will now upload the `ckmc.csv` file to a spreadsheet that already contains the `adult.data` file, a sample of the U.S. census data with ML labels.

Analyzing the output of the KMC algorithm

In the last section, we produced the `ckmc.csv` file. We can now compare the results obtained by the KMC and the results produced by the ML algorithms used to create `adult.data`, the original trained U.S. census data file used in this chapter.

We will first load the `adult.data` file, as displayed in the following three screenshots. The **adult data** tab of the spreadsheet of `data_analysis.xlsx` is available in the directory of this chapter. The following table contains the first columns:

Age	Workclass	fnlwgt	Education	Education-Num	Marital-Status	Occupation
37	Private	284582	Masters	14	Married-civ-spouse	Exec-managerial

This table contains the following columns:

Relationship	Race	Sex	Capital-Gain	Capital-Loss	Hours-per-week
Wife	White	Female	0	0	40

The last columns of the `adult.data` file contain the controversial data for which we need to make a decision regarding its usage:

Relationship	Race	Sex	Capital-Gain	Capital-Loss	Hours-per-week	Country

Now, we insert the label of the initial dataset, Over-50K, and the three columns of `ckmc.csv`, the output of the KMC verification program:

Over-50K	kage	kednum	Centroid
<=50K	37	14	1
>50K	31	14	1

We will analyze two samples to explain the results, starting with sample 1.

Sample 1 – Filtering by age 30 to 39 and 14 years of education

We will filter the data using the spreadsheet's filters to focus on the people who are between 30 and 39 years old. We also select 14 years of education in the Education-Num field. 14 years is about what it takes to obtain a bachelor's or a master's degree.

When we look at the first 4 records, we see that our KMC predicts 1, >50K for all 4 records:

Race	Sex	Country	Over-50K	kage	kednum	centroid
White	Female	United-States	<=50K	37	14	1
White	Female	United-States	>50K	31	14	1
White	Male	United-States	<=50K	33	14	1
White	Male	Iran	>50K	38	14	1

However, you will notice the algorithms used to predict that the income of the people are not stable with these features.

The `adult.names` file contains a description of the ML algorithms used and the error rate. For example, the following excerpt of `adult.names` provides a description of the work accomplished:

```
|    Algorithm               Error
|  -- ----------------        -----
|  1  C4.5                    15.54
|  2  C4.5-auto               14.46
|  3  C4.5 rules              14.94
|  4  Voted ID3 (0.6)         15.64
|  5  Voted ID3 (0.8)         16.47
|  6  T2                      16.84
|  7  1R                      19.54
|  8  NBTree                  14.10
|  9  CN2                     16.00
| 10  HOODG                   14.82
| 11  FSS Naive Bayes         14.05
| 12  IDTM (Decision table)   14.46
| 13  Naive-Bayes             16.12
| 14  Nearest-neighbor (1)    21.42
| 15  Nearest-neighbor (3)    20.35
More...
```

We will name these algorithms the USC algorithms (U.S. census algorithms) in this section.

For each result, we will state that the >50K column prediction is positive when income is >50K and negative if the income is <=50K.

The Over-50K column resulting from the original data leads to several questions:

- Line 1 shows a positive result for the KMC but not for the USC.

- Could race be a discriminating feature? Not in this case, since all four lines contain White as the feature for race.

- Could work class be a discriminating feature? Not in this case, since the first two lines are private and USC does not produce the same label.

- Could the sex of the person make a difference? Not in this case, since the first two lines are Female, and the two other lines are Male.

- Could the country of origin make a difference? Not in this case, because the fourth person in this sample comes from Iran and shows a positive result for USC.

- The relationship or marital status makes no sense, so it is ignored for this case.

Clearly, the KMC shows a logical result in this age group for people who have a master's degree or above. However, USC cannot explain why the results are not stable.

In this case, our implementation of XAI has led to several interesting questions on how to predict the income of the people based on the information provided.

Let's add a controversial feature, such as race.

Sample 2 – Filtering by age 30 to 39, 14 years of education, and "race"="black" or "race"="white"

On lines 13,372 and 13,378, we have two interesting observations:

Wife	Black	Female	United-States	>50K	38	14	1
Unmarried	White	Female	United-States	<=50K	34	14	1

Race (Black or White) makes no sense here. Black is positive for USC and negative for White. Opposite cases can be found for USC. The KMC algorithm provides positive values that seem logical.

We could examine hundreds of samples and still not reach conclusive proof that features other than age and the level of education provide highly accurate results.

Let's conclude this analysis.

Conclusion of the analysis

We have explored the original adult.data file and have reached the following conclusions:

- The U.S. census data represents best what it was designed for: a census of the population of the United States
- The adult.data U.S. census sample contains labeled data showing how to use ML algorithms for various tasks
- The adult.data file provides a unique dataset for XAI

The team that used the U.S. census data to test ML programs did an excellent job of showing how AI can be applied to datasets.

XAI shows that the data contained in the adult.data file is insufficient to predict the income of a person.

Using a customized what-if approach with Facets Dive and a KMC, we explored two key features of the `adult.data` file: age and the number of years of education. The results were logical and showed no bias. However, better results could be obtained with more information on a person.

It appears that in real-life projects, two more key features are required to produce better income predictions:

- The level of consistency between the education of a person and their work experience. If a person has a master's degree in mathematics, for example, but works as a librarian for some reason or another, there will be a significant income variance.

- The number of successful years of experience in a given field is a crucial factor when recruiting a person.

We know that age, level of education, years of successful experience, and the level of consistency between our education and our job constitute the pillars of our market value.

 Many cultural factors, along with our personalities, influence how successful we are in getting a higher income, or if we choose a lower income for a better quality of life.

We now know that key information is missing in the `adult.data` dataset and the controversial fields do not really explain the differences between the labels.

We will thus transform the controversial columns into cultural columns that provide interesting information on a person, if the person consents to offering this private data.

Transforming the input data

We will now suppress the controversial data, keeping the same number of fields but replacing the field names with other cultural information before using Google's WIT tool. The motivation isn't to obtain better numerical results. These fields provide a better, more human background to a person that can help predict if that person's income is high or low. The present practice of the market is to ignore discriminatory information on a person and focus on the real qualities required to get a job done.

The original data contained the following columns:

```
csv_columns = ["Age", "Workclass", "fnlwgt", "Education",
               "Education-Num", "Marital-Status", "Occupation",
               "Relationship", "Race", "Sex", "Capital-Gain",
               "Capital-Loss", "Hours-per-week", "Country",
               "Over-50K"]
```

The transformed data contains the following columns:

```
csv_columns = ["Age", "Purchasing", "fnlwgt", "Education",
               "Education-Num", "media", "Occupation", "transport",
               "reading", "traveling", "Capital-Gain",
               "Capital-Loss", "Hours-per-week", "Country",
               "Over-50K"]
```

The following descriptions of the transformed features are merely speculative at this point. We would have to obtain real data from a random sample of a cultural survey. Then we would have to implement ML algorithms to see which features have an impact on income predictions. We would also have to add more features if the results weren't accurate.

We consider the following new fields as an excellent way to approach XAI for educational purposes without having to use controversial information:

- **Workclass becomes purchasing**: Purchasing contains information on purchasing habits. The behavior of a person who mostly goes to markets and not supermarkets can be an income indicator, for example. We define our new Purchasing field as:

  $Purchase$ = {shops, markets, malls, supermarkets}

- **Marital-Status becomes media**: Media describes the way a person accesses music and movies. We define our new media field as:

  $Media$ = {DVD, live, social_networks, television, theaters, websites}

  A person who mostly goes to a theater to see a movie spends more money than a person who mostly watches movies on television.

- **Relationship becomes transport**: Transport shows how a person goes from one location to another. A person who drives an expensive car and never takes a bus spends more money than a person who either walks or takes a bus. We define our new transport field as:

  $Transport$ = {walking, running, cycling, bus, car}

- **Race becomes reading**: A person who reads books and magazines versus a person who only reads websites could be more educated. We define our new reading field as:

Reading = {books, magazines, television, websites}

- **Sex becomes traveling preferences, in terms of physical activities**: One person might mostly prefer action, such as surfing, running, swimming, and other structured physical activities. Another person might mostly prefer to discover new horizons, such as treks in distant mountains or jungles. Swimming at a local pool costs less than treks in distant countries, for example. We define our new traveling field as:

Traveling = {action, adventures}

Note that some of the features of the original content are still present in some of these fields, creating some useful noise in the dataset.

Our customized what-if method leads to the suppression of controversial fields in the adult.data dataset and we replaced them with cultural features that will not offend anybody. On top of that, our cultural features make more sense when analyzing a person's level of income.

We will now explore WIT applied to an entertaining ethical dataset.

WIT applied to a transformed dataset

We carried out a full what-if XAI investigation from scratch. We then transformed the data of the U.S. census sample. Now, let's explore the transformed data using Google's WIT tool.

The first step is to load our transformed dataset from GitHub, or you can choose to use Google Drive by setting repository to "google":

```
# @title Importing data <br>
# Set repository to "github"(default) to read the data
# from GitHub <br>
# Set repository to "google" to read the data
# from Google {display-mode: "form"}
import os
from google.colab import drive


# Set repository to "github" to read the data from GitHub
# Set repository to "google" to read the data from Google
repository = "github"
```

```
if repository == "github":
  !curl -L https://raw.githubusercontent.com/PacktPublishing/Hands-
On-Explainable-AI-XAI-with-Python/master/Chapter05/adult_train.csv
--output "adult_train.csv"
  dtrain = "/content/adult_train.csv"
  print(dtrain)


if repository == "google":
  # Mounting the drive. If it is not mounted, a prompt
  # will provide instructions.
  drive.mount('/content/drive')
  # Setting the path for each file
  dtrain = '/content/drive/My Drive/XAI/Chapter05/adult_train.csv'
  print(dtrain)
```

We comment out the former CSV column definitions and define our feature names:

```
# @title Read training dataset from CSV {display-mode: "form"}

import pandas as pd

# Set the path to the CSV containing the dataset to train on.
csv_path = dtrain

# Set the column names for the columns in the CSV.
# If the CSV's first line is a header line containing
# the column names, then set this to None.
csv_columns = ["Age", "Purchasing", "fnlwgt", "Education",
               "Education-Num", "media", "Occupation", "transport",
               "reading", "traveling", "Capital-Gain",
               "Capital-Loss", "Hours-per-week", "Country",
               "Over-50K"]
'''
csv_columns = ["Age", "Workclass", "fnlwgt", "Education",
               "Education-Num", "Marital-Status", "Occupation",
               "Relationship", "Race", "Sex", "Capital-Gain",
               "Capital-Loss", "Hours-per-week", "Country",
               "Over-50K"]
'''
```

We now display the transformed data:

```
# Read the dataset from the provided CSV and print out
# information about it.
df = pd.read_csv(csv_path, names=csv_columns, skipinitialspace=True)
df
```

The following output shows our transformed data:

	Age	Purchasing	fnlwgt	Education	Education-Num	media	Occupation
0	39	shops	77516	Bachelors	13	live	Adm-clerical
1	50	markets	83311	Bachelors	13	DVD	Exec-managerial
2	38	malls	215646	HS-grad	9	social_networks	Handlers-cleaners
3	53	malls	234721	11th	7	DVD	Handlers-cleaners
4	28	malls	338409	Bachelors	13	DVD	Prof-specialty
...	...	...	...	...	...	...	...
10353	33	malls	126414	Bachelors	13	DVD	Other-service
10354	27	malls	43652	Bachelors	13	live	Adm-clerical
10355	47	supermarkets	227244	Bachelors	13	DVD	Protective-serv
10356	29	malls	160731	HS-grad	9	DVD	Craft-repair
10357	33	malls	287878	Some-college	10	DVD	Other-service

Figure 5.9: Transformed data

The program now specifies the label column, which has not been transformed. We respect the original labeling of the dataset and the comments from the Google team:

```
# @title Specify input columns and column to predict
# {display-mode: "form"}
import numpy as np

# Set the column in the dataset you wish for the model to predict
label_column = 'Over-50K'

# Make the label column numeric (0 and 1), for use in our model.
# In this case, examples with a target value of '>50K' are
# considered to be in the '1' (positive) class and all other
# examples are considered to be in the '0' (negative) class.
make_label_column_numeric(df, label_column, lambda val: val == '>50')
```

Now, we insert our cultural features in place of the original data:

```
# Set list of all columns from the dataset we will use for
# model input.
```

```
input_features = ['Age', 'Purchasing', 'Education', 'media',
                  'Occupation', 'transport', 'reading', 'traveling',
                  'Capital-Gain', 'Capital-Loss', 'Hours-per-week',
                  'Country']
```

Our customized XAI investigation showed that we need additional data to make accurate income predictions. We thus applied an ethical approach—the controversial fields have been removed. The cultural data is random because we have seen that they are not significant when compared to the level of education. We know that a person with a master's degree or a Ph.D. has a higher probability of earning more than a person with a tenth-grade education. This feature will weigh heavily on the income level.

We now have an ethical dataset to explore Google's innovative WIT with.

The program now creates a list with all of the input features:

```
features_and_labels = input_features + [label_column]
```

The data has to be converted into datasets that are compatible with TensorFlow estimators:

```
# @title Convert dataset to tf.Example protos
# {display-mode: "form"}
examples = df_to_examples(df)
```

We now run the linear classifier as implemented by Google's team:

```
# @title Create and train the linear classifier
# {display-mode: "form"}
num_steps = 2000 # @param {type: "number"}

# Create a feature spec for the classifier
feature_spec = create_feature_spec(df, features_and_labels)

# Define and train the classifier
train_inpf = functools.partial(tfexamples_input_fn, examples,
                               feature_spec, label_column)
classifier = tf.estimator.LinearClassifier(
    feature_columns=create_feature_columns(input_features,
        feature_spec))
classifier.train(train_inpf, steps=num_steps)
```

We then run the **deep neural network (DNN)** as implemented by Google's team:

```
# @title Create and train the DNN classifier {display-mode: "form"}
num_steps_2 = 2000 # @param {type: "number"}

classifier2 = tf.estimator.DNNClassifier(
    feature_columns=create_feature_columns(input_features,
        feature_spec), hidden_units=[128, 64, 32])
classifier2.train(train_inpf, steps=num_steps_2)
```

We will explore TensorFlow's DNN and others in more detail in *Chapter 6, AI Fairness with Google's What-If Tool (WIT)*.

For now, move on and display the trained dataset in Google's implementation of Facets Dive.

We choose the number of data points we wish to explore and the height of the tool:

```
num_datapoints = 2000    # @param {type: "number"}
tool_height_in_px = 1000 # @param {type: "number"}
```

We import the visualization `witwidget` modules:

```
from witwidget.notebook.visualization import WitConfigBuilder
from witwidget.notebook.visualization import WitWidget
```

For our example, we'll use our transformed dataset to test the model:

```
dtest = dtrain
# Load up the test dataset
test_csv_path = dtest
test_df = pd.read_csv(test_csv_path, names=csv_columns,
                    skipinitialspace=True, skiprows=1)
make_label_column_numeric(test_df, label_column,
                        lambda val: val == '>50K.')
test_examples = df_to_examples(test_df[0:num_datapoints])
```

We finally set up the tool and display the WIT visualization interface:

```
config_builder = WitConfigBuilder(
    test_examples[0:num_datapoints]).set_estimator_and_feature_spec(
    classifier, feature_spec).set_compare_estimator_and_feature_spec(
    classifier2, feature_spec).set_label_vocab(
    ['Under 50K', 'Over 50K'])
a = WitWidget(config_builder, height=tool_height_in_px)
```

You are ready to explore the results with Google's implementation of Facets in WIT from a user's perspective:

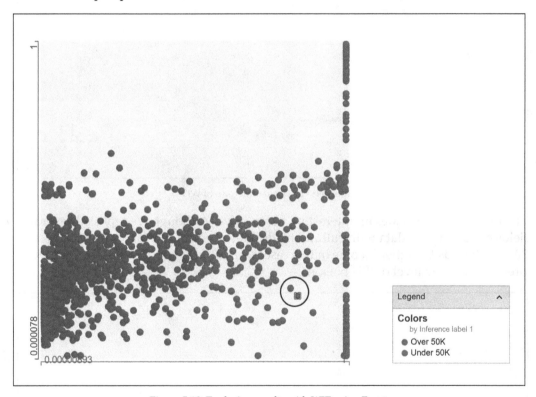

Figure 5.10: Exploring results with WIT using Facets

The data point chosen is a >50K point in the blue (see color image) area. We will now look at the features of this person:

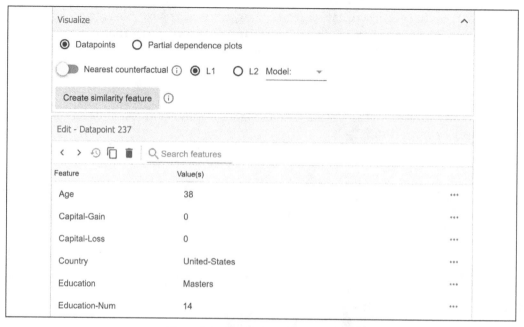

Figure 5.11: The feature interface of WIT

The information provides an interesting perspective. Although we replaced several fields of the original data with cultural fields, higher education for a person between 30 and 39 leads to higher income in this case. Our cultural features did not alter the predicted income level of this person:

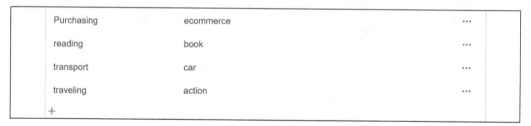

Figure 5.12: Cultural features in WIT that did not modify the predictions

We know that we cannot expect sufficiently accurate results until we add other fields such as the number of years of job experience in the area, or the presence of a college degree.

We can use WIT to prove this by activating the nearest counterfactual data point:

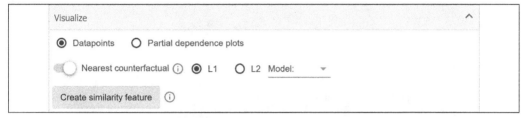

Figure 5.13: Activating the nearest counterfactual option

A new point appears in the <=50K area of the visualization module:

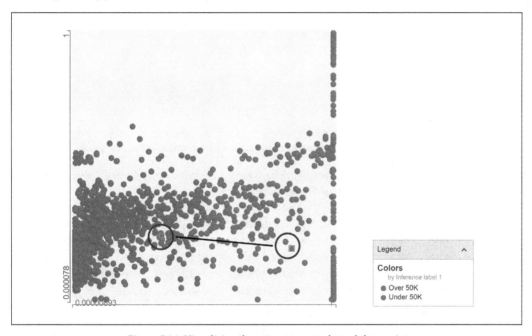

Figure 5.14: Visualizing the nearest counterfactual data point

This excellent tool has displayed a data point that should have been >50 but isn't. You can investigate hundreds of data points and find out which features count the most for a given model.

The information of the first data point we chose automatically displays the counterfactual data point so that we can compare the features:

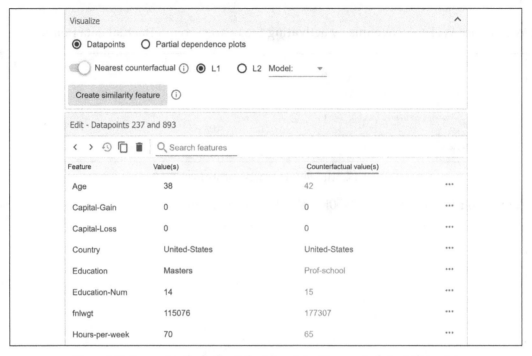

Figure 5.15: Comparing the features of a data point with a counterfactual data point

We can make some observations without drawing any conclusions until we have more information on the careers of these two people:

- The counterfactual age value is not in the 30-39 age group we targeted. However, this is not a valid explanation since the graph in the *Analyzing the training data with Facets* section of this chapter showed that the 42-50 age group with 14+ years of education constitutes a higher proportion of >50K earners than the 34-42 age group with 14+ years of education.

- They both have studied for 14+ years.

- One person works 70 hours and the other 65 hours. That does not mean much, with just a 5-hour difference. We have no information to confirm that those 5 hours are paid as overtime work. We would need to have this information to be able to make such a conclusion.

- We don't know how much they both actually earn. Maybe the counterfactual data point represents a person who makes 50K, which puts the value in the <=50K class. Perhaps the person who makes >50K only earns 50.5K. The border between the two classes is very precise, although the data isn't.

We recommend that you spend as much time as necessary drawing exciting what-if conclusions that will boost your XAI expertise.

In this section, we loaded the dataset and transformed and defined the new features. We then ran a linear estimator and a DNN. We displayed the data points in WIT's visualization module to investigate factual and counterfactual data points.

Summary

In this chapter, we first explored the moral and ethical issues involved in an AI project. We asked ourselves whether using certain features could offend the future users of our program.

We examined the legal issues of some of the information in a dataset from a legal perspective. We discovered that the legal use of information depends on who processes it and how it is collected. The United States government, for example, is entitled to use data on certain features of a person for a U.S. census survey.

We found that even if a government can use specific information, this doesn't mean that a private corporation can use it. This is illegal for many other applications. Both U.S. and European legislators have enacted strict privacy laws and make sure to apply them.

The ML perspective showed that the key features, such as age and the level of education, provide interesting results using a KMC algorithm. We built a KMC algorithm and trained on age and level of education. We saved the model and ran it to produce our labels. These labels provided a logical explanation. If you have a high level of education, such as 14+ years of overall education, for example, you are more likely to have a higher income than somebody with less education.

The KMC algorithm detected that higher education in age groups with some years of experience provides a higher income. However, the same customized XAI approach showed that additional features were required to predict the income level of a given person.

We suppressed the controversial features of the original dataset and inserted random cultural features.

We trained the transformed data with a linear classifier and a DNN, leaving the initial labels as they were.

Finally, we used WIT's visualization modules to display the data. We saw how to use WIT to find explanations for factual and counterfactual data points.

In the next chapter, *AI Fairness with Google's What-If Tool (WIT)*, we will build an ethical XAI investigation program.

Questions

1. Moral considerations mean nothing in AI as long as it's legal. (True | False)
2. Explaining AI with an ethical approach will help users trust AI. (True | False)
3. There is no need to check whether a dataset contains legal data. (True | False)
4. Using machine learning algorithms to verify datasets is productive. (True | False)
5. Facets Dive requires an ML algorithm. (True | False)
6. You can anticipate ML outputs with Facets Dive. (True | False)
7. You can use ML to verify your intuitive predictions. (True | False)
8. Some features in an ML model can be suppressed without changing the results. (True | False)
9. Some datasets provide accurate ML labels but inaccurate real-life results. (True | False)
10. You can visualize counterfactual datapoints with WIT. (True | False)

References

Google's WIT income classification example can be found at https://pair-code. github.io/what-if-tool/index.html#demos

Further reading

For more on k-means clustering, see the following link:

https://scikit-learn.org/stable/modules/generated/sklearn.cluster.KMeans. html

6

AI Fairness with Google's What-If Tool (WIT)

Google's **PAIR (People + AI Research)** designed the **What-If Tool (WIT)**, a visualization tool designed to investigate the fairness of an AI model. Usage of WIT leads us directly to a critical ethical and moral question: *what do we consider as fair?* WIT provides the tools to represent what we view as bias so that we can build the most impartial AI systems possible.

Developers of **machine learning (ML)** systems focus on accuracy and fairness. WIT takes us directly to the center of human-machine pragmatic decision-making. In *Chapter 2, White Box XAI for AI Bias and Ethics*, we discovered the difficulty each person experiences when trying to make the right decision. MIT's Moral Machine experiment brought us to the core of ML ethics. We represented life and death decision-making by humans and autonomous vehicles.

The PAIR team is dedicated to people-centric AI systems. Human-centered AI systems will take us beyond mathematical algorithms into an innovative world of human-machine interactions.

In this chapter, we will explore WIT's human-machine interface and interaction functionality.

We will start by examining the COMPAS dataset from an ethical and legal perspective. We will define the difference between **explainable AI (XAI)**, and the AI interpretability required in some cases.

We will then get started with WIT, import the dataset, preprocess the data, and create the structures to train and test a **deep neural network (DNN)** model.

After training the model, we will create a **SHapley Additive exPlanations (SHAP)** explainer based on Python code that we developed in *Chapter 4, Microsoft Azure Machine Learning Model Interpretability with SHAP*. We will begin to interpret the model with a SHAP plot.

Finally, we will implement WIT's datapoint explorer and editor human-machine interactive interface. WIT contains Facets functionality, as we learned in *Chapter 3, Explaining Machine Learning with Facets*. We will discover how to use WIT to decide what we think is fair and what we find biased in ML datasets and model predictions.

This chapter covers the following topics:

- Datasets from ethical and legal perspectives
- Creating a DNN model with TensorFlow
- Creating a SHAP explainer and plotting the features of the dataset
- Creating the WIT datapoint explorer and editor
- Advanced Facets functionality
- Ground truth
- Cost ratio
- Fairness
- The ROC curve and AUC
- Slicing
- The PR curve
- The confusion matrix

Our first step will be to view the dataset and project from an ethical AI perspective.

Interpretability and explainability from an ethical AI perspective

It comes as no surprise that Google's WIT AI fairness example notebook comes with a biased dataset. It is up to us to use WIT to point out the unethical or moral dilemmas contained in the COMPAS dataset.

COMPAS stands for **Correctional Offender Management Profiling for Alternative Sanctions**. Judges and parole officers are said to score the probability of recidivism for a given defendant.

In this section, our task will be to transform the dataset into an unbiased, ethical dataset. We will analyze COMPAS with people-centered AI before importing it.

We will first describe the ethical and legal perspectives. Then we will define AI explainability and interpretability for our COMPAS example. Finally, we will prepare an ethical dataset for our model by improving the feature names of the dataset.

Our ethical process fits the spirit of Google's research team when they designed WIT for us to detect bias in datasets or models.

But first, let's go through the ethical perspective.

The ethical perspective

The COMPAS dataset contains unethical data that we will transform into ethical data before using the dataset.

On Kaggle, the *Context* section, as of March 2020, states that the algorithms favor white defendants and discriminate against black defendants: `https://www.kaggle.com/danofer/compass`.

If you read Kaggle's text carefully, you will notice that it also mentions white defendants and black inmates. The correct formulation should always at least be equal, stating "white and black defendants."

The whole aspect of color should be ignored, and we should only mention "defendants."

The ambiguities we just brought up have legal consequences, and are related to deep social tensions that need to end.

Let's now explain why this is important from a legal perspective as well.

The legal perspective

If you try to use this type of dataset in Europe, for example, you will potentially face charges for racial discrimination or illegal information gathering as described in the *General Data Protection Regulation (GDPR), Article 9*:

> *"Art. 9 GDPR Processing of special categories of personal data*
>
> *Processing of personal data revealing racial or ethnic origin, political opinions, religious or philosophical beliefs, or trade union membership, and the processing of genetic data, biometric data for the purpose of uniquely identifying a natural person, data concerning health or data concerning a natural person's sex life or sexual orientation shall be prohibited."*

Source: https://gdpr-info.eu/, https://gdpr-info.eu/art-9-gdpr/

There are many exceptions to this law. However, you will need legal advice before attempting to collect or use this type of data.

We can now go further and ask ourselves why we would need to engage in unethical and biased datasets to explore WIT, Facets, and SHAP.

The straightforward answer is that we must be proactive when we explain and interpret AI.

Explaining and interpreting

In many cases, the words "explaining" and "interpreting" AI describe the same process. We can thus feel free to use the words indifferently. Most of the time, we do not have to worry about semantics. We just need to get the job done.

However, in this section, the difference between these two expressions is critical.

At first, we *interpret* laws, such as GDPR, Article 9. In a court of law, laws are interpreted and then applied.

Once the law is *interpreted*, a judge might have to *explain* a decision to a defendant.

An AI specialist can end up in a court of law trying to explain why an ML program was interpreting data in a biased and unethical manner.

To avoid these situations, we will transform the COMPAS dataset into ethical, educational data.

Preparing an ethical dataset

In this section, we will rename the columns that contain unethical column names.

The original COMPAS file used in the original WIT notebook was named `cox-violent-parsed_filt.csv`.

I renamed it by adding a suffix: `cox-violent-parsed_filt_transformed.csv`.

I also modified the feature names.

The original feature names that we will not be using were the following:

```
# input_features = ['sex_Female', 'sex_Male', 'age',
#                    'race_African-American', 'race_Caucasian',
#                    'race_Hispanic', 'race_Native American',
#                    'race_Other', 'priors_count', 'juv_fel_count',
#                    'juv_misd_count', 'juv_other_count']
```

The whole people-centered approach of WIT leads us to think about the bias such a dataset constitutes from ethical and legal perspectives.

I replaced the controversial names with income and social class features in the `input_features` array that we will create in the *Preprocessing the data* section of this chapter:

```
input_features = ['income_Lower', 'income_Higher', 'age',
                  'social-class_SC1', 'social-class_SC2',
                  'social-class_SC3', 'social-class_SC4',
                  'social-class_Other', 'priors_count',
                  'juv_fel_count', 'juv_misd_count',
                  'juv_other_count']
```

The new input feature names make the dataset ethical and still retain enough information for us to analyze accuracy and fairness with SHAP, Facets, and WIT.

Let's analyze the new input features one by one:

1. `'income_Lower'`: I selected a column with relatively high feature values. Objectively, a person with low income and no resources has a higher risk of being tempted by crime than a multi-millionaire.

2. `'income_Higher'`: I selected a column with relatively low feature values. Objectively, how many people with income over USD 200,000 try to steal a car or a television? How many professional soccer players, baseball players, and tennis players try to rob a bank?

It is evident in any country around the world that a richer person will tend to commit fewer major physical crimes than a poor person. However, some wealthy people do commit crimes, and almost all poor people are law-abiding citizens.

It can easily be seen that genetic factors do not make even a marginal contribution to the probability of committing a crime.

When a judge or parole officer makes a decision, the capacity of the defendant to get and keep a job is far more important than genetic factors.

Naturally, this is my firm opinion and belief as the author of this chapter! Others might have other opinions. That is the whole point of WIT. It takes us right to where humans have difficulties agreeing on ethical perspectives that vary from one culture to another!

3. `'age'`: This becomes an essential feature for people over 70 years old. It's difficult to imagine a hit-and-run crime committed by a 75-year-old defendant!

4. `'social-class_SC1'`: The social class we belong to makes quite a difference when it comes to physical crime. I'm using the term "physical" to exclude white-collar tax evasion crime, which is another domain in itself.

   There are now four social classes in the feature list. In this social class (`'social-class_SC1'`), access to education was limited or very difficult. Statistically, almost everyone in this category never committed a crime. However, the ones that did helped build up the statistics against this social class.

   Defining what this social class represents goes well beyond the scope of this book. Only sociologists could attempt to explain what this means. I left this feature in this notebook. In real life, I would take it out, as well as `'social-class_SC3'` and `'social-class_SC4'`. The motivation is simple. All social classes have predominantly law-abiding citizens and a few that lose their way.

   These features do not help. However, `'social-class_SC2'`, as I define it, does.

5. `'social-class_SC2'`: From a mathematical point of view, this is the only social class that makes a significant difference.

   I fit people with valuable knowledge in this class: college graduates in all fields, and people with less formal education but with useful skills for society (plumbers and electricians, for example).

   I also include people with strong beliefs that work pays and crime doesn't.

Competent, objective judges and parole officers assess these factors when making a decision. As in any social class, the majority of actors in a judicial system try to be objective. As for the others, it brings us back to cultural and personal bias.

The difficulties brought up in this section fully justify people-centered XAI! We can easily see the tensions that can arise from my comments in this section. Life is a constant MIT Moral Machine experiment!

6. `'social-class_SC3'`: See `'social-class_SC1'`.

7. `'social-class_SC4'`: See `'social-class_SC1'`.

8. `'social-class_Other'`: See `'social-class_SC1'`.

9. **The count features – `'priors_count'`, `'juv_fel_count'`, `'juv_misd_count'`, `'juv_other_count'`:** These features are worth consideration. The arrest record of a person contains objective information. If a person's rap sheet contains thirty lines for a person aged 20 versus one parking ticket offense for another person, this means something.

    However, these features provide information but also depend on what the present charges or behavior are at the time a decision must be made by a judge or parole officer.

We can safely contend that even with a more ethical dataset, I have raised as many issues as the ones I was trying to solve!

We now have the following considerations, for example:

- Am I biased by my own education and culture?
- Am I right, or am I wrong?
- Do others agree with me?
- Do other people with other perspectives disagree with my views?
- Would a victim of discrimination want to see the biased features anyway?
- Would a person that does not think the feature names are discriminating agree?

I can only conclude by saying that I expressed my doubts just as WIT expects us to investigate.

You are free to view this dataset in many other different ways!

In any case, the transformed dataset contains the information to take full advantage of all of the functionality of the program in this chapter.

Let's now get started with WIT.

Getting started with WIT

In this section, we will install WIT, import the dataset, preprocess the data, and create data structures to train and test the model.

Open `WIT_SHAP_COMPAS_DR.ipynb` in Google Colaboratory, which contains all of the modules necessary for this chapter.

We must first check the version of TensorFlow of our runtime. Google Colaboratory is installed with TensorFlow 1.x and TensorFlow 2.x. Google provides sample notebooks that use either TensorFlow 1.x or TensorFlow 2.x. In this case, our notebook needs to use TensorFlow 2.x.

Google provides a few lines of code for TensorFlow 1.x as well, plus a link to read for more information on the flexibility of Colab regarding TensorFlow versions:

```
# https://colab.research.google.com/notebooks/tensorflow_version.ipynb
# tf1 and tf2 management
# Restart runtime using 'Runtime' -> 'Restart runtime...'
%tensorflow_version 1.x
import tensorflow as tf
print(tf.__version__)
```

In our case, the first cell for this notebook is as follows:

```
import tensorflow
print(tensorflow.__version__)
```

The output will be as follows:

```
2.2.0
```

Installing WIT with SHAP takes one line of code:

```
# @title Install What-If Tool widget and SHAP library
!pip install --upgrade --quiet witwidget shap
```

We now import the modules required for `WIT_SHAP_COMPAS_DR.ipynb`:

```
# @title Importing data <br>
# Set repository to "github"(default) to read the data
# from GitHub <br>
# Set repository to "google" to read the data
# from Google {display-mode: "form"}
```

```
import pandas as pd
import numpy as np
import tensorflow as tf
import witwidget
import os
from google.colab import drive
import pickle

from tensorflow.keras.layers import Dense
from tensorflow.keras.models import Sequential

from sklearn.utils import shuffle
```

We can now import the dataset.

Importing the dataset

You can import the dataset from GitHub or your Google Drive.

In WIT_SHAP_COMPAS_DR.ipynb, repository is set to "github":

```
# Set repository to "github" to read the data from GitHub
# Set repository to "google" to read the data from Google
repository = "github"
```

The dataset file will be retrieved from GitHub:

```
if repository == "github":
    !curl -L https://raw.githubusercontent.com/PacktPublishing/Hands-On-
Explainable-AI-XAI-with-Python/master/Chapter06/cox-violent-parsed_
filt_transformed.csv --output "cox-violent-parsed_filt_transformed.csv"

    # Setting the path for each file
    df2 = "/content/cox-violent-parsed_filt_transformed.csv"
    print(df2)
```

However, you can choose to download cox-violent-parsed_filt_transformed.csv from GitHub and upload it to your Google Drive.

In that case, set repository to "google":

```
if repository == "google":
    # Mounting the drive. If it is not mounted, a prompt will
    # provide instructions
    drive.mount('/content/drive')
```

You can also choose your own directory name and path, for example:

```
# Setting the path for each file
df2 = '/content/drive/My Drive/XAI/Chapter06/cox-violent-parsed_filt_
transformed.csv'
print(df2)


df = pd.read_csv(df2)
```

The next step consists of preprocessing the data.

Preprocessing the data

In this section, we will preprocess that data before training the model. We will first filter the data that contains no useful information:

```
# Preprocess the data
# Filter out entries with no indication of recidivism or
# no compass score
df = df[df['is_recid'] != -1]
df = df[df['decile_score'] != -1]
```

We will now rename our key target feature `'is_recid'` so that it can easily be visualized in WIT:

```
# Rename recidivism column
df['recidivism_within_2_years'] = df['is_recid']
```

The program now creates a numeric binary value for the `'COMPASS_determination'` feature that we will also visualize as a prediction in WIT:

```
# Make the COMPASS label column numeric (0 and 1),
# for use in our model
df['COMPASS_determination'] = np.where(df['score_text'] == 'Low',
                                        0, 1)
```

These two columns are considered as dummy columns:

```
df = pd.get_dummies(df, columns=['income', 'social-class'])
```

The program now applies the transformations described in the *Preparing an ethical dataset* section of this chapter.

We will ignore the former column names:

```
# Get list of all columns from the dataset we will use
# for model input or output.
# input_features = ['sex_Female', 'sex_Male', 'age',
#                   'race_African-American', 'race_Caucasian',
#                   'race_Hispanic', 'race_Native American',
#                   'race_Other', 'priors_count', 'juv_fel_count',
#                   'juv_misd_count', 'juv_other_count']
```

We will now insert our transformed ethical feature names as well as the two target labels:

```
input_features = ['income_Lower', 'income_Higher', 'age',
                  'social-class_SC1', 'social-class_SC2',
                  'social-class_SC3', 'social-class_SC4',
                  'social-class_Other', 'priors_count',
                  'juv_fel_count', 'juv_misd_count',
                  'juv_other_count']
to_keep = input_features + ['recidivism_within_2_years',
                            'COMPASS_determination']
```

to_keep contains the feature names and two labels. 'COMPASS_determination' is the training label. We will use 'recidivism_within_2_years' to measure the performance of the model.

We now finalize the preprocessing phase:

```
to_remove = [col for col in df.columns if col not in to_keep]
df = df.drop(columns=to_remove)
input_columns = df.columns.tolist()
labels = df['COMPASS_determination']
```

We now display the first lines of the dataset:

```
df.head()
```

The output will appear in a structured way:

	age	juv_fel_count	juv_misd_count	juv_other_count	priors_count
0	69	0	0	0	0
1	69	0	0	0	0
3	34	0	0	0	0
4	24	0	0	1	4
5	24	0	0	1	4

Figure 6.1: The fields of the dataset and sample data

We are all set to create the data structures to train and test the model.

Creating data structures to train and test the model

In this section, we create the data structures to train and test the model.

We first drop the training label, 'COMPASS_determination' and the measuring label, 'recidivism_within_2_years':

```
df_for_training = df.drop(columns=['COMPASS_determination',
                                   'recidivism_within_2_years'])
```

Now create the train data and test data structures:

```
train_size = int(len(df_for_training) * 0.8)
train_data = df_for_training[:train_size]
train_labels = labels[:train_size]
test_data_with_labels = df[train_size:]
```

We have transformed the data, loaded it, preprocessed it, and created data structures to train and test the model.

We will now create a DNN model.

Creating a DNN model

In this section, we will create a dense neural network using a Keras sequential model. The scope of the WIT example in this notebook is to explain the behavior of a model through its input data and outputs. However, we will outline a brief description of the DNN created in this section.

In a dense neural network, all of the neurons of a layer are connected to all of the layers of the previous layer, as shown in *Figure 6.2*:

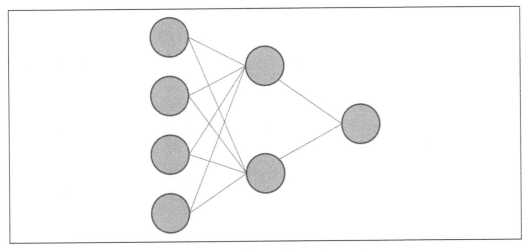

Figure 6.2: Dense layers of a neural network

The graph shows that the first layer contains four neurons, the second layer two neurons, and the last layer will produce a binary result of 1 or 0 with its single neuron.

 Each neuron in a layer will be connected to all the neurons of the previous layer.

In this model, each layer contains fewer neurons than the previous layer leading to a single neuron, which will produce a 0 or 1 output to make a prediction.

We now create the model and compile it:

```
# Create the model
# This is the size of the array we'll be feeding into our model
# for each example
input_size = len(train_data.iloc[0])

model = Sequential()
model.add(Dense(200, input_shape=(input_size,), activation='relu'))
model.add(Dense(50, activation='relu'))
model.add(Dense(25, activation='relu'))
model.add(Dense(1, activation='sigmoid'))
```

We see that although all of the neurons of a layer are connected to all of the neurons of the previous layer, the number of neurons per layer diminishes: from 200, to 50, 25, and then 1, the binary output.

The neurons of a sequential model are activated by two approaches:

- `activation='relu'`: For a neuron x, the **rectified linear unit (ReLU)** function will return the following:

$$f(x) = \max(0, x)$$

- `activation='sigmoid'`: For a neuron x, the logistic sigmoid function will return the following:

$$f(x) = \frac{1}{1 + e^{-x}}$$

You can add a summary:

```
model.summary()
```

The output will confirm the architecture of your model:

```
Model: "sequential"

Layer (type)                 Output Shape              Param #
=================================================================
dense (Dense)                (None, 200)               2600

dense_1 (Dense)              (None, 50)                10050

dense_2 (Dense)              (None, 25)                1275

dense_3 (Dense)              (None, 1)                 26
=================================================================
Total params: 13,951
Trainable params: 13,951
Non-trainable params: 0
```

Figure 6.3: The architecture of the model of the neural network

The model requires a loss function and optimizer. The loss function calculates the distance between the model's predictions and the binary labels it should predict. The optimizer finds the best way to change the weights and biases at each iteration:

```
model.compile(loss='mean_squared_error', optimizer='adam')
```

- `'loss'`: The `mean_squared_error` loss function is a mean square regression loss. It calculates the distance between the predicted value of a sample i defined as $\hat{y}_i$ and y_i. The optimizer will use this value to modify the weights of the layers. This iterative process will continue until the accuracy of the model improves enough for the model to stop training the dataset.

- `'optimizer'`: Adam is a stochastic optimizer that can automatically adjust to update parameters using adaptive estimates.

In this section, we briefly went through the DNN estimator. Once again, the primary goal of the WIT approach in this notebook is to explain the model's predictions based on the input data and the output data.

The compiled model now requires training.

Training the model

In this section, we will train the model and go through the model's parameters.

The model trains the data with the following parameters:

```
# Train the model
model.fit(train_data.values, train_labels.values, epochs=4,
          batch_size=32, validation_split=0.1)
```

- `train_data.values` contains the training values.
- `train_labels.values` contains the training labels to predict.
- `epochs=4` will activate the optimization process four times over a number of samples. The loss should diminish or at least remain sufficient and stable.
- `batch_size=32` is the number of samples per gradient update.
- `validation_split=0.1` will split the training set, the fraction of the dataset to be used for training, to `0.1`.

The sequential Keras model has trained the data. Before running WIT, we will create a SHAP explainer to interpret the trained model's predictions with a SHAP plot.

Creating a SHAP explainer

In this section, we will create a SHAP explainer.

We described SHAP in detail in *Chapter 4, Microsoft Azure Machine Learning Model Interpretability with SHAP*. If you wish, you can go through that chapter again before moving on.

We pass a subset of our training data to the explainer:

```
# Create a SHAP explainer by passing a subset of our training data
import shap
sample_size = 500
```

```
if sample_size > len(train_data.values):
   sample_size = len(train_data.values)
explainer = shap.DeepExplainer(model,
    train_data.values[:sample_size])
```

We will now generate a plot of Shapley values.

The plot of Shapley values

In *Chapter 4, Microsoft Azure Machine Learning Model Interpretability with SHAP*, we learned that Shapley values measure the marginal contribution of a feature to the output of an ML model. We also created a plot. In this case, the SHAP plot contains all of the predictions, not only one prediction at a time.

As in *Chapter 4*, we will retrieve the Shapley values of the dataset and create a plot:

```
# Explain the SHAP values for the whole dataset
# to test the SHAP explainer.
shap_values = explainer.shap_values(train_data.values[:sample_size])
# shap_values
shap.initjs()
shap.force_plot(explainer.expected_value[0].numpy(), shap_values[0],
                train_data, link="logit")
```

We can now analyze the outputs of the model displayed in a SHAP plot.

Model outputs and SHAP values

In this section, we will begin to play with AI fairness, which will prepare us for WIT.

The default display shows the features grouped by feature prediction similarity:

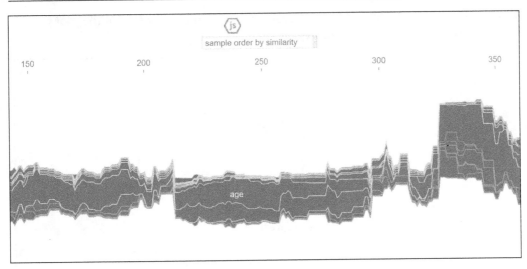

Figure 6.4: SHAP plot

You can change the plot by selecting a feature at the top of the plot. Select **social-class_SC2**, for example:

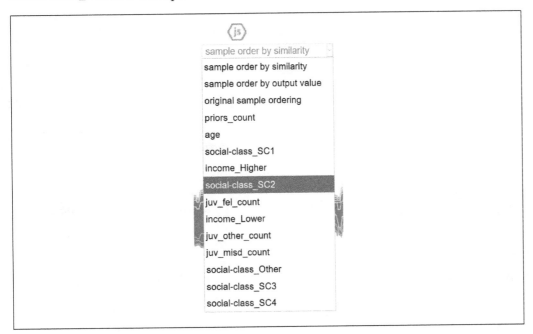

Figure 6.5: Selecting social-class_SC2 from the feature list

To observe the model's predictions, choose a feature on the left side of the plot for the *y* axis. Select **model output value**, for example:

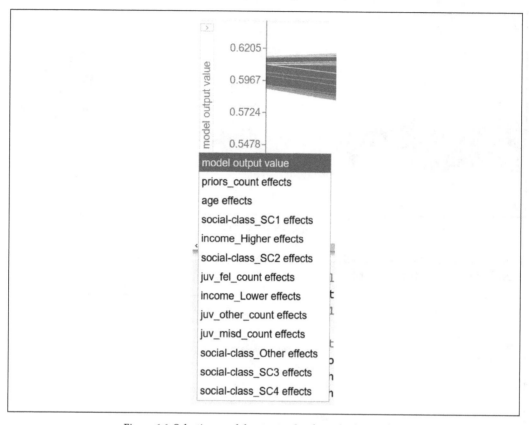

Figure 6.6: Selecting model output value from the feature list

In the *Preparing an ethical dataset* section of this chapter, the value of `social-class_SC2` represents the level of education of a person, a defendant. A population with a very high level of education has fewer chances of committing physical crimes.

If we select **model output value** the plot will display the recidivism prediction of the model.

In this scenario, we can see the positive values decrease (shown in red in the color image) and the negative values (blue in the color image) increase:

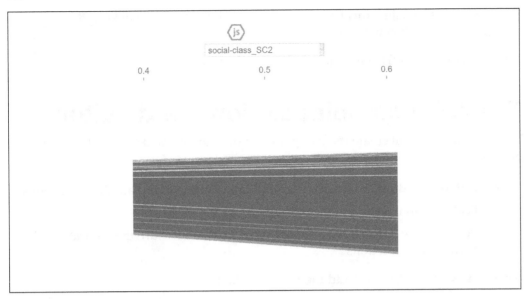

Figure 6.7: SHAP predictions plot

However, if you change the feature to observe to **juv_fel_count**, you will see that this feature makes the positive (shown in red in the color image) predictions increase:

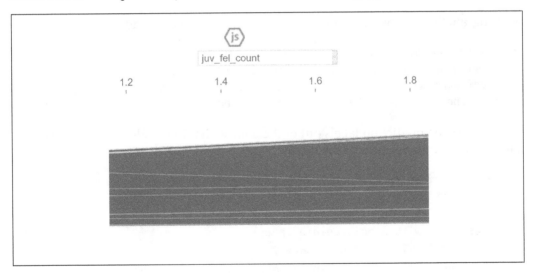

Figure 6.8: juv_fel_count plot

These examples remain educational simulations. However, we will keep this example in mind when we explore WIT.

Let's first create the WIT datapoint explorer and editor.

The WIT datapoint explorer and editor

In this section, we will create the datapoint editor. Then we will explain the model's predictions with the following tools:

- **Datapoint editor**, an interface to edit datapoints and explain the predictions
- **Features**, an interface to visualize the feature statistics
- **Performance & Fairness**, a robust set of tools to measure the accuracy and fairness of predictions

We will now create WIT and add the SHAP explainer.

Creating WIT

In this section, we will create and configure WIT.

The program first selects the number of datapoints to visualize and explore:

```
# @title Show model results and SHAP values in WIT
from witwidget.notebook.visualization import WitWidget,
WitConfigBuilder
num_datapoints = 1000 # @param {type: "number"}
```

We then take the prediction labels out of the data so that the model can analyze the contributions of the features to the model:

```
# Column indices to strip out from data from WIT before
# passing it to the model!.
columns_not_for_model_input = [
    test_data_with_labels.columns.get_loc(
        "recidivism_within_2_years"),
    test_data_with_labels.columns.get_loc("COMPASS_determination")
]
```

The program creates the functions and retrieves the model's predictions and the Shapley values for each inference:

```
# Return model predictions and SHAP values for each inference.
def custom_predict_with_shap(examples_to_infer):
  # Delete columns not used by model
  model_inputs = np.delete(np.array(examples_to_infer),
                           columns_not_for_model_input,
                           axis=1).tolist()


  # Get the class predictions from the model.
  preds = model.predict(model_inputs)
  preds = [[1 - pred[0], pred[0]] for pred in preds]



  # Get the SHAP values from the explainer and create a map
  # of feature name to SHAP value for each example passed to
  # the model.
  shap_output = explainer.shap_values(np.array(model_inputs))[0]
  attributions = []
  for shap in shap_output:
    attrs = {}
    for i, col in enumerate(df_for_training.columns):
      attrs[col] = shap[i]
    attributions.append(attrs)
  ret = {'predictions': preds, 'attributions': attributions}
  return ret
```

Finally, we select the examples for SHAP in WIT, build the WIT interactive interface, and display WIT:

```
examples_for_shap_wit = test_data_with_labels.values.tolist()
column_names = test_data_with_labels.columns.tolist()

config_builder = WitConfigBuilder(
    examples_for_shap_wit[:num_datapoints],
    feature_names=column_names).set_custom_predict_fn(
        custom_predict_with_shap).set_target_feature(
            'recidivism_within_2_years')

ww = WitWidget(config_builder, height=800)
```

We have created WIT and added SHAP. Let's start by exploring datapoints with the datapoint editor.

The datapoint editor

The datapoint editor will appear with the predicted datapoints, with the labels of the dataset and WIT labels as well:

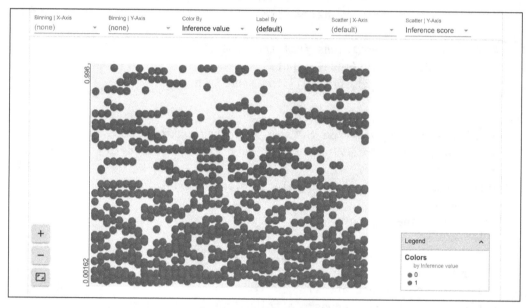

Figure 6.9: Datapoint editor

We already covered the functionality of the datapoint editor in *Chapter 3, Explaining Machine Learning with Facets*. WIT relies on Facets for this interactive interface. If necessary, take the time to go back to *Chapter 3, Explaining Machine Learning with Facets* for additional information.

In this section, we will focus on the Shapley values of the features as described in *Chapter 4, Microsoft Azure Machine Learning Model Interpretability with SHAP*. If necessary, take the time to go back to *Chapter 4, Microsoft Azure Machine Learning Model Interpretability with SHAP* for the mathematical explanation of SHAP and to check the Python examples implemented.

To view the Shapley values of a datapoint, first click on a negative prediction (shown in blue in the color image):

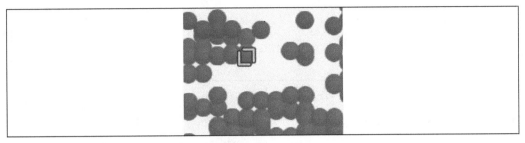

Figure 6.10: Selecting a datapoint

On the left of the screen, the features of the datapoint you selected will appear in the following format:

Feature	Value(s)	Attribution value(s)
priors_count	7	0.2726
income_Higher	1	0.0955
social-class_SC2	1	0.0347
social-class_Other	0	0.0074
social-class_SC4	0	0
social-class_SC3	0	-0.0004
juv_misd_count	0	-0.0066
juv_other_count	0	-0.008
juv_fel_count	0	-0.0115

Figure 6.11: Shapley values of a datapoint

The **Attribution value(s)** column contains the Shapley value of each feature. The Shapley value of a feature represents its marginal contribution to the model's prediction. In this case, we have a true negative for the fact that income_Higher and social-class_SC2 (higher education) contributed to the prediction as one of the ground truths expressed in the *Preparing an ethical dataset* section of this chapter.

We verify this by scrolling down to see the labels of the datapoint:

| COMPASS_determinati on | 0 |
| recidivism_within_2_ye ars | 0 |

Figure 6.12: Prediction labels

Our true negative seems correct.

However, since we know this dataset is biased from the start, let's find a counterfactual datapoint by clicking on **Nearest counterfactual**:

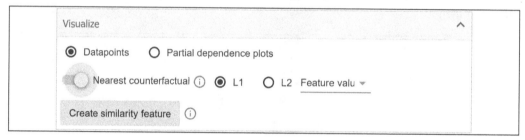

Figure 6.13: Activating Nearest counterfactual

The nearest counterfactual will appear (shown in red in the color image):

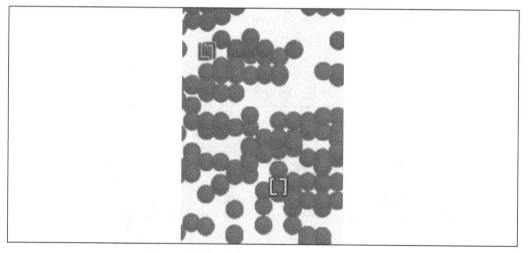

Figure 6.14: Displaying the nearest counterfactual

In our scenario, this is a false positive. Let's play with *what-ifs*.

First, we find a datapoint with `social-class_SC2` (higher education) and `income_Lower` in the positive area (predicted recidivism):

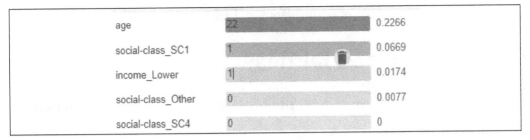

Figure 6.15: Shapley values of the features

The Shapley value of `income_Lower` is high. Let's set `income_Lower` to `0`:

Figure 6.16: Editing a datapoint

You will immediately see a datapoint with a negative prediction (no recidivism) appear.

Try to change the values of other datapoints to visualize and explain how the model thinks.

We can also explore statistical data for each feature.

Features

If you click on **Features**, you might recognize the data displayed:

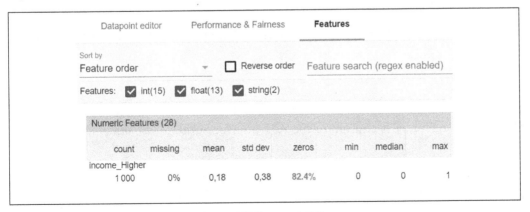

Figure 6.17: Feature statistics

We covered these columns in *Chapter 3, Explaining Machine Learning with Facets*. You can refer to *Chapter 3* if necessary.

Let's now learn how to analyze performance and fairness.

Performance and fairness

In this section, we will verify the performance and fairness of a model through ground truth, cost ratio, fairness, ROC curves, slicing, PR curves, and the confusion matrix of the model.

To access the performance and fairness interface, click on **Performance & Fairness**:

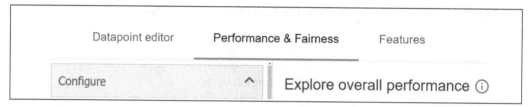

Figure 6.18: Performance & Fairness interface

A world of XAI tools opens to us!

We will begin with the ground truth, a key feature.

Ground truth

The ground truth is the feature that you are trying to predict. The primary target of this dataset is to determine the probability of recidivism of a person: `recidivism_within_2_years`. WIT contains functions to measure the ground truth that are described in this section.

We defined this in the *Creating data structures to train and test the model* section of this chapter:

```
df_for_training = df.drop(columns=['COMPASS_determination',
                                   'recidivism_within_2_years'])
```

The prediction feature is chosen for the WIT interface in the *Show model results and SHAP values in WIT* cell:

```
feature_names=column_names).set_custom_predict_fn(
    custom_predict_with_shap).set_target_feature(
        'recidivism_within_2_years')
```

You can now select the prediction in the drop-down list as shown in the following screenshot:

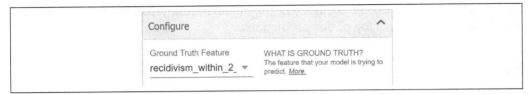

Figure 6.19: Ground truth of a model

Let's verify the cost ratio before visualizing the status of the ground truth of the process.

Cost ratio

A model rarely produces 100% accurate results. The model can produce **true positives (TP)** or **false positives (FP)**, for example. The predictions of this model are supposed to help a judge or a parole officer, for example, make a decision. However, FPs can lead a parole officer to decide to send a person back to prison, for example. Likewise, a **false negative (FN)** can lead a judge, for example, to set a guilty defendant free on parole.

This is a moral dilemma, as described in *Chapter 2, White Box XAI for AI Bias and Ethics*. An FP could send an innocent person to prison. An FN could set a guilty person free to commit a crime.

We can fine-tune the cost ratio to optimize the *classification thresholds* that we will explain in the following *Fairness* section.

The cost ratio can be defined as follows:

$$\text{cost ratio} = \frac{FP}{FN}$$

The default value of the cost ratio is set to 1:

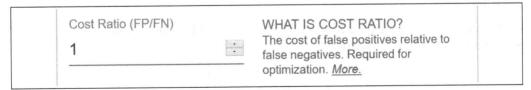

Figure 6.20: Cost ratio for AI fairness

In this case, if the cost ratio is set to 1, FP = FN.

However, other scenarios are possible. For example, if cost ratio = 4, then FP = cost ratio × FN = 4 × FN. The FP will cost four times as much as an FN.

The cost ratio will display the accuracy of the model in numerical terms. We now need to determine the slicing of our predictions.

Slicing

Slicing contributes to evaluating the model's performance. Each datapoint has a value for a feature. Slicing will group the datapoints. Each group will contain the value of the feature we select. Slicing will influence fairness, so we must choose a significant feature.

In our scenario, we will try to measure the model's performance by selecting **income_Higher** (being a binary feature, 0 or 1, the values are stored in two *Buckets*):

Figure 6.21: Slicing feature

You can choose a secondary feature once you have explored the interface with one slicing option. For this scenario, the option will be **<none>**:

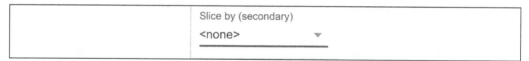

Figure 6.22: Secondary slicing feature

We need to choose a fairness option before visualizing the model's performance based on our choice.

Let's now add fairness to WIT to visualize the quality of the predictions.

Fairness

AI fairness will make the user trust our ML systems. WIT provides several parameters to monitor AI fairness.

You can measure fairness with thresholds. On a range of 0 to 1, what do you believe? At what point do you consider a prediction a TP?

For example, do you believe a prediction of 0.4 that would state that a professional NBA basketball player who owns 15 luxury cars just stole a little family car? No, you probably wouldn't.

Would you believe a prediction of 0.6 that a person who as a Ph.D. harassed another person? Maybe you would. Would you believe this same prediction for this person but with a value of 0.1? Probably not.

In WIT, you can control the threshold above which you consider the predictions as TPs just like you would in real-life situations.

WIT thresholds are automatically calculated using the cost ratio and slicing. If the ratio and the data slices are changed manually, then WIT will revert to custom thresholds:

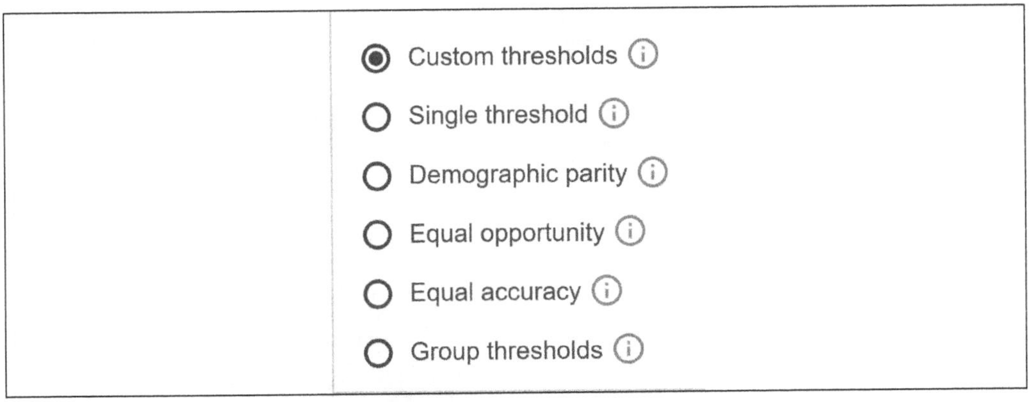

Figure 6.23: Threshold options

If you select **Single threshold**, the threshold will be optimized with the single cost ratio chosen for all of the datapoints.

The other threshold options might require sociological expertise and special care, such as demographic parity and equal opportunity. In this section, we will let WIT optimize the thresholds.

For our scenario, we will not modify the default value of the fairness thresholds.

We have selected the parameters for ground truth, cost ratio, slicing, and fairness. We can now visualize the ROC curve to measure the output of the predictions.

The ROC curve and AUC

ROC is a metric that evaluates the quality of the model's predictions.

ROC stands for **receiver operating characteristic** curve.

For example, we selected 'recidivism_within_2_years' as the ground truth we would like to measure.

We will first display ROC with slicing set to **<none>** to view the influence of the features' combined values:

Figure 6.24: No slicing

ROC represents the TP rate on the *y* axis and the FP rate on the *x* axis, as shown in the following screenshot in *Figure 6.25*:

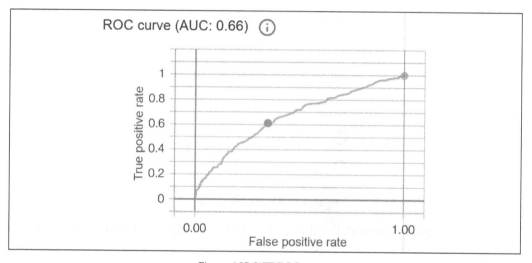

Figure 6.25: WIT ROC curve

The **area under the curve (AUC)** represents the TP area. If the TP rate never exceeded 0.2, for example, the AUC would have a much smaller value. As in any curve, the area beneath the curve remains small when the values of the *y* axis remain close to 0.

The threshold values appear in a pop-up window if you explore the curve with your mouse up to the optimized threshold (the point on the curve):

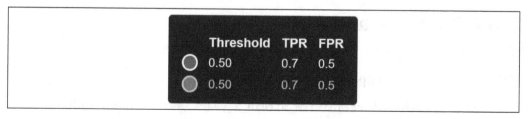

Figure 6.26: Threshold information

The threshold states that fairness applies at that point when TPs reach `0.6`.

Let's now activate slicing with the `income_Higher` feature, as shown in the *Slicing* section of this chapter. The `count` column indicates the number of datapoints containing the binary value of the feature:

Custom thresholds for 2 values of income_Higher ⓘ			Sort by Count ▾				
Feature Value	Count	Threshold ⓘ		False Positives (%)	False Negatives (%)	Accuracy (%)	F1
▸ 0	824	——●—— 0.5		27.9	13.2	58.9	0.62
▸ 1	176	——●—— 0.5		23.3	11.4	65.3	0.64

Figure 6.27: Visualizing model outputs

On the right side of the interface, we can consult the FPs and FNs, and the accuracy of the model.

If we click on `0`, the ROC curve of the performance of the model for `income_Higher` appears:

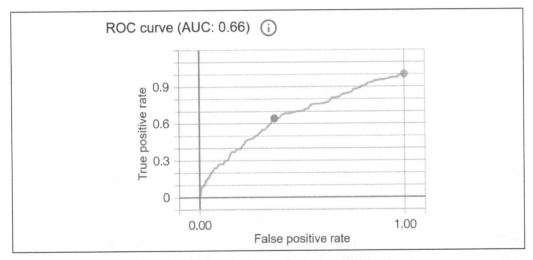

Figure 6.28: WIT ROC curve

We can now measure the model's performance with a ROC curve. However, the PR curve in the next section displays additional information.

The PR curve

PR stands for **precision-recall** curves. They plot precision against recall at classification thresholds.

We have defined thresholds. In this section, we will define precision and recall.

Let's start by looking at a plot:

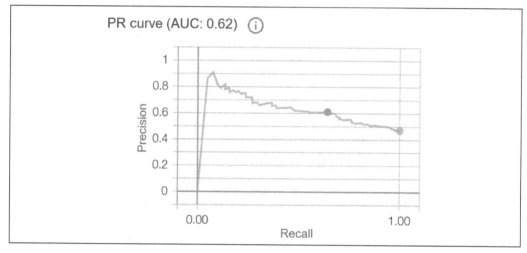

Figure 6.29: PR curve

The y axis contains precision defined as a ratio between TPs and FP:

$$precision = \frac{TP}{TP + FP}$$

Precision thus measures how well a model can distinguish a positive sample from a negative sample without mislabeling samples.

The x axis contains recall defined as a ratio between TPs and FNs:

$$recall = \frac{TP}{TP + FN}$$

An FN can be considered as a positive sample. Recall thus measures how well a model can distinguish all positive samples from the other datapoints.

We have defined a PR matrix that we see in the plot. As for ROC curves, the higher the curve goes upward, the better.

A confusion matrix will provide an additional visualization of the model's performance.

The confusion matrix

A confusion matrix shows the accuracy of a model's performance in one table. The table contains the TPs, FPs, TNs, and FNs.

In WIT, the rows contain the actual labels of the predictions, and the columns contain the predictions:

Confusion Matrix (i)

	Predicted Yes		Predicted No		Total	
Actual Yes	30.3%	(250)	16.9%	(139)	47.2%	(389)
Actual No	19.3%	(159)	33.5%	(276)	52.8%	(435)
Total	49.6%	(409)	50.4%	(415)		

Figure 6.30: WIT confusion matrix

We can visualize the performance of the model in one glance by looking at the **Predicted Yes** and **Actual Yes** rate, for example, which is 22.2%. The **Predicted No** and **Actual No** rate is 39.8%.

The values in this table are rounded to one decimal, which makes the result a bit imprecise. The total of true and false values of each classification should sum up to about 100. However, we do not need more precision to analyze the predictions, find the weak spots of a model, and explain them.

In this section, we created WIT and explored several tools to interpret and explain the accurate predictions (the TPs), the FPs, TNs, and FNs.

Summary

In this chapter, we went right to the core of XAI with WIT, a people-centric system. Explainable and interpretable AI brings humans and machines together.

We first analyzed a training dataset from an ethical perspective. A biased dataset will only generate biased predictions, classifications, or any form of output. We thus took the necessary time to examine the features of COMPAS before importing the data. We modified the column feature names that would only distort the decisions our model would make.

We carefully preprocessed our now-ethical data, splitting the dataset into training and testing datasets. At that point, running a DNN made sense. We had done our best to clean the dataset up.

The SHAP explainer determined the marginal contribution of each feature. Before running WIT, we already proved that the COMPAS dataset approach was biased and knew what to look for.

Finally, we created an instance of the WIT to explore the outputs from a fairness perspective. We could visualize and evaluate each feature of a person with Shapley values. Then we explored concepts such as ground truth, cost ratio, ROC curves, AUC, slicing, PR curves, confusion matrices, and feature analysis.

The set of tools offered by WIT measured the accuracy, fairness, and performance of the model. The interactive real-time functionality of WIT puts you right in the center of the AI system.

WIT shows that people-centered AI systems will outperform the now-outdated ML solutions that don't have any humans involved. People-centered AI systems will take systems' ethical and legal standards, and accuracy to a higher level of quality.

In the next chapter, *A Python Client for Explainable AI Chatbots*, we will go further in our quest for human-machine AI by experimenting with XAI by building a chatbot from scratch.

Questions

1. The developer of an AI system decides what is ethical or not. (True | False)
2. A DNN is the only estimator for the COMPAS dataset. (True | False)
3. Shapley values determine the marginal contribution of each feature. (True | False)
4. We can detect the biased output of a model with a SHAP plot. (True | False)
5. WIT's primary quality is "people-centered." (True | False)
6. A ROC curve monitors the time it takes to train a model. (True | False)
7. AUC stands for "area under convolution." (True | False)
8. Analyzing the ground truth of a model is a prerequisite in ML. (True | False)
9. Another ML program could do XAI. (True | False)
10. The WIT "people-centered" approach will change the course of AI. (True | False)

References

- The **General Data Protection Regulation (GDPR)** can be found at `https://gdpr-info.eu/` and `https://gdpr-info.eu/art-9-gdpr/`.

- The COMPAS dataset can be found on Kaggle at `https://www.kaggle.com/danofer/compass`.

Further reading

- More on WIT can be found at `https://pair-code.github.io/what-if-tool/`.

- More information on the background of COMPAS, as recommended by Google, can be found at the following links:
    - `https://www.propublica.org/article/machine-bias-risk-assessments-in-criminal-sentencing`
    - `https://www.propublica.org/article/how-we-analyzed-the-compas-recidivism-algorithm`
    - `http://www.crj.org/assets/2017/07/9_Machine_bias_rejoinder.pdf`

- More information on Keras sequential models can be found at `https://keras.io/models/sequential/`.

- The AI Fairness 360 toolkit contains demos and tutorials not only on measuring unwanted bias, but also mitigating bias using several different types of algorithms, and can be found at `http://aif360.mybluemix.net/`.

7

A Python Client for Explainable AI Chatbots

In the previous chapters, we have explored several interactions between all types of users and machines. It is now time to introduce chatbots in our **explainable AI (XAI)** process. Progressively, personal assistants will replace keyboards. As more and more connected objects enter the **Internet of things (IoT)** market, chatbots will emerge as a useful communication tool.

In this chapter, we will implement a Python client to write a flexible XAI program for a user to interact with a Dialogflow AI expert agent. We will start by installing the Python client for Dialogflow on a local machine.

We will then create a Dialogflow agent on Dialogflow using Google's intuitive interface. The agent will simulate a human support agent that will answer user requests. The local Python client cannot communicate with Google Dialogflow online without APIs and services.

Activating the Google APIs and services will provide a private key that we will install on the local machine. This private key will be accessed through our Python client program when we open a session.

Our Python client program will then communicate with Dialogflow. We will create a test dialog in Python. We will then add an intent to Dialogflow, creating a training phrase and a response. This intent will be tested. Once the intent works, we will add a follow-up dialog to our intent.

Our dialog will now be ready to interact with the output of a **Markov decision process (MDP)** in real time. We will be simulating a decision process in which a trained MDP model produces outputs. However, other sources of data will conflict with the decisions of the machine learning program. Real-time data often creates problems for trained machine learning algorithms.

The user will be able to interrupt the machine learning algorithm to ask the chatbot to explain what is going on and why these conflicts are occurring. The chatbot will provide explanations and recommendations.

Finally, we will explore a **conversational user interface (CUI)** XAI dialog with Dialogflow. We will also deploy our chatbot on Google Assistant.

This chapter covers the following topics:

- Installing the Python client for Google Dialogflow
- Creating a Google Dialogflow agent
- Enabling Google APIs and services
- Implementing the Google Dialogflow Python client
- Adding XAI to the Google Dialogflow Python client
- Creating a dialog function in Python and Dialogflow
- The architecture of an XAI dialog
- Training phrases of the intent
- The responses to an intent
- How to follow up an intent
- Inserting interactions in the MDP
- Interacting with Dialogflow with the Python client
- CUI XAI dialog using Google Dialogflow
- A Jupyter Notebook XAI dialog
- Testing the XAI agent on Google Assistant

We will first start by building a Python client program for Google Dialogflow.

The Python client for Dialogflow

You can create an XAI dialog only using the cloud version of Google Dialogflow. You can even load your data online and access it from there with Jupyter Notebooks, as we will do in the subsequent sections of this chapter.

However, in some cases, a company might refuse to upload any form of data it considers sensitive on a cloud platform such as Google, Amazon, Microsoft, IBM, or others. Sensitive information such as blueprint data on the research of a new type of airplane or pharmaceutical research sometimes involves investments of hundreds of millions of dollars. In those cases, the company might accept using Dialogflow if the data remains in the company but Dialogflow will only make general explanations and recommendations.

In cases where a project does not contain sensitive data, the Python client for Dialogflow provides flexibility.

In this section, we will install the Python client for Dialogflow, create a Dialogflow agent, and enable the APIs and services. We will then write a Python program that communicates with Dialogflow.

> The goal of this chapter is not to specifically use Python and Dialogflow but to learn how to implement XAI chatbots. The Google framework in this chapter, Google's APIs, and interfaces are constantly evolving. Furthermore, the trend is to migrate services to pay-as-you-go cloud platforms. *Focus on the method, the ideas, and the way to implement XAI interactive interfaces that you can adapt to any present or future framework.*

Let's start by first installing the Python client for Google Dialogflow.

Installing the Python client for Google Dialogflow

Installing the Python client for Google Dialogflow might vary from one environment to another.

It is recommended to install the library in a virtual environment using `virtualenv`: `https://virtualenv.pypa.io/en/latest/`.

Once you have chosen your environment, either virtual or not, run the following command to install the Python client:

```
pip install dialogflow
```

If you want to use other installation strategies, you can go through the documentation at `https://dialogflow-python-client-v2.readthedocs.io/en/latest/`

We now need to create an agent in Google Dialogflow.

Creating a Google Dialogflow agent

To create an agent, sign in to Google Dialogflow at `https://dialogflow.com/`

If you are new to Google Dialogflow, follow the instructions to sign in.

Once you are signed in, you can create an agent. If you are new to Google Dialogflow, you will see a **CREATE AGENT** button on the welcome window. If you already have created agents, scroll down the agent list in the menu on the left, and choose **Create new agent**.

Choose a name for your agent. In my case, its name is **XAI.** Dialogflow will create everything we need for the agent automatically. When it's finished, we will have the cloud environment we need:

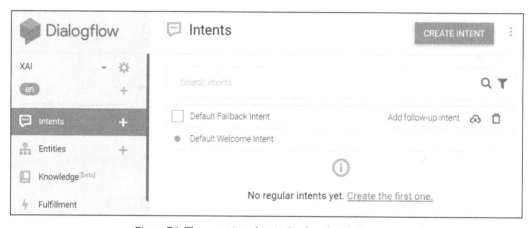

Figure 7.1: The agent interface is displayed with its menu

Once the agent is created, a menu of possible actions appears.

We will now check the main default settings by clicking on the gear icon at the top left of the window:

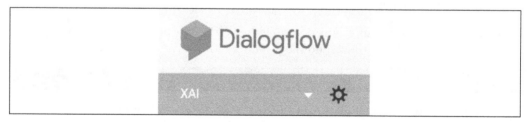

Figure 7.2: Accessing the settings of the agent

The main default options for your agent are displayed. I recommend you do not change them until you have a dialog up and running:

- **DESCRIPTION**: This is optional. You will fill it in later once everything is working.
- **DEFAULT TIME ZONE**: Your default time zone will appear automatically.
- **Project ID**: Your unique project ID number.
- **Service Account**: The service account code for integration purposes.

Among the other options, you will see a logging option checked:

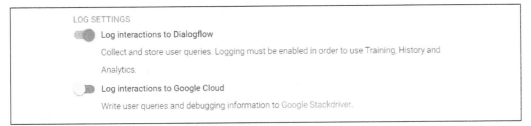

Figure 7.3: Logging activated

Make good use of the options! Some logging data might require a privacy policy you will have to share with your users. As we saw in *Chapter 2*, *White Box XAI for AI Bias and Ethics*, if you are going online with this agent, you should check your legal obligations with your legal advisor first.

In the **Languages** tab, the default language should be **English — en**:

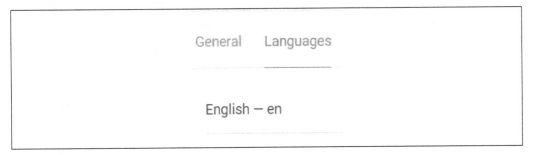

Figure 7.4: Default language

Our Python client will communicate in English with Dialogflow. Do not change the language until you have finished this chapter and verified that everything works as described.

We have now created an agent and changed no options at all.

To test the agent, click on the test console at the top right and enter Hi:

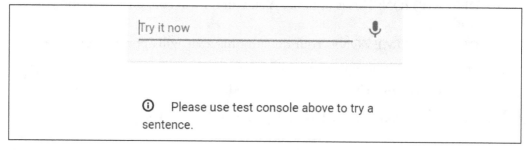

Figure 7.5: Test console

The test console is a precious tool to use every time we enter new information. We need to make sure our chatbot works before letting others use it.

The agent's default response will appear:

Figure 7.6: Testing a dialog

The default response in my case was, `Hello! How can I help you?`

We will now enable the APIs and services before adding any other dialogs to the agent.

Enabling APIs and services

The primary goal of this chapter is still to write an XAI Python client. As such, at first, we will change none of the options and add no new dialogs until our basic Python client works.

The Python client requires APIs and services to be activated:

 **Warning**

Read the conditions to activate the APIs and services for your account before continuing this section. Make sure you understand how Google Cloud Platform billing works and keep any possible cost to the lowest amount possible if you do not obtain free access. Google Cloud Platform account policies are beyond the scope of this book. The policies chosen by a user are personal choices.

1. Once you are ready and logged into Dialogflow, go to your Google Cloud Platform: `https://console.cloud.google.com/`.

   A link to your service account will appear on the general settings page of your project:

Figure 7.7: Project properties

2. Click on the **Service Account** link, and you will see a page with your email and a link to your service account details under **Email**:

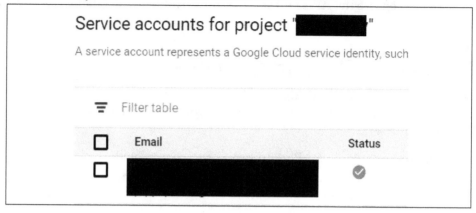

Figure 7.8: Service account

> **Note**
>
> The interface may evolve as Google improves its products and services. However, the principles remain the same to obtain the information we need for our Python client.

3. The integration link below **Email** will lead you to a dialog integration page. On this page, your service account status should be active:

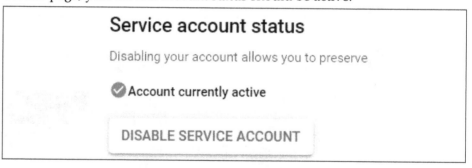

Figure 7.9: Service account status

4. Your Python program will require a private key to access your Dialogflow agent. We thus need a JSON file containing a private key on our machine. To obtain this file, first, click on the **EDIT** button to enter the editing mode:

Figure 7.10: Dialogflow integrations

5. Then click on **+ CREATE KEY**:

Figure 7.11: Creating a key in Dialogflow integrations

6. Make sure the key type is JSON and then click on **CREATE**:

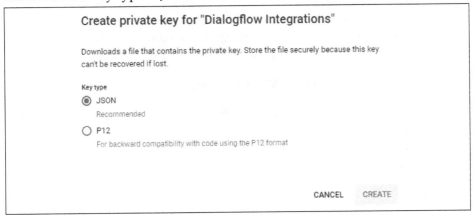

Figure 7.12: Private key

7. You will now be able to save the key to your computer, and a confirmation window will appear:

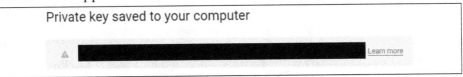

Figure 7.13: Private key saved message

8. Once the file is on your computer, you can rename it `private_key.json`, for example. We can now write our Python client to access Dialogflow from our machine.

The Google Dialogflow Python client

In this section, we will write a dialog for one of our agent's intents on Dialogflow. An intent means literally what you intend to obtain from a dialog. As in all dialogs, person A says something, and person B will provide a response. In our case, person A is our Python program and person B is the Dialogflow agent.

We are creating an automatic dialog between two machines through an intent.

An intent works as follows:

1. **Input**: It expects the query named `training_phrase`. It is named "training phrase" because Dialogflow uses machine learning to train the intent with different types of spelling, misspelling, and pronunciation. An intent can contain many training phrases for the same meaning to adapt to the different ways we send queries for the same message.

2. **Output**: If the intent detects one of the possible inputs, a training phrase, then it will send a response. An intent can contain several responses for the same meaning to make the dialog resemble human dialogs.

We will be using `python_client_01.py` for this section:

1. Let's build a Python client program by first importing the `dialogflow_v2` API library:

```
import os
import dialogflow_v2 as dialogflow
from google.api_core.exceptions import InvalidArgument
```

Do not use the v1 version of Dialogflow's API because it is obsolete.

2. Now, we must enter our credentials. Refer to the names and codes we created in the previous section:

```
os.environ["GOOGLE_APPLICATION_CREDENTIALS"] =
    '[YOUR private_key.json]'
DIALOGFLOW_PROJECT_ID = '[YOUR PROJECT_ID]'
```

3. Use English to start with since the default agent was set to English:

```
DIALOGFLOW_LANGUAGE_CODE = 'en'   # '[LANGUAGE]'
```

4. You can invent your `SESSION_ID` and enter it here:

```
SESSION_ID = '[MY_SESSION_ID]'
```

5. We now send a query to Dialogflow, starting with the one we tested online:

```
our_query = "Hi"
```

The query and response code represents a standard example that should work fine with our default agent.

The program starts by creating the session variables:

```
# session variables
session_client = dialogflow.SessionsClient()
session = session_client.session_path(DIALOGFLOW_PROJECT_ID,
                                      SESSION_ID)
```

Then it creates our query:

```
# Our query
our_input = dialogflow.types.TextInput(text=our_query,
    language_code=DIALOGFLOW_LANGUAGE_CODE)
query = dialogflow.types.QueryInput(text=our_input)
```

It now tries to communicate with Dialogflow and will use the `InvalidArgument` module we imported in the first lines of the program to send us messages if it fails:

```
# try or raise exceptions
try:
    response = session_client.detect_intent(session=session,
                                            query_input=query)
except InvalidArgument:
    raise
```

If no exception is thrown, then Dialogflow will send the information we request back:

```
print("Our text:", response.query_result.query_text)
print("Dialogflow's response:",
      response.query_result.fulfillment_text)
print("Dialogflow's intent:",
      response.query_result.intent.display_name)
```

The output should be the following:

```
Our text: Hi
Dialogflow's response: Hi! How are you doing?
Dialogflow's intent: Default Welcome Intent
```

Dialogflow's response might vary since the default welcome intent (side menu | **Intents | Default Welcome Intent**) response contains several random possibilities:

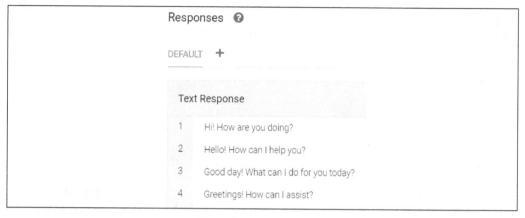

Figure 7.14: Text responses

If you run your Python client program several times, you will see that the answers change as well.

The same goes for our query. The default welcome intent contains several possible inputs we can send to our query:

Figure 7.15: Training phrases

There are more training phrases than the ones displayed in the preceding figure. Before going to the next section, try different training phrases using the our_input variable.

Enhancing the Google Dialogflow Python client

In this section, we will enhance our program to prepare it for the XAI dialog we will build using the functions we wrote in the previous sections.

For this section, use python_client_02.py.

The goal of this section is to transform the query and response dialog of python_client_01.py into a function that can be called by various XAI requests a user might make.

Creating a dialog function

The import and credential code at the beginning of the program remains unchanged. We will simply create a function that will receive our our_query variable and return the response:

```python
def dialog(our_query):
    # session variables
    session_client = dialogflow.SessionsClient()
    session = session_client.session_path(DIALOGFLOW_PROJECT_ID,
                                          SESSION_ID)

    # Our query
    our_input = dialogflow.types.TextInput(text=our_query,
        language_code=DIALOGFLOW_LANGUAGE_CODE)
    query = dialogflow.types.QueryInput(text=our_input)

    # try or raise exceptions
    try:
        response = session_client.detect_intent(session=session,
                                                query_input=query)

    except InvalidArgument:
        raise

    return response.query_result.fulfillment_text
```

We now will add the call to the function and print the response:

```
our_query = "Hi" # our query
print(our_query)
vresponse = dialog(our_query)
print(vresponse)
```

The output should be one of the responses of our intent. In one case, one possible dialog is as follows:

```
Hi
Good day! What can I do for you today?
```

There is more code, but let's stay focused on the method of creating a chatbot XAI with whatever framework you choose to use in the present or future.

We are now ready to implement an XAI dialog.

The constraints of an XAI implementation on Dialogflow

In some cases, a company will not agree to have its data published to a cloud server at all for security reasons. The company might want to separate out each function of a software solution. Many scenarios are possible. The following organizational setup represents one of those possibilities:

- A data server in one secure private location
- A service server in another location, handling algorithms, processing data, and making calculations
- A user interface server with the outside world, meaning various locations of subsidiaries within the same corporation

In this section, we will respect the philosophy of the security policy of some corporations with the following components:

- Google Dialogflow will contain a general set of intents (training phrases and responses) explaining AI. Dialogflow will not contain sensitive information.
- Google Colaboratory will simulate the use of a local server. In real life, the server might be in a private data center, not a public cloud server. Our Google Colaboratory virtual machine will play the role of a private server.

- Our program, `XAI_Chatbot.ipynb`, will simulate the use of private information on our private server but will communicate with Google Dialogflow for XAI.

The Python client will manage our XAI functionality on our private server.

Let's create an intent in Dialogflow that will provide general explanations on a machine learning algorithm.

Creating an intent in Dialogflow

An intent contains training phrases (inputs) and responses (outputs). To create an intent, click on **Intents** in the agent's menu, as shown in the following screenshot:

Figure 7.16: Intents in the menu

When the intent page appears, click on **CREATE INTENT**:

Figure 7.17: Create intent

An intent page will appear. We now need to fill in some key fields for this intent to work.

Enter `explain MDP` as the intent name and then click on the **SAVE** button:

Figure 7.18: Intent name

Your intent has been created, but it is empty.

We will now create a training phrase – the possible phrases a user can write or say.

The training phrases of the intent

The training phrases are the input phrases we expect a user to enter.

To add a training phrase or training phrases, click on **ADD TRAINING PHRASES**:

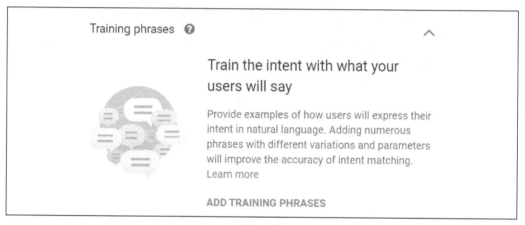

Figure 7.19: Training phrases

Add a few variations of a user phrase expressing that the user would like to understand the MDP algorithm. You must think of the various ways you might ask the same question or express something with a sentence:

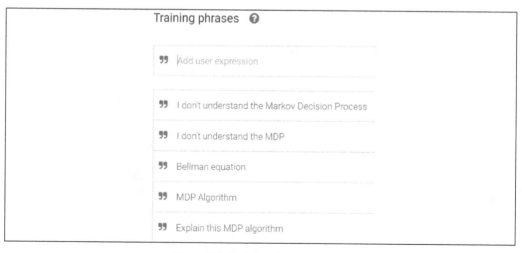

Figure 7.20: Training phrases entered

You have provided some possible user phrases. You must now think of some possible answers that will satisfy the user.

The response of an intent

The response section of an intent is a critical part of your dialog. If the response means nothing, the user might just abandon the conversation with no explanation.

That being said, let's provide a response. Scroll down to the response section and add a response and save it, as follows:

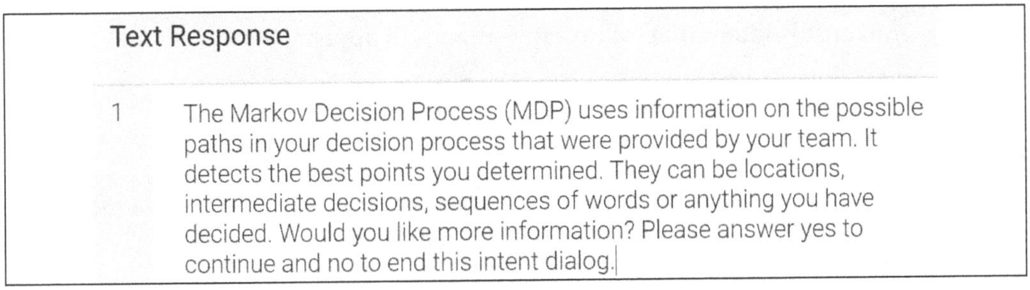

Text Response
1   The Markov Decision Process (MDP) uses information on the possible paths in your decision process that were provided by your team. It detects the best points you determined. They can be locations, intermediate decisions, sequences of words or anything you have decided. Would you like more information? Please answer yes to continue and no to end this intent dialog.

Figure 7.21: Response

As you can see, the user needs to answer *yes* or *no*. This way, you limit the user's choice of answers to your question. Otherwise, you will have to think of all of the possible inputs the user can enter. You have closed the door to an open dialog, which can lead to confusion.

The user will now answer the question. We need to follow this answer up. It's called a **follow-up**.

Defining a follow-up intent for an intent

Following up an intent means that we have not left it. Dialogflow will remember the previous training phrase and response. Dialogflow thus knows how to manage the *context* of a conversation. If not, there would be no way to know what question the user asked.

To add a follow-up intent, click on the **Intents** menu again and you will see the intent named **explain MDP** that we just created:

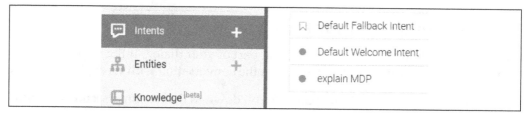

Figure 7.22: Follow-up intent

If you hover over this intent, the follow-up option will appear:

Figure 7.23: Creating a follow-up intent

Click on **Add follow-up intent**. A drop-down list will appear showing our **yes** and **no** options:

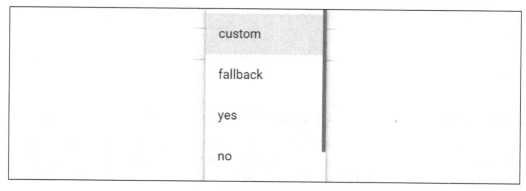

Figure 7.24: Follow-up options

We will click on **yes**. It will create an intent *remembering* the original intent it is related to:

Figure 7.25: The name of the follow-up intent

As you can see, the **yes** answer will be related to the **explain MDP** intent.

Remember, if a user sends **yes** to Dialogflow without using a follow-up intent, it could trigger any of the intents that start with a yes training phrase! We don't want that. We want Dialogflow to remember which intent this follow-up question is related to.

This *context* process of remembering the previous interactions with a user is exactly like in a conversation between humans when somebody says "yes" to a specific question.

When you click on the follow-up intent, **explain MDP - yes**, you will see the context of the intent you just created being displayed:

Figure 7.26: Yes follow-up dialog

Our XAI agent has just given an intuitive explanation of what an MDP is. However, the XAI agent provides a deeper explanation because the user answered *yes*.

First, we want to enter the training phrases section of the intent. However, Dialogflow has already done that for us, as shown in the following screenshot:

Figure 7.27: Training phrases

Note that there are more possibilities than the ones in the preceding screenshot.

Now, all we must do is to create our response. The following response is an example of how an MDP can be implemented with a chatbot:

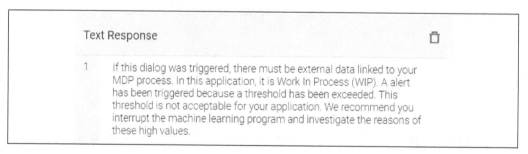

Figure 7.28: Text response

As a reminder, we can define the MDP process as a machine learning algorithm. It is a stochastic decision process framework. It will take a point A in a decision process and decide which is the best next step out of several possible decisions such as B, C, or D. The MDP might decide that C is the best next step, so the system will go from A to C.

The decision is based on a reward matrix that rewards the best decision and learns from it. This can be a machine in a factory, a person in a warehouse, a distribution location, or any other element in a decision process.

The response contains vital information for the user. For example, suppose the application and MDP were designed to manage a threshold. Suppose the user manages hundreds of developers. A team of six developers, for example, is writing code in a sequence, sharing their tasks. Once a development task is over, the program goes through another phase.

The *threshold* of these six developers is 8 × 6 = 48 hours.

In this development team, the number of hours remaining to finish their work is the **work in progress (WIP)**.

If the WIP is very low, then the developers will be sitting around waiting for work to come their way. If six developers are at work for 8 hours a day, and they only have 1 hour of work to do, they are far from the threshold. 6 hours of work to do out of 48 hours isn't much. If they are well managed, they have a backlog of long-term work or other tasks they can code.

However, if the same six workers have a total of 90 hours of work to do, then their WIP has been exceeded and an alert level has been reached. The user must find what went wrong. Maybe the problem is due to the machine learning algorithm's parameters. Maybe there are more developers required. Maybe the developers did not use the right method.

In any case, the user would like to stop the algorithm instead of waiting until it's finished. For this session, the dialog will stop now to let the user interact with the program.

Just below the response, for this session, we will set this response as the last interaction with the user:

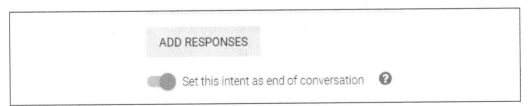

Figure 7.29: Setting the intent as the end of the conversation

The dialog is ready on the cloud side. We will now go back to the Python client to improve it.

The XAI Python client

Suppose we built a reinforcement program, the MDP application, and delivered it to a customer. The MDP program would receive an encoded reward matrix and be trained to find optimal scheduling sequences for teams producing any product or service. The output would then be decoded for further use.

In this section, we will be interacting with the output of an MDP program using our Python client and the Dialogflow agent we created online. The output produces sequences of tasks that move from one developer or group of developers to another in a development unit of production.

Open `XAI_Chatbot.ipynb`. The program starts with the code we previously wrote to activate the Python client for Dialogflow. Dialogflow is installed. The content of `python_client_02.py` is inserted. Then the MDP code was inserted into this notebook, without any user interaction elements. In this section, we are focusing on interactions with the output, not the training process.

We can sum up the first part of `XAI_Chatbot.ipynb` as follows:

- The installation of Dialogflow
- The Dialogflow session code taken from `python_client_02.py` (`python_client_03.py` is a maintenance program to see whether the API works)
- The MDP code.

Before inserting interactions into our Python client, we must upload our private key to Google Colaboratory.

First, make sure Dialogflow is installed. The first cell contains the following:

```
!pip install dialogflow
```

Then comment this `pip` instruction.

The following cell will display the present working directory:

```
!pwd
```

In this case, the directory is `/content`.

Click on the file manager button on the left and upload `private_key.json` from your local machine:

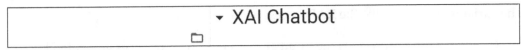

Figure 7.30: File manager

Once it's uploaded, make sure it's in the `content` directory or the directory displayed with the following command:

```
!pwd
```

We are now ready to insert interactions into the MDP program.

Inserting interactions in the MDP

The second part of `XAI_Chatbot.ipynb` starts with the following title:

```
Improving the program by introducing a decision-making process
```

We will have a generic decoder array named `conceptcode`. In our example, `conceptcode` will contain letters from `A` to `F`. Each letter will represent a developer or group of developers. We will not go into the detail of the specific organization of this company. We will limit ourselves to observing sequences of work being passed from one team to another.

At the same time, the WIP is fed into the algorithm through an array named `WIP`. `WIP` contains six elements set to `0` at the beginning of the process. Each element represents the WIP of the corresponding group of developers in `conceptcode`.

For example, `WIP = [80, 0, 0, 0, 0, 0]` means that team A has 80 hours of WIP, that is, of work remaining to do.

Our code starts by inserting `conceptcode` and `WIP`:

```
"""# Improving the program by introducing a decision-making process"""
conceptcode = ["A", "B", "C", "D", "E", "F"]
WIP = [0, 0, 0, 0, 0, 0]
```

We now add the following:

```
print("Sequences")
maxv = 1000
mint = 450
maxt = 500
```

```
# sh = qL.zeros((maxv, 2))
for i in range(0, maxv):
```

The variables used to drive the XAI process are as follows:

- `maxv = 1000` represents the number of scheduling sequences generated by a scheduling process derived from the MDP we described in the *Defining a follow-up intent for an intent* section of this chapter
- `mint = 450` represents the lower value of the threshold window; it is the sum of all the remaining work for a given team in each sequence
- `maxt = 500` represents the higher value of the threshold window; it is the sum of all the remaining work for a given team in each sequence

The lower and higher values of the threshold represent the threshold's interval, its window. The threshold is not a precise value but rather a fuzzy window of values that trigger a WIP overload alert.

The program generates random values for the WIP array:

```
for w in range(0, 6):
  WIP[w] = random.randint(0, 100)
print(WIP)
print("\n")
```

We are simulating the real-time load of the developers in each sequence of tasks in the production unit, for example.

When the sum of the WIP of a team in a sequence enters the threshold window, the alert is triggered, and a dialog is initiated between the user and the AI program. The user requires explanations on the algorithm and the decision rules agreed upon when the algorithm was designed:

```
if (np.sum(WIP) > mint and np.sum(WIP) < maxt):
  print(mint, maxt)
  print("Alert!", np.sum(WIP))
  print("Mention MDP or Bellman in your comment, please")
  while our_query != "no" or our_query != "bye":
    our_query = input("Enter your comment or question:")
    if our_query == "no" or our_query == "bye":
      break;
    # print(our_query)
    vresponse = dialog(our_query)
    print(vresponse)
  decision = input("Do you want to continue(enter yes) or
```

```
stop(enter no) to work with your department before letting the program
make a decision:")
        if(decision=="no"):
            break
```

If the user decides to let the AI program continue, the system might constrain the threshold window:

```
mint = 460
maxt = 470
```

The origin of each scheduling sequence is random to simulate the status of the production teams at a given time:

```
nextc = -1
nextci = -1
origin = ql.random.randint(0, 6)
print(" ")
print(conceptcode[int(origin)])

for se in range(0, 6):
    if (se == 0):
        po = origin
    if (se > 0):
        po = nextci
    for ci in range(0, 6):
        maxc = Q[po, ci]
        maxp = Qp[po, ci]
        if (maxc >= nextc):
            nextc = maxc
            nextp = maxp
            nextci = ci
            conceptprob[int(nextci)]=nextp
    if (nextci == po):
        break;
    print(conceptcode[int(nextci)])
print("\n")
```

conceptcode ensures that the results are decoded for the user. Let's see what a dialog could be.

Interacting with Dialogflow with the Python client

In the previous section, a dialog was triggered by an alert. We will now analyze the output.

In the following example, one production unit, C, was in a scheduling sequence for a given task. However, the WIP values of the other production units related to the project C is working on were considered and displayed under C:

```
C
[23, 72, 75, 74, 45, 77]
```

In the following example, two production units, D-C, were in a scheduling sequence for a given task. However, the WIP values of the other production units related to the project that D-C were working on were considered and displayed under D-C:

```
D
C
[94, 90, 8, 39, 35, 31]
```

In the following example, three production units, E-D-C, were in a scheduling sequence for a given task. However, the WIP values of the other production units related to the project E-D-C were working on were considered and displayed under E-D-C:

```
E
D
C
[99, 81, 98, 2, 89, 100]
```

In this case, the total WIP of the project these developers are working on entered the alert threshold. The threshold values are displayed. The user now activates the dialog intents we created in Dialogflow. The Python client program also contains a dialog:

```
450 500
Alert! 469
Mention MDP or Bellman in your comment, please
Enter your comment or question: what is Bellman
The Markov Decision Process (MDP) uses information on the possible
paths in your decision process that were provided by your team.
It detects the best points you determined. They can be locations,
intermediate decisions, sequences of words, or anything you have
decided. Would you like more information? Please answer yes to continue
and no to end this intent dialog.
```

```
Enter your comment or question: yes

If this dialog was triggered, there must be external data linked to
your MDP process. In this application, it is Work In Progress (WIP). An
alert has been triggered because a threshold has been exceeded. This
threshold is not acceptable for your application. We recommend you
interrupt the machine learning program and investigate the reasons for
these high values.
Enter your comment or question: no

Do you want to continue (enter yes) or stop (enter no) to work with
your department before letting the program make a decision: no
```

The user, the manager of the production team, has obtained an explanation about the program and interacted with it before waiting until the end of a complete MDP scheduling session. Introducing a user to an automatic AI process has the following double effect:

- Explaining the AI
- Creating a strong relationship with an AI algorithm by converting it into a white box automatic process.

We have described a text dialog between a Python client and Dialogflow. The inputs and outputs were in written form. This toy example that simulates possible dialogs shows the many ideas and ways you can implement solutions in real work scenarios.

We will now explore the CUI functionality of our agent in Google Dialogflow.

A CUI XAI dialog using Google Dialogflow

A CUI can be designed in four different ways:

- Voice input and voice response
- Voice input and text response
- Text input and voice response
- Text input and text response

We have already seen how to test a chatbot in Dialogflow's test console.

Let's implement a text or voice input and a text response on a website.

Dialogflow integration for a website

In this section, we will explore two scenarios for a website:

- Voice input and text response
- Text input and text response

First, click on **Integrations** in your agent's menu:

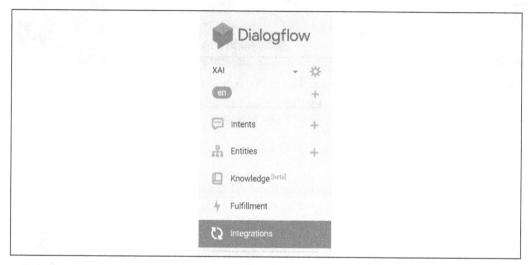

Figure 7.31: Dialogflow integration

You will see several integration modules. Click on **Web Demo**:

Figure 7.32: Web integration

Web Demo is not activated. We must first activate it as shown in the following screenshot:

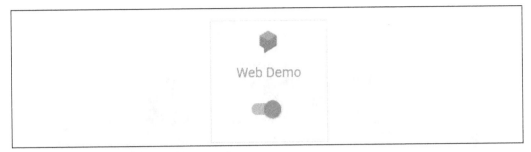

Figure 7.33: Web Demo activated

Once you have activated **Web Demo**, a pop-up window will display a link that you can copy and paste in your browser to access a ready-to-use web page with the agent on it:

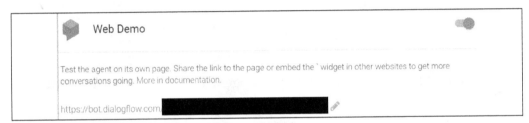

Figure 7.34: Web URL

You can also copy the following script into a web page of your choice:

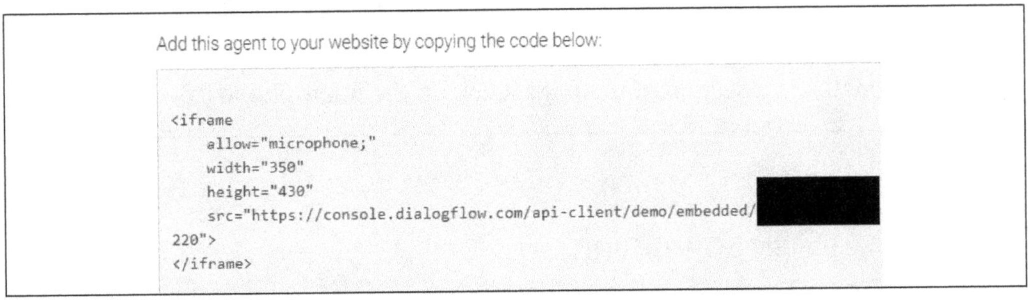

```
Add this agent to your website by copying the code below:

<iframe
    allow="microphone;"
    width="350"
    height="430"
    src="https://console.dialogflow.com/api-client/demo/embedded/
220">
</iframe>
```

Figure 7.35: Adding an agent to a website

If you use the link and not the embedding code, you will reach your agent, as shown in the following screenshot:

Figure 7.36: Dialog interface

You can share and email the link or embed the agent as you wish. We will now test the CUI functionality of our agent.

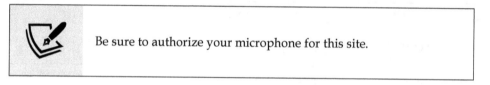

Be sure to authorize your microphone for this site.

In the **Ask something...** section of the page, click on the microphone icon:

Figure 7.37: Asking something

Say *hello*, for example.

Your chatbot will answer with the following text:

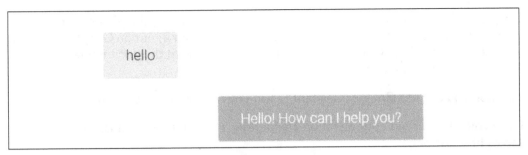

Figure 7.38: Chatbot dialog

The agent might answer with other responses. If you type hello, you will also obtain a text response.

You can create an agent manager that will contain links to multiple agents.

A Jupyter Notebook XAI agent manager

We might have to create multiple XAI agents for different aspects of an AI project. In that case, we can add an agent manager. Go to the last cell of XAI_Chatbot.ipynb.

Once it's uploaded, drag and drop it into the content directory or the directory displayed by the following command:

```
!pwd
```

In the last cell of the notebook, there are two options.

The first option is to consult:

```
[ML Explanation Consult](https://console.dialogflow.com/api-client/
demo/embedded/[YOUR AGENT HERE])
```

The second option is to consult and share:

```
[ML Explanation Consult and Share](https://bot.dialogflow.com/https://
console.dialogflow.com/api-client/demo/embedded/[YOUR AGENT HERE])
```

You can create an XAI chatbot menu for several agents, depending on the AI theme you wish to activate. You can change the titles, add comments, and add links. You can also create HTML pages to manage your agents.

We will now see how to explore the CUI of our agent further with Google Assistant.

Google Assistant

Google Assistant will take your agent to every smartphone on the planet that has Google Assistant installed on it. You can even deploy your agent on Google Assistant and then access it from Google Home, for example. Consult the documentation on Dialogflow to go from testing to production.

But first, you can use Google Assistant to test your agent's CUI capability.

Once you have chosen your agent on Dialogflow, click on **Google Assistant** at the top right of the page:

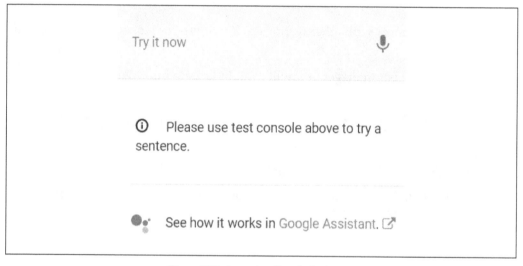

Figure 7.39: Accessing Google Assistant

Dialogflow will first update your actions:

Figure 7.40: Updating actions

There are many functions, but let's focus on testing the CUI:

Figure 7.41: CUI with Google Assistant

Make sure to authorize access to your device's microphone for this page.

For the first question, say `hello talk to my test app`, and you will receive both audio and text answers:

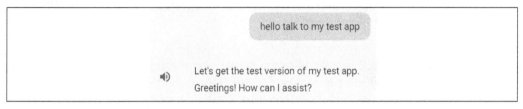

Figure 7.42: CUI dialog

Then type `hello`, and you will again receive both audio and text responses:

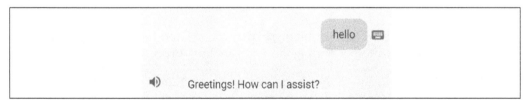

Figure 7.43: CUI dialog

You have just tested the four scenarios of a CUI dialog:

- Voice input and voice response
- Voice input and text response
- Text input and voice response
- Text input and text response

We have now implemented an XAI Python client for Dialogflow and explored how to use a CUI to obtain information from our XAI agent. You can explore Dialogflow further through Google's documentation and design complex integrations. For example, instead of using a Python client to access Python code, you can communicate with a server through Dialogflow as well.

You can add hundreds of intents to your agent, create new agents, and add new XAI Python Dialogflow clients to improve the relationship between humans and machines.

Summary

In this chapter, we built a Python client that can interact with Google Dialogflow. Our XAI chatbot can manage alert functions in the output of a machine learning algorithm.

Before implementing our chatbot, the trained machine learning algorithm would produce outputs. The user would have to wait until the ML program was finished and then activate an interactive interface.

An XAI interface, though interesting, might come too late in a decision-making process. Hundreds of automatic decisions may have been made before the user could intervene. Even if the XAI interface provides excellent explanations, bad decisions may have been made. These bad decisions must thus be analyzed, the parameters modified, and the program run again. If the errors were not damaging, then the problem can be solved with some additional configuration. But if the errors were critical, then an XAI interaction *before* the machine learning program ends is very productive.

Our XAI chatbot addressed two problems: explaining AI and interrupting an AI program in real time to interact with its decision-making process.

To reach our goals, we installed the Python client program on a local machine. We also installed it on Google Colaboratory in a Jupyter Notebook. We created a Dialogflow agent and activated the Google APIs and services. A private key in a JSON file was downloaded and used to establish a session between the Python client and Dialogflow.

We also built a CUI chatbot functionality for our XAI agent and explored how to deploy it on Google Assistant. Personal assistants will progressively replace keyboard interactions in many cases as smart objects become increasingly part of our everyday lives.

In the next chapter, *Local Interpretable Model-Agnostic Explanations (LIME)*, we will explore new ways to interpret a model's predictions using only its input and output data.

Questions

1. It is possible to create a dialog with Python and Dialogflow. (True | False)

2. You can customize your XAI dialog with a Python client. (True | False)

3. You do not need to set anything up in Dialogflow if you use a Python client. (True | False)

4. Intents are optional in Dialogflow. (True | False)

5. A training phrase is a response in a dialog. (True | False)

6. Context is a way of enhancing an XAI dialog. (True | False)

7. A follow-up question is a way of managing the context of a dialog. (True | False)

8. Small talk improves the emotional behavior of a dialog. (True | False)

9. Small talk can be directly set up in Dialogflow. (True | False)

Further reading

- For more on installing the Python client library for Dialogflow, see the following two links:
    - https://dialogflow-python-client-v2.readthedocs.io/en/latest/
    - https://cloud.google.com/dialogflow/docs/reference/libraries/python

- For more on the Dialogflow API, visit https://dialogflow-python-client-v2.readthedocs.io/en/latest/gapic/v2/api.html.

- For more on creating chatbots with Google Dialogflow, consider the book *Artificial Intelligence By Example, Second Edition*, by Denis Rothman, Packt, 2020.

- The documentation for Dialogflow can be found at https://cloud.google.com/dialogflow/docs?hl=en

8

Local Interpretable Model-Agnostic Explanations (LIME)

The expansion of **artificial intelligence (AI)** relies on trust. Users will reject **machine learning (ML)** systems they cannot trust. We will not trust decisions made by models that do not provide clear explanations. An AI system must provide clear explanations, or it will gradually become obsolete.

Local Interpretable Model-agnostic Explanations (LIME)'s approach aims at reducing the distance between AI and humans. LIME is people-oriented like SHAP and WIT. LIME focuses on two main areas: trusting a model and trusting a prediction. LIME provides a unique **explainable AI (XAI)** algorithm that interprets predictions locally.

I recommend a third area: trusting the datasets. A perfect model and accurate predictions based on a biased dataset will destroy the bond between humans and AI. We have detailed the issue of ethical data in several chapters in this book, such as in *Chapter 6, AI Fairness with Google's What-If Tool (WIT)*. In this chapter, instead of explaining why a dataset needs to meet ethical standards, I chose neutral datasets with information on electronics and space to avoid culturally biased datasets.

In this chapter, we will first define LIME and its unique approach. Then we will get started with LIME on Google Colaboratory, retrieve the data we need, and vectorize the datasets.

We will then create five machine learning models to demonstrate LIME's model-agnostic algorithm, train the model, and measure the predictions produced.

We will run an experimental AutoML module to compare the scores of the five ML models. The experimental AutoML module will run the ML models and choose the best one for the dataset. It will then automatically use the best model to make predictions and explain them with LIME.

Finally, we will build the LIME explainer to interpret the predictions with text and plots. We will see how the LIME explainer applies local interpretability to a model's predictions.

This chapter covers the following topics:

- Introducing LIME
- Running LIME on Google Colaboratory
- Retrieving and vectorizing datasets
- An experimental AutoML module
- Creating classifiers with a model-agnostic approach
- Random forest
- Bagging
- Gradient boosting
- Decision trees
- Extra trees
- Prediction metrics
- Vectorizing pipelines
- Creating a LIME explainer
- Visualizing LIME's text explanations
- LIME XAI plots

Our first step will be to understand AI interpretability with LIME.

Introducing LIME

LIME stands for **Local Interpretable Model-agnostic Explanations**. LIME explanations can help a user trust an AI system. A machine learning model often trains at least 100 features to reach a prediction. Showing all these features in an interface makes it nearly impossible for a user to analyze the result visually.

In *Chapter 4, Microsoft Azure Machine Learning Model Interpretability with SHAP,* we used SHAP to calculate the marginal contribution of a feature to the model and for a given prediction. The Shapley value of a feature represents its contribution to one or several sets of features. LIME has a different approach.

LIME wants to find out whether a model is *locally faithful regardless of the model*. Local fidelity verifies how a model represents the features around a prediction. Local fidelity might not fit the model globally, but it explains how the prediction was made. In the same way, a global explanation of the model might not explain a local prediction.

For example, we helped a doctor conclude that a patient was infected by the West Nile virus in *Chapter 1, Explaining Artificial Intelligence with Python*.

Our global feature set was as follows:

features = {colored sputum, cough, fever, headache, days, france, chicago, class}

Our global assumption was that the following main features led to the conclusion with a high probability value that the patient was infected with the West Nile virus:

features = {bad cough, high fever, bad headache, many days, chicago=true}

Our predictions relied on that ground truth.

But was this global ground truth always verified locally? What if a prediction was true for the West Nile virus with a slightly different set of features — how could we explain that locally?

LIME will explore the local vicinity of a prediction to explain it and analyze its local fidelity.

For example, suppose a prediction was a true positive for the West Nile virus but not precisely for the same reasons as our global model. LIME will search the vicinity of the instance of the prediction to explain the decision the model made.

In this case, LIME could find a high probability of the following features:

Local explanation = {high fever, mild sputum, mild headache, chicago=true}

We know that a patient with a high fever with a headache that was in Chicago points to the West Nile virus. The presence of chills might provide an explanation as well, although the global model had a different view. Locally, the prediction is faithful, although globally, our model's output was positive when many days and bad cough were present, and mild sputum was absent.

The prediction is thus locally faithful to the model. It has inherited the global feature attributes that LIME will detect and explain locally.

In this example, LIME did not take the model into account. LIME used the global features involved in a prediction and the local instance of the prediction to explain the output. In that sense, LIME is a model-agnostic model explainer.

We now have an intuitive understanding of what LIMEs are. We can now formalize LIME mathematically.

A mathematical representation of LIME

In this section, we will translate our intuitive understanding of LIME into a mathematical expression of LIME.

The original, global representation of an instance x can be represented as follows:

$$x \in \mathbb{R}^d$$

However, an interpretable representation of an instance is a binary vector:

$$x' \in \{0,1\}^{d'}$$

The interpretable representation determines the local presence or absence of a feature or several features.

Let's now consider the model-agnostic property of LIME. g represents a machine learning model. G represents a set of models containing g among other models:

$$g \in G$$

As such, LIME's algorithm will interpret any other model in the same manner.

The domain of g being a binary vector, we can represent it as follows:

$$g, \{0,1\}^{d^n}$$

Now, we face a difficult problem! The complexity of $g \in G$ might create difficulties in analyzing the vicinity of an instance. We must take this factor into account. We will note the complexity of an interpretation of a model as follows:

$$\Omega(g)$$

We encountered such a complexity program in *Chapter 2, White Box XAI for AI Bias and Ethics*, when interpreting decision trees. When we began to explain the structure of a decision tree, we found that "the default output of a default decision tree structure challenges a user's ability to understand the algorithm." In *Chapter 2*, we fine-tuned the decision tree's parameters to limit the complexity of the output to explain.

We thus need to measure the complexity of a model with $\Omega(g)$. High model complexity can hinder AI explanations and interpretations of a probability function $f(x)$. $\Omega(g)$ must be reasonably low enough for humans to be able to interpret a prediction.

$f(x)$ defines the probability that x belongs to the binary vector we defined previously, as follows:

$$x' \in \{0,1\}^{d'}$$

The model can thus also be defined as follows:

$$f: \mathbb{R}^d \rightarrow \mathbb{R}$$

Now, we need to add an instance z to see how x fits in this instance. We must measure the locality around x. For example, consider the features (in bold) in the two following sentences:

- **Sentence 1**: *We danced all night; it was like in the movie Saturday Night **Fever**, or that movie called **Chicago** with that murder scene that sent **chills** down my spine. I listened to music for **days** when I was a teenager.*

- **Sentence 2**: *Doctor, when I was in **Chicago**, I hardly noticed a **mosquito** bit me, then when I got back to France, I came down with a **fever**.*

Sentence 2 leads to a West Nile virus diagnosis.

However, a model g could predict that **Sentence 1** is a true positive as well.

The same could be said of the following **Sentence 3**:

- **Sentence 3**: *I just got back from Italy, have a bad **fever**, and **difficulty breathing**.*

Sentence 3 leads to a COVID-19 diagnosis that could be a false positive or not. I will not elaborate while in isolation in France at the time this book is being written. It would not be ethical to make mathematical models for educational purposes in such difficult times for hundreds of millions of us around the world.

In any case, we can see the importance of a proximity measurement between an instance z and the locality around x. We will define this proximity measurement as follows:

$$\Pi_x(z)$$

We now have all the variables we need to define LIME, except one important one. How faithful is this prediction to the global ground truth of our model? Can we explain why it is trustworthy? The answer to our question will be to determine how unfaithful a model g can be when calculating f in the locality Π_x.

For all we know, a prediction could be a false positive! Or the prediction could be a false negative! Or even worse, the prediction could be a true positive or negative for the wrong reasons. This shows how unfaithful g can be.

We will measure unfaithfulness with the letter $\mathcal{L}$.

$\mathcal{L}(f, g, \Pi_x)$ will measure how unfaithful g is when making approximations of f in the locality we defined as Π_x.

We must minimize unfaithfulness with $\mathcal{L}(f, g, \Pi_x)$ and find how to keep the complexity $\Omega(g)$ as low as possible.

Finally, we can define an explanation $\mathcal{E}$ generated by LIME as follows:

$$\mathcal{E}(x) = \underset{g \in G}{\text{argmin}}\, \mathcal{L}(f, g, \Pi_x) + \Omega(g)$$

LIME will draw samples weighted by Π_x to optimize the equation to produce the best interpretation and explanations $\mathcal{E}(x)$ regardless of the model implemented.

LIME can be applied to various models, fidelity functions, and complexity measures. However, LIME's approach will follow the method we have defined.

For more on LIME theory, consult the *References* section at the end of this chapter.

We can now get started with this intuitive view and mathematical representation of LIME in mind!

Getting started with LIME

In this section, we will install LIME using `LIME.ipynb`, a Jupyter Notebook on Google Colaboratory. We will then retrieve the 20 newsgroups dataset from `sklearn.datasets`.

We will read the dataset and vectorize it.

The process is a standard scikit-learn approach that you can save and use as a template for other projects in which you implement other scikit-learn models.

We have already used this process in *Chapter 4, Microsoft Azure Machine Learning Model Interpretability with SHAP*. In this chapter, we will not examine the dataset from an ethical perspective. I chose one with no ethical ambiguity.

We will directly install LIME, then import and vectorize the dataset.

Let's now start by installing LIME on Google Colaboratory.

Installing LIME on Google Colaboratory

Open `LIME.ipynb`. We will be using `LIME.ipynb` throughout this chapter. The first cell contains the installation command:

```
# @title Installing LIME
try:
    import lime
except:
    print("Installing LIME")
    !pip install lime
```

The try/except will try to import `lime`. If `lime` is not installed, the program will crash. In this code, except will trigger `!pip install lime`.

Google Colaboratory deletes some libraries and modules when you restart it, as well as the current variables of a notebook. We then need to reinstall some packages. This piece of code will make the process seamless.

We will now retrieve the datasets.

Retrieving the datasets and vectorizing the dataset

In this section, we will import the program's modules, import the dataset, and vectorize it.

We first import the main modules for the program:

```
# @title Importing modules
import lime
import sklearn
import numpy as np
from __future__ import print_function
import sklearn
import sklearn.ensemble
import sklearn.metrics
from sklearn.ensemble import BaggingClassifier
from sklearn.neighbors import KNeighborsClassifier
from sklearn.ensemble import GradientBoostingClassifier
from sklearn.tree import DecisionTreeClassifier
from sklearn.ensemble import ExtraTreesClassifier
```

sklearn is the primary source of the models used in this program. sklearn also provides several datasets for machine learning. We will import the 20 newsgroups dataset:

```
# @title Retrieving newsgroups data
from sklearn.datasets import fetch_20newsgroups
```

A quick investigation of the source of this dataset is good practice, although the newsgroup we will choose contains no obvious ethical issues. The 20 newsgroups dataset contains thousands of newsgroups documents widely used for machine learning purposes. Scikit-learn offers more real-world datasets that you can explore with this program at https://scikit-learn.org/stable/datasets/index.html#real-world-datasets.

We now import two newsgroups from the dataset and label them:

```
categories = ['sci.electronics', 'sci.space']
newsgroups_train = fetch_20newsgroups(subset='train',
                                      categories=categories)
newsgroups_test = fetch_20newsgroups(subset='test',
                                     categories=categories)
class_names = ['electronics', 'space']
```

The models in this notebook will classify the content of these newsgroups in two classes: 'electronics' and 'space'.

The program classifies the datasets using vectorized data.

The text is vectorized and transformed into token counts, as explained and displayed in *Chapter 4, Microsoft Azure Machine Learning Model Interpretability with SHAP*:

```
# @title Vectorizing
vectorizer = sklearn.feature_extraction.text.TfidfVectorizer(
    lowercase=False)
train_vectors = vectorizer.fit_transform(newsgroups_train.data)
test_vectors = vectorizer.transform(newsgroups_test.data)
```

The dataset has been imported and vectorized. We can now focus on an experimental AutoML module.

An experimental AutoML module

In this section, we will implement ML models in the spirit of LIME. We will play by the rules and try not to influence the outcome of the ML models, whether we like it or not.

The LIME explainer will try to explain predictions no matter which model produces the output or how.

Each model g will be treated equally as part of G, our set of models:

$$g \in G$$

We will implement five machine learning models with their default parameters, as provided by scikit-learn's example code.

We will then run all five machine learning models in a row and select the best one with an agnostic scoring system to make predictions for the LIME explainer.

Each model will be created with the same template and scoring method.

This experimental model will only choose the best model. If you wish to add features to this experiment, you can run epochs. You can develop functions that will change the parameters of the module during each epoch to try to improve it.

For this experiment, we do not want to influence outputs by tweaking the parameters.

Let's create the template we will be using for all five models.

Creating an agnostic AutoML template

In this section, we will create five models using the following template I initially designed for a random forest classifier.

The AutoML experiment begins by creating two optimizing variables. It is a small AutoML experiment limited to the goal of this section.

best will contain the score of the best model at the end of the evaluation phase, as follows:

```
# @title AutoML experiment: Score measurement variables
best = 0 # best classifier score
```

clf will contain the name of the best model at the end of the evaluation phase, as follows:

```
clf = "None" # best classifier name
```

The score can vary from one run to another because of the randomized sampling methods involved.

The program creates each model, then trains and evaluates its performance using the following template:

```
# @title AutoML experiment: Random forest
rf1 = sklearn.ensemble.RandomForestClassifier(n_estimators=500)
rf1.fit(train_vectors, newsgroups_train.target)
pred = rf1.predict(test_vectors)
```

Before we continue, we need to describe how a random forest model makes predictions. In *Chapter 2, White Box XAI for AI Bias and Ethics,* we went through the theoretical definition of a decision tree. A random forest is an ensemble algorithm. An ensemble algorithm takes several machine learning algorithms to improve its performance. It usually produces better results than a single algorithm.

A random forest fits a number of decision trees, makes random subsamples of the dataset, and uses averaging to increase the performance of the model. In this model, n_estimators=500 represents a forest of 500 trees.

Each classifier of the five classifiers has its own name: {rf1, rf2, rf3, rf4, rf5}

Each trained classifier has its own metrics: {score1, score2, score3, score4, score5}

sklearn.metrics.f1_score evaluates each model's score, as follows:

```
score1 = sklearn.metrics.f1_score(newsgroups_test.target,
                                  pred, average='binary')
```

If the score of a model exceeds the best score of the preceding models, it becomes the best model:

```
if score1 > best:
    best = score1
    clf = "Random forest"
    print("Random forest has achieved the top score!", score1)
else:
    print("Score of random forest", score1)
```

If score1 > best, best will become the best score and clf the name of the best model. best memorizes score1, which is displayed as the top-ranking score.

If the model has achieved the best score, its performance is displayed as follows:

```
Random forest has achieved the top score! 0.7757731958762887
```

Each model will apply the same template.

We have implemented the random forest classifier. We will now create the bagging classifier.

Bagging classifiers

A bagging classifier is an ensemble meta-estimator that fits the model using random samples of the original dataset. In this model, the classifiers are based on the k-nearest neighbors classifier described in *Chapter 1, Explaining Artificial Intelligence with Python*:

```
# @title AutoML experiment: Bagging
rf2 = BaggingClassifier(KNeighborsClassifier(),
                    n_estimators=500, max_samples=0.5,
                    max_features=0.5)
rf2.fit(train_vectors, newsgroups_train.target)
pred = rf2.predict(test_vectors)
score2 = sklearn.metrics.f1_score(newsgroups_test.target,
                                pred, average='binary')
if score2 > best:
  best = score2
  clf = "Bagging"
  print("Bagging has achieved the top score!", score2)
else:
  print("Score of bagging", score2)
```

Note a key parameter: n_estimators=500. If you do not set this parameter to 500, the default value is only 10 base estimators for the ensemble. If you leave it that way, the random forest classifier will end up as the best model, and bagging will produce a poor accuracy value.

However, if you set the number of base classifiers to 500, like for the random forest, then it will exceed the performance of the random forest classifier.

Also note that if you do not set the base classifier to KNeighborsClassifier(), the default classifier is a decision tree.

`max_samples=0.5` represents the maximum proportion of samples that the classifier will draw to train each estimator.

`max_features=0.5` represents the maximum number of features that an estimator will draw to train each sample.

The bagging model achieved a better score in this case than the random forest model with the same number of estimators:

```
Bagging has achieved the top score! 0.7942583732057416
```

Let's now add a gradient booster classifier to our experiment.

Gradient boosting classifiers

A gradient boosting classifier is an ensemble meta-estimator like the preceding models. It uses a differentiable loss function to optimize its estimators, generally decision trees.

`n_estimators=500` will run 500 estimators to optimize its performance:

```
# @title AutoML experiment: Gradient boosting
rf3 = GradientBoostingClassifier(random_state=1, n_estimators=500)
rf3.fit(train_vectors, newsgroups_train.target)
pred = rf3.predict(test_vectors)
score3 = sklearn.metrics.f1_score(newsgroups_test.target,
                                  pred, average='binary')
if score3 > best:
  best = score3
  clf = "Gradient boosting"
  print("Gradient boosting has achieved the top score!", score3)
else:
  print("Score of gradient boosting", score3)
```

The performance of the gradient boosting model does not beat the preceding models:

```
Score of gradient boosting 0.7909319899244333
```

Let's add a decision tree to the experiment.

Decision tree classifiers

The decision tree classifier only uses one tree. It makes it difficult to beat the ensemble models.

In *Chapter 2, White Box XAI for AI Bias and Ethics*, we already went through the theoretical definition of a decision tree and its parameters.

In this project, the program creates the model with default models:

```
# @title AutoML experiment: Decision tree
rf4 = DecisionTreeClassifier(random_state=1)
rf4.fit(train_vectors, newsgroups_train.target)
pred = rf4.predict(test_vectors)
score4 = sklearn.metrics.f1_score(newsgroups_test.target,
                                  pred, average='binary')

if score4 > best:
  best = score4
  clf = "Decision tree"
  print("Decision tree has achieved the top score!", score4)
else:
  print("Score of decision tree", score4)
```

As expected, a single decision tree cannot beat ensemble estimators for this dataset:

```
Score of decision tree 0.7231352718078382
```

Finally, let's add an extra trees classifier.

Extra trees classifiers

The extra trees model appears as a good approach for this dataset. This meta-estimator fits a number of randomized decision trees using subsamples of the dataset and averaging methods to obtain the best performance possible.

As for the preceding meta-estimators, let's set n_estimators=500 so that each meta-estimator in our experiment generates the same number of estimators:

```
# @title AutoML experiment: Extra trees
rf5 = ExtraTreesClassifier(n_estimators=500, random_state=1)
rf5.fit(train_vectors, newsgroups_train.target)
pred = rf5.predict(test_vectors)
score5 = sklearn.metrics.f1_score(newsgroups_test.target,
                                  pred, average='binary')

if score5 > best:
  best = score5
  clf = "Extra trees"
  print("Extra trees has achieved the top score!", score5)
else:
  print("Score of extra trees", score5)
```

The extra trees model produces the best performance:

```
Extra Trees has achieved the Top Score! 0.818297331639136
```

We have now run the five models of our prototype of an AutoML experiment.

We will now use our program to interpret the scores.

Interpreting the scores

In this section, we will display the scores achieved by the five models. You can try to improve the performance of a model by fine-tuning the parameters.

You can also add several other models to measure their performance.

In this chapter, we will focus on the LIME model-agnostic explainer and let the program select the model that produces the best performance.

The program displays the AutoML experiment summary:

```
# @title AutoML experiment: Summary
print("The best model is", clf, "with a score of:", round(best, 5))
print("Scores:")
print("Random forest          :", round(score1, 5))
print("Bagging                :", round(score2, 5))
print("Gradient boosting      :", round(score3, 5))
print("Decision tree          :", round(score4, 5))
print("Extra trees            :", round(score5, 5))
```

The output displays the summary:

```
The best model is Extra Trees with a score of: 0.8183
Scores:
Random forest      : 0.77577
Bagging            : 0.79426
Gradient boosting  : 0.79093
Decision tree      : 0.72314
Extra trees        : 0.8183
```

The best model is stored in `clf`.

We have now found the best model for this dataset. We can start making and displaying predictions.

Training the model and making predictions

In this section, we will decide whether we will take the AutoML experiment's choice into account or not. Then we will run the final model chosen, train it, and finalize the prediction process.

The interactive choice of classifier

The notebook now displays a form where you can specify to activate the automatic process or not.

If you choose to set **AutoML** to **On** in the dropdown list, then the best model of the AutoML experiment will become the default model of the Notebook.

If not, choose **Off** in the AutoML dropdown list:

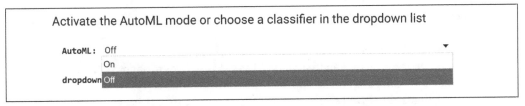

Figure 8.1: Activating AutoML or manually selecting a classifier

If you select **Off**, select the model you wish to choose for the LIME explainer in the dropdown list:

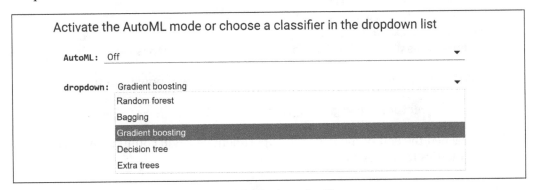

Figure 8.2: Selecting a classifier

Double-click on the form to view the code that manages the automatic process and the interactive selection:

```
# @title Activate the AutoML mode or
# choose a classifier in the dropdown list
AutoML = 'On' # @param ["On", "Off"]
dropdown = 'Gradient boosting' # @param ["Random forest",
#                                        "Bagging",
#                                        "Gradient boosting",
#                                        "Decision tree",
#                                        "Extra trees"]

if AutoML == "On":
  dropdown = clf

if clf == "None":
  dropdown = "Decision tree"

if dropdown == "Random forest":
  rf = sklearn.ensemble.RandomForestClassifier(n_estimators=500)
if dropdown == "Bagging":
  rf = BaggingClassifier(KNeighborsClassifier(), n_estimators=500,
                         max_samples=0.5, max_features=0.5)
if dropdown == "Gradient boosting":
  rf = GradientBoostingClassifier(random_state=1, n_estimators=500)
if dropdown == "Decision tree":
  rf = DecisionTreeClassifier(random_state=1)
if dropdown == "Extra trees":
  rf = ExtraTreesClassifier(random_state=1, n_estimators=500)
```

The AutoML experiment model or the model you chose will now train the data:

```
rf.fit(train_vectors, newsgroups_train.target)
```

We have reached the end of the AutoML experiment. We will continue by creating prediction metrics for the estimator.

Finalizing the prediction process

In this section, we will create prediction metrics and a pipeline with a vectorizer, and display the model's predictions.

The model chosen will be the AutoML experiment's choice if the automatic mode was turned on, or the model you select if the automatic mode was off.

First, we will start by creating the final prediction metrics for the selected model:

```
# @title Prediction metrics
pred = rf.predict(test_vectors)
sklearn.metrics.f1_score(newsgroups_test.target,
                         pred, average='binary')
```

The selected model's score will be displayed:

```
0.818297331639136
```

This score will vary every time you or the AutoML experiment changes models. It might also vary due to the random sampling processes during the training phase.

The program now creates a pipeline with a vectorizer to make predictions on the raw text:

```
# @title Creating a pipeline with a vectorizer
# Creating a pipeline to implement predictions on raw text lists
# (sklearn uses vectorized data)
from lime import lime_text
from sklearn.pipeline import make_pipeline
c = make_pipeline(vectorizer, rf)
```

Interception functions

We will now test the predictions. I added two records in the dataset to control the way LIME will explain them:

```
# @title Predictions
# YOUR INTERCEPTION FUNCTION HERE
newsgroups_test.data[1] = "Houston, we have a problem with our ice-
cream out here in space. The ice-cream machine is out of order!"
newsgroups_test.data[2] = "Why doesn't my TV ever work? It keeps
blinking at me as if I were the TV, and it was watching me with a
webcam. Maybe AI is becoming autonomous!"
```

Note the following comment in the code:

```
# YOUR INTERCEPTION FUNCTION HERE
```

I will refer to them as the "interception records" in the *The LIME explainer* section.

You add an interception function here or at the beginning of the program to insert phrases you wish to test. To do this, you can consult the *Intercepting the dataset* section of *Chapter 4, Microsoft Azure Machine Learning Model Interpretability with SHAP*.

The program will print the text, which is in index 1 of the data object in this case. You can set it to another value to play with the model. However, in the next section, a form will make sure you do not choose an index that exceeds the length of the list. The prediction and text are displayed as follows:

```
print(newsgroups_test.data[1])
print(c.predict_proba([newsgroups_test.data[1]]))
```

The output shows the text and the prediction for both classes:

```
Houston, we have a problem with our ice-cream out here in space. The
ice-cream machine is out of order!
[[0.266 0.734]]
```

We now have a trained model and have verified a prediction.

We can activate the LIME explainer to interpret the predictions.

The LIME explainer

In this section, we will implement the LIME explainer, generate an explanation, explore some simulations, and interpret the results with visualizations.

However, though I eluded ethical issues by selecting bland datasets, the predictions led to strange explanations!

Before creating the explainer in Python, we must sum up the tools we have before making interpretations and generating explanations.

We represented an equation of LIME in the *A mathematical representation of LIME* section of this chapter:

$$\mathcal{E}(x) = \underset{g \in G}{\operatorname{argmin}} \mathcal{L}(f, g, \Pi_x) + \Omega(g)$$

argmin searches the closest area possible around a prediction and finds the features that make a prediction fall into one class or another.

LIME will thus explain how a prediction was made, whatever the model is and however it reached that prediction.

Though LIME does not know which model was chosen by our experimental AutoML, we do. We know that we chose the best model, g, among five models in a set named G:

$$g \in G$$

LIME does not know that we ran ensemble meta-estimators with 500 estimators and obtained reasonably good results in our summary:

```
The best model is Extra Trees with a score of: 0.8183
Scores:
Random Forest:        : 0.77577
Bagging               : 0.79426
Gradient Boosting     : 0.79093
Decision Tree         : 0.72314
Extra Trees           : 0.8183
```

We concluded that g = "Extra Trees" was the best model in G:

$$G = \{\text{"Random Forest", "Bagging", "Gradient Boosting", "Decision Trees", "Extra Trees"}\}$$

The extra trees classifier achieved a score of 0.81, which laid the ground for good and solid explanations.

We even created an interception function in the *Interception functions* section just like we did in *Chapter 4, Microsoft Azure Machine Learning Model Interpretability with SHAP*.

We should now expect the LIME explainer to highlight valuable features as we did in *Chapter 4, Microsoft Azure Machine Learning Model Interpretability with SHAP*, with our intercepted dataset.

But will we obtain the explanations we expected? We will see.

First, we need to create the LIME explainer and generate explanations.

Creating the LIME explainer

In this section, we will create the LIME explainer, select a text to explain, and generate an explanation.

The program first creates the explainer:

```
# @title Creating the LIME explainer
from lime.lime_text import LimeTextExplainer
explainer = LimeTextExplainer(class_names=class_names)
```

The explainer used the names of the classes defined when we imported the dataset:

```
class_names = ['electronics', 'space']
```

The program calculates the length of the dataset:

```
pn = len(newsgroups_test.data)
print("Length of newsgroup", pn)
```

In this case, the output is as follows:

```
Length of newsgroup 787
```

You can now select an index of the list in a form:

```
                     Selecting a text to explain

                          index: 5  _____
```

Figure 8.3: Selecting an index of the list

If you double-click on the form after choosing an index that exceeds the length of the dataset, the default value of the index will be 1:

```
# @title Selecting a text to explain
index = 5 # @param {type: "number"}
idx = index
if idx > pn:
  idx = 1


print(newsgroups_test.data[idx])
```

You can now see the content of this element of the list, as shown in this excerpt of a message:

```
From: cmh@eng.cam.ac.uk (C.M. Hicks)
Subject: Re: Making up odd resistor values required by filters
Nntp-Posting-Host: club.eng.cam.ac.uk
Organization: cam.eng
Lines: 26


idh@nessie.mcc.ac.uk (Ian Hawkins) writes:

>When constructing active filters, odd values of resistor are often
required
>(i.e. something like a 3.14 K Ohm resistor).(It seems best to choose
common
>capacitor values and cope with the strange resistances then demanded).
```

The content of an index may change from one run to another due to the random sampling of the testing dataset.

Finally, the program generates an explanation for this message:

```
# @title Generating the explanation
exp = explainer.explain_instance(newsgroups_test.data[idx],
                           c.predict_proba, num_features=10)
print('Document id: %d' % idx)
print('Probability(space) =',
      c.predict_proba([newsgroups_test.data[idx]])[0,1])
print('True class: %s' % class_names[newsgroups_test.target[idx]])
```

The output shows the document index, along with probability and classification information:

```
Document id: 5
Probability(space) = 0.45
True class: electronics
```

We created the explainer, selected a message, and generated an explanation.

We will now interpret the results produced by the LIME explainer.

Interpreting LIME explanations

In this section, we will interpret the results produced by the LIME explainer. I used the term "interpret" for a good reason.

To explain generally refers to making something clear and understandable. XAI can do that with the methods and algorithms we have implemented in this book.

In this section, we will see that *explainable AI, AI explainability,* or *explaining AI* are the best terms to describe a process by which a machine makes a prediction clear to a user.

To *interpret* implies more than just *explaining*. Interpreting means more than just looking at the context of a prediction and providing explanations. When we humans interpret something, we construe, we seek connections beyond the instance we are observing, beyond the context, and make connections that a machine cannot imagine.

XAI clarifies a prediction. Interpreting explanations requires the unique human imaginative ability to connect a specific theme to a wide range of domains. Machines explain, humans *construe*.

To make things easier, in this book, I will continue to use "interpreting" AI loosely as a synonym for "explaining" AI.

However, bear in mind that it will take your human ability of interpretation and construal to understand the following sections.

Explaining the predictions as a list

The article in the *Further reading* section, *"Why Should I Trust You?": Explaining the Predictions of Any Classifier*, concludes that if something does not fit what we expected when we chose to use some newsgroups, the authors find that the model's predictions cannot be trusted.

In this section, we will try to understand why.

The program displays LIME's explanation as a list:

```
# @title Explain as a list
exp.as_list()
```

The output of the explanation of index 5 that we selected is no less than stunning!

Take a close look at the list of words that LIME highlighted and that influenced the prediction:

```
[('given', 0.07591981678565418),
 ('space', 0.05907439931403264),
 ('program', 0.031052797629092826),
 ('values', -0.01962286424974262),
 ('want', -0.0190854700026052057),
 ('took', 0.018065064825319777),
 ('such', 0.017583164138156998),
 ('resistor', -0.015927676300306223),
 ('reported', 0.011573402045350527),
 ('was', 0.0076483181262587616)]
```

Each word has a negative or positive impact on the prediction. But this means nothing, as we will see now.

If we drop the "space" class name, we will get the following set W of LIME's explanations:

$$W = \{\text{"given", "program", "value", "want", "took", "resistor", "reported", "was"}\}$$

"resistor" could apply to a spacecraft or a radio.

If we try one of our interception function sentences, we obtain an overfitted explanation. Go back, choose 1 in the **Selecting a text to explain** form, and then rerun the program.

We first read the sentence:

```
Houston, we have a problem with our ice-cream out here in space. The
ice-cream machine is out of order!
```

Then we look at LIME's explanation:

```
[('space', 0.2234448477494966),
 ('we', 0.05818967308950206),
 ('in', 0.015367276432916372),
 ('ice', -0.015137670461620763),
 ('of', 0.014242945006601808),
 ('our', 0.012470992672708379),
 ('with', -0.010137856356371086),
 ('Houston', 0.009826506741944144),
 ('The', 0.00836296328281397),
 ('machine', -0.0033670468609339615)]
```

We drop the "space" class name and create a set W' containing LIME's explanation. We will order the explanation as closely as possible to the original sentence:

$$W' = \{\text{"Houston", "we", "with", "our", "in", "the", "ice", "machine", "of"}\}$$

This explanation makes no sense either. Key features are not targeted.

If you try several index numbers randomly, you will find pertinent explanations from time to time.

However, at this point, we trust anything we see, so let's visualize LIME's explanations with a plot.

Explaining with a plot

In this section, we will visualize the explanations of the text in index 5 again. We will find nothing new. However, we will have a much better view of LIME's explanation.

First, LIME removes some of the features to measure the effect on the predictions:

```
# @title Removing some features
print('Original prediction:',
      rf.predict_proba(test_vectors[idx])[0, 1])
tmp = test_vectors[idx].copy()
tmp[0, vectorizer.vocabulary_['Posting']] = 0
tmp[0, vectorizer.vocabulary_['Host']] = 0
print('Prediction removing some features:',
      rf.predict_proba(tmp)[0, 1])
print('Difference:', rf.predict_proba(tmp)[0, 1] -
                      rf.predict_proba(test_vectors[idx])[0, 1])
```

This function will help a user simulate various local scenarios.

The output, in this case, does not change the prediction:

```
Original prediction: 0.334
Prediction removing some features: 0.336
Difference: 0.0020000000000000018
```

We now create the plot:

```
# @title Explaining with a plot
fig = exp.as_pyplot_figure()
```

The plot displays what we already know, but in a visually clear form:

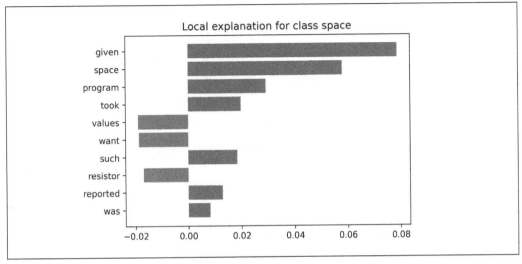

Figure 8.4: A local explanation for a prediction

We can see that words that relate to the positive impact on the class name space make no sense, such as: "given", "took", "such", "was", and "reported".

On the negative side, things aren't better with "want", for example.

This plot confirms the conclusions we will reach after the last verification.

We will now visualize the summary of the explanation in our notebook:

```
# @title Visual explanations
exp.show_in_notebook(text=False)
```

Let's save the explanations and display them in the HTML output:

```
# @title Saving explanation
exp.save_to_file('/content/oi.html')
```

```
# @title Showing in notebook
exp.show_in_notebook(text=True)
```

The visual HTML output contains the visual LIME explanations.

On the left, we can visualize the prediction probabilities:

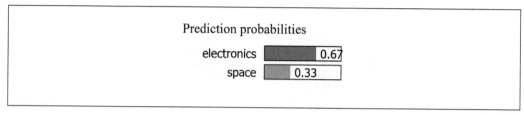

Figure 8.5: The probabilities of a prediction

In the center, we can see the text explanations in a clear visual format:

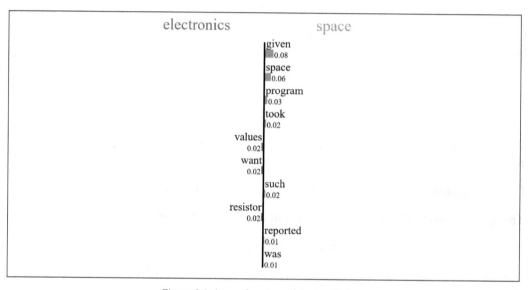

Figure 8.6: An explanation of the prediction

On the right side of the HTML output, we can consult the original text of this prediction and LIME explanation, as shown in this excerpt:

|Is there a PD program out there that will work out how best to make up such
|a resistance, given fixed resistors of the standard 12 values per decade?.(1,
|1.2,1.5,1.8,2.2,3.3 etc). It is a common enough problem, yet I cant
|recall seing a program that tells that Rx+Ry//Rz gives Rq, starting with
|q and finding prefered values x,y and z.

I once wrote such a program (in BBC basic...) It was very crude, and took
around 5 seconds to do an exhaustive search (with a small amount of
intelligence), and told you the best combination |Rq and the best below Rq.

Figure 8.7: The original text of the prediction

LIME's explanation is shown in the text by highlighting the words used for the explanations. Each color (see color image) reflects the values calculated by LIME.

Conclusions of the LIME explanation process

We can draw several conclusions from the LIME process we implemented:

- LIME proves that even accurate predictions cannot be trusted without XAI
- Local interpretable models will measure to what extent we can trust a prediction
- Local explanations might show that the dataset cannot be trusted to produce reliable predictions
- XAI can prove that a model cannot be trusted or that it is reliable
- LIME's visual explanations can be an excellent way to help a user gain trust in an AI system

Note that in the third conclusion, the wording is *might show*. We must be careful because of the number of parameters involved in such a model. For example, in *Chapter 12, Cognitive XAI*, we will implement other approaches and investigate this third conclusion.

We can make only one global conclusion:

Once a user has an explanation that doesn't meet expectations, the next step will be to investigate and contribute to the improvement of the model. No conclusion can be made before investigating the causes of the explanations provided.

In this section, we proved that XAI is a prerequisite for any AI project, not just an option.

Summary

In this chapter, we confirmed that an AI system must base its approach on trust. A user must understand predictions and on what criteria an ML model produces its outputs.

LIME tackles AI explainability locally, where misunderstandings hurt the human-machine relationship. LIME's explainer does not satisfy itself with an accurate global model. It digs down to explain a prediction locally.

In this chapter, we installed LIME and retrieved newsgroup texts on electronics and space. We vectorized the data and created several models.

Once we implemented several models and the LIME explainer, we ran an experimental AutoML module. The models were all activated to generate predictions. The accuracy of each model was recorded and compared to its competitors. The best model then made predictions for LIME explanations.

Also, the final score of each model showed which model had the best performance with this dataset. We saw how LIME could explain the predictions of an accurate or inaccurate model.

The successful implementation of random forests, bagging, gradient boosting, decision trees, and extra trees models demonstrated LIME's model-agnostic approach.

Explaining and interpreting AI requires visual representations. LIME's plots transform the complexity of machine learning algorithms into clear visual explanations.

LIME shows once again that AI explainability relies on three factors: the quality of a dataset, the implementation of a model, and the quality of a model's predictions.

In the next chapter, *The Counterfactual Explanation Method*, we will discover how to explain a result with an *unconditional method*.

Questions

1. LIME stands for Local Interpretable Model-agnostic Explanations. (True | False)

2. LIME measures the overall accuracy score of a model. (True | False)

3. LIME's primary goal is to verify if a local prediction is faithful to the model. (True | False)

4. The LIME explainer shows why a local prediction is trustworthy or not. (True | False)

5. If you run a random forest model with LIME, you cannot use the same model with an extra trees model. (True | False)

6. There is a LIME explainer for each model. (True | False)

7. Prediction metrics are not necessary if a user is satisfied with predictions. (True | False)

8. A model that has a low accuracy score can produce accurate outputs. (True | False)

9. A model that has a high accuracy score provides correct outputs. (True | False)

10. Benchmarking models can help choose a model or fine-tune it. (True | False)

References

The reference code for LIME can be found at the following link:

`https://github.com/marcotcr/lime`

Further reading

- For more on LIME, see the following:

    - `https://homes.cs.washington.edu/~marcotcr/blog/lime/`
    - *"Why Should I Trust You?": Explaining the Predictions of Any Classifier,* `https://arxiv.org/pdf/1602.04938v1.pdf`

- For more on scikit-learn, see `https://scikit-learn.org`

9

The Counterfactual Explanations Method

The EU **General Data Protection Regulation (GDPR)** states that an automatic process acting on personal data must be explained. *Chapter 2, White Box XAI for AI Bias and Ethics*, described the legal obligations that **artificial intelligence** (**AI**) faces. If a plaintiff requires an explanation for a decision that a **machine learning** (**ML**) application made, the editor of the AI system must justify its output.

In the previous chapters, we used a *bottom-to-top* method to understand an **explainable AI** (**XAI**) method. We displayed the source code. We then saw how the data was loaded, vectorized, preprocessed, and split into the training/test datasets. We described the mathematical representation of some of the ML and deep learning algorithms in the programs. We also defined the parameters of the ML models.

In *Chapter 4, Microsoft Azure Machine Learning Model Interpretability with SHAP*, we calculated the Shapley value of a feature to determine its marginal contribution to a positive or negative prediction.

In *Chapter 8, Local Interpretable Model-Agnostic Explanations (LIME)*, we scanned the vicinity of an instance to explain a prediction locally.

Counterfactual explanations look at AI from another perspective. In a real-life situation, an editor who may have invested considerable resources in an AI system does not want to make it public. The legal obligation to explain an ML process in detail can become a threat to the very survival of the editor's business. Yet an explanation must be provided.

The counterfactual explanation approach introduces a new dimension: *unconditionality*. Unconditional explanations take us a step further. We will go beyond positive and negative predictions. We will look at a result irrespective of whether or not it was fully automated.

Counterfactual explanations do not require opening and looking inside a "black box" algorithm, the preprocessing phases, and whether they were automated. We do not need to understand the algorithm, read its code, or even know what the model does at all.

Counterfactual explanations require a new challenging approach for an AI specialist, a *top-to-bottom* approach.

In this chapter, we will begin to view counterfactual explanations through distances between two predictions and examine their features. We will have a user's perspective when objectively stating the position of two features regardless of their classification or origin (automated or semi-automated).

We will then leave the top layer of the counterfactual explanation, moving to explore the logic and metrics of counterfactual explanations.

Finally, we will then reach the code level and describe the architecture of this deep learning model.

This chapter covers the following topics:

- Visualizing counterfactual distances in the **What-If Tool (WIT)**
- Running `Counterfactual_Explanations.ipynb` in Google Colaboratory
- Defining conditional XAI
- Defining belief in a prediction
- Defining the truth of a prediction
- Defining justification
- Defining sensitivity
- L1 norm distance functions
- L2 norm distance functions
- Custom distance functions
- How to invoke the **What-If Tool**
- Custom predictions for WIT
- XAI as the future of AI

Our first step will be to explore the counterfactual explanations method with examples.

The counterfactual explanations method

In this chapter and section, we will be exploring AI explanations in a unique way. We will not go through the "getting started" developer approach and then explore the code in sequential steps from beginning to end.

We will start from a user's perspective when faced with factual and counterfactual data that require an immediate explanation.

Let's now see which dataset we are exploring and why.

Dataset and motivations

Sentiment analysis is one of the key aspects of AI. Bots analyze our photos on social media to find out who we are. Social media platforms scan our photos daily to find out who we are. Our photos enter the large data structures of Google, Facebook, Instagram, and other data-collecting giants.

Smiling or not on a photo makes a big difference in sentiment analysis. Bots make inferences on this.

For example, if a bot detects 100 photos of people, which contain 0 smiles and 50 frowns, that means something. If a bot detects 100 pictures of a person with 95 smiles, this will mean something else.

A chatbot with a connected webcam will react according to facial expressions. If a person is smiling, the chatbot will be chirpy. If not, the chatbot might begin the conversation with careful small talk.

In this chapter, we will be exploring the CelebA dataset, which contains more than 200,000 celebrity images with 40 annotated attributions each. This dataset can be used for all types of computer vision tasks, such as face recognition or smile detection.

This chapter focuses on counterfactual data points for smile detection.

We will now visualize counterfactual distances in WIT.

Visualizing counterfactual distances in WIT

Open `Counterfactual_Explanations.ipynb` in Google Colaboratory. The notebook is an excellent Google WIT tutorial to base counterfactual explanations on. In this section, we will use WIT's counterfactual interface as an AI expert who demands an explanation for certain results produced by an AI system.

The WIT widget is installed automatically at the start of the program.

The program first automatically imports `tensorflow` and prints the version:

```
import tensorflow as tf
print(tf.__version__)
```

You will be asked to restart the notebook. Restart the program (from the **Runtime** menu) and then click on **Run all**.

Then, automatically install the widget:

```
# @title Install the What-If Tool widget if running in Colab
# {display-mode: "form"}
!pip install witwidget
```

We will not be running the program cell by cell in this top-to-bottom approach. We will run the whole program and start analyzing the results interactively. To do so, open **Runtime** in the menu bar and click on **Run all**:

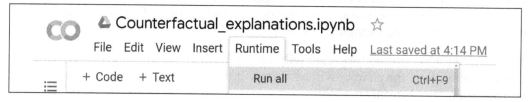

Figure 9.1: Running the program

Once the program has gone through all of the cells, scroll down to the bottom of the notebook until you reach the *Invoke What-If Tool for the data and model* cell.

You will see a region on the right side of the screen with smiling faces and not-so-smiling faces. To view the images in color, set **Color By** to **(none)**:

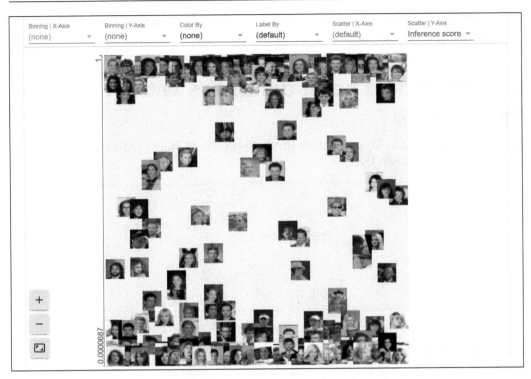

| Binning | X-Axis | Binning | Y-Axis | Color By | Label By | Scatter | X-Axis | Scatter | Y-Axis |
| (none) | (none) | (none) | (default) | (default) | Inference score |

Figure 9.2: Displaying images as data points

On the left side of WIT's interface, you should see an empty screen waiting for you to click on a data point and begin analyzing the data points:

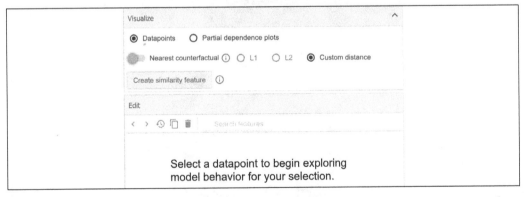

Figure 9.3: The WIT interface

This top-to-bottom process leads us to explore WIT with the default settings going down the interface, level by level.

Exploring data point distances with the default view

The data points are displayed by their prediction value. Choose **Inference value** in the **Label By** drop-down list:

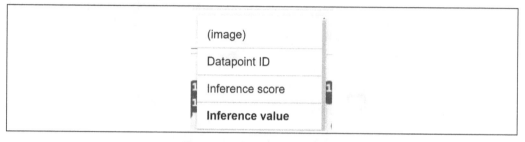

Figure 9.4: Choosing a label name

The data point labels appear with their prediction value:

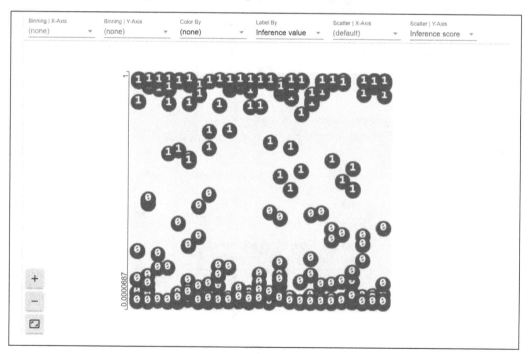

Figure 9.5: Inference values of the data points

Now, set **Label By** to **(none)** and **Color By** to **Inference value**. This time, the images will appear again with one color for images classified as smiling (top images) and another for the not smiling (bottom) images. The higher the image, the higher the probability the person is smiling:

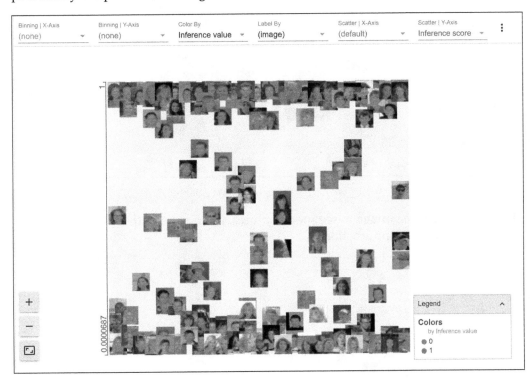

Figure 9.6: Displaying the data points by the color of the prediction value

To begin a counterfactual investigation, click on one of the images:

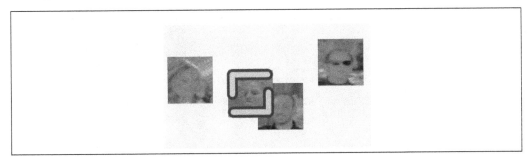

Figure 9.7: Selecting a data point

The features of the data point will appear on the left side of the interface:

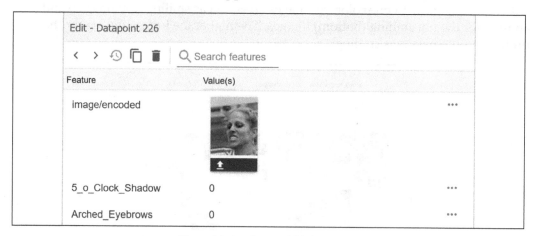

Figure 9.8: Attributes of the data point

Scroll down under the image to see more features. Now activate the **Nearest counterfactual** data point function:

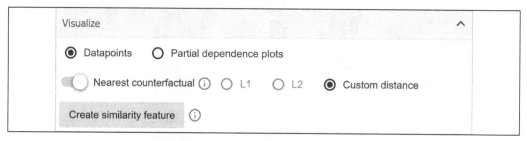

Figure 9.9: Activating the Nearest counterfactual function

We now see the counterfactual features of the counterfactual datapoint next to the data point we selected. The closest counterfactual data point is a person classified as "smiling":

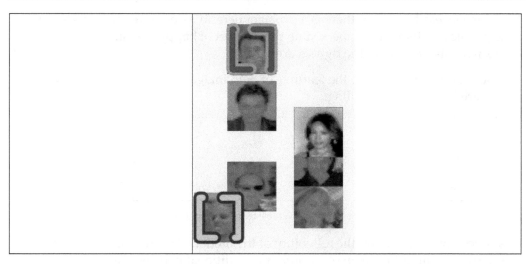

Figure 9.10: Visualizing the data point and its counterfactual data point

We now see the attributes of the image of the "smiling" person on the left side of the interface:

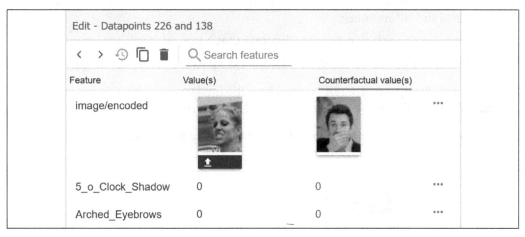

Figure 9.11: Comparing the attributes of two data points

A human can easily see that there is a problem here! We do not really know what these people are doing! Is the person on the left sort of happy and smiling? Who knows what the person on the right is doing?

If we scroll down to compare the features of both images, we can see that both images are labeled as not smiling:

Sideburns	0	0	•••
Smiling	0	0	•••
Straight_Hair	0	0	•••

Figure 9.12: Two possible features of an image

This raises several issues on the reliability of the model. First, we can imagine some issues from a counterfactual explanations' unconditional perspective for the person of the left:

- This picture does not really prove the person is smiling or not smiling.
- This person could have this sort of expression when expressing a happy, "Yes, I did it!" moment.
- Why choose such a picture to illustrate that a person is smiling or not?
- How can a mouth covered by a hand end up in the **Smiling** category?

Maybe we are wrong and are not interpreting the image correctly. You can play around with WIT. That's the whole purpose of the interface.

To check, set **Label By** to **Inference value** and **Color By** to **Inference score**:

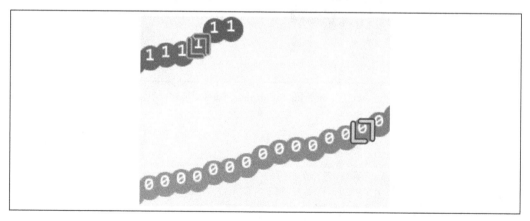

Figure 9.13: Showing the prediction value of a data point and its counterfactual data point

The inference value of the person on the right is clearly 1.

If we apply this to other domains, we see how unconditional counterfactual explanations will provide the legal basis for many lawsuits in the coming years:

- Suppose 1 represents a person who obtained a loan from a bank, and 0 represents a person who did not obtain the same type of loan. It is impossible to know if the positive prediction can be verified or not. The prediction was made without sufficient information. The person who did not get the loan will undoubtedly win a damage suit and also win punitive damages as well.
- Suppose 1 represents a cancer diagnosis and 0 a clean health diagnosis although they have similar attributes.

Imagine as many other similar situations as you can before continuing this chapter using an unconditional counterfactual explanation approach.

We can now sum up this first top level:

- **Unconditional**: We are not concerned about where this data comes from or about the AI model used. We want to know why one person "obtains" a "smile" (it could be anything else) and why another one doesn't. In this case, the explanation is far from convincing for the AI model involved. Of course, the whole point of this notebook is to show that accurate AI training performances cannot be trusted without XAI.
- **Counterfactual**: We take a data point at random. We choose a counterfactual point. We decide whether the counterfactual point is legitimate or not.

In a court of law, the AI model proposed here would be in serious trouble. However, the notebook was designed precisely to help us understand the importance of the unconditional counterfactual explanations' method.

XAI has gone from being a cool way to explain AI to a legal obligation with significant consequences, as stated by the GDPR:

> *"(71) The data subject should have the right not to be subject to a decision, which may include a measure, evaluating personal aspects relating to him or her* **which is based solely on automated processing** *and which produces legal effects concerning him or her or similarly significantly affects him or her, such as automatic refusal of an online credit application or e-recruiting practices without any human intervention.*
>
> *.../...*
>
> *In any case, such processing should be subject to suitable safeguards, which should include specific information to the data subject and the right* **to obtain human intervention,** *to express his or her point of view, to obtain an explanation of the decision reached after such assessment and to challenge the decision."*
>
> *Regulation 2016/679, GDPR, recital 71, 2016 O.J. (L 119) 14 (EU)*

Counterfactual explanations meet these legal requirements.

We will now go to a lower level. We need to go deeper into the logic of counterfactual explanations.

The logic of counterfactual explanations

In this section, we will first go through the logic of counterfactual explanations and define the key aspects of the method.

Counterfactual explanations can first be defined through three key traditional concepts and a fourth concept added by ML theory:

- Belief
- Truth
- Justification
- Sensitivity

Let's begin with *belief.*

Belief

If we do not believe a prediction, it will shake the foundations of the AI system we are using.

Belief is a bond of trust between a subject S and a proposition p. Belief does not require truth or justification. It can be stated as follows:

> If p is believable, S believes p.

A subject S requires no information other than belief to conclude that p is true.

For example, S, based on human experience, can believe four assertions based on the following image:

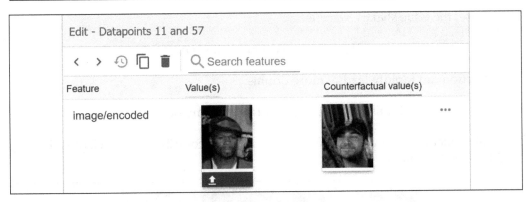

Figure 9.14: Comparing the images

- **p is true**: The person on the left is not smiling.
- **p is true**: The statement that the person on the left is smiling is false.
- **p is true**: The person on the right is smiling.
- **p is true**: The statement that the person on the right is not smiling is false.

If an AI system makes these assertions, S will believe them.

However, in the following case, S's belief in the AI system might be shaken.

The following screenshot is difficult to believe. The inference score of the person on the left is 0 (not smiling), and the inference score of the person on the right is 1 (smiling):

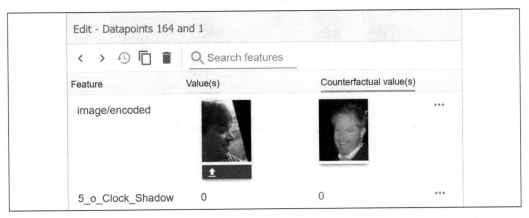

Figure 9.15: A false negative and a true positive

In this case, the issue shakes *S*'s belief:

If *p* is false, *S* cannot believe *p*.

This assertion can rapidly lead to more doubts:

If this *p* is false, *S* cannot believe any other *p*.

The counterfactual distances between the two people contribute to a lack of belief in the AI system's ability to predict:

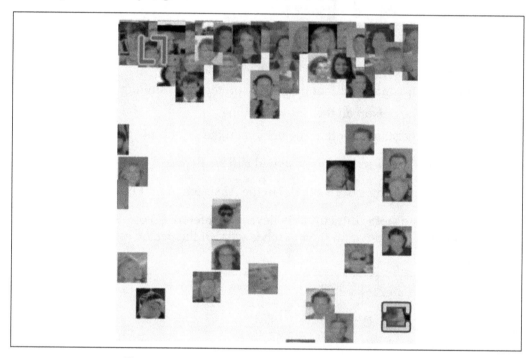

Figure 9.16: Visualizing the distance between two data points

The distance between the two smiling people goes beyond *S*'s belief in the system.

We will now see the contribution of *truth* when analyzing counterfactual explanations.

Truth

Suppose *S*, the subject observing an AI system, believes *p*, the assertion made by the system.

Even if S believes p, p must be true, leading to the following possibilities:

- S believes p; p is false.
- S believes p; p is true.

When applying counterfactual XAI methods, the following best practice rules apply:

- Without belief, S will not trust an apparent truth.
- Belief does not imply truth.

Take a moment to observe the following screenshot:

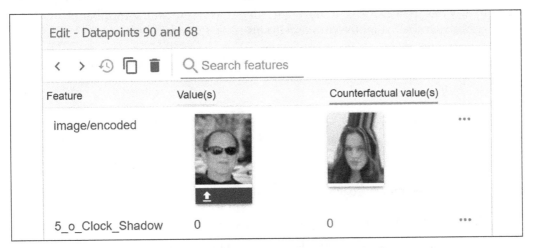

Figure 9.17: Detecting whether or not a person is smiling

The notebook's model makes the following assertions:

p: The person on the left is smiling, and the person on the right is not smiling.

In this situation, S believes p, however, is p true?

If you looked closely at the image of the person on the left, the person could be smiling or could be blinded by sunlight, squinting, and tightening his face.

However, the prediction score for this image is 1 (true, the person is smiling).

At this point, the counterfactual explanation situation can be summed up as follows:

S believes p.

p can be the truth.

However, p must now be *justified*.

Justification

If an AI system fails to provide sufficient explanations, we could refer to the good practice required by GDPR:

> *"In any case, such processing should be subject to suitable safeguards, which should include specific information to the data subject and the right* **to obtain human intervention**, *to express his or her point of view, to obtain an explanation of the decision reached after such assessment and to challenge the decision."*

> *Regulation 2016/679, GDPR, recital 71, 2016 O.J. (L 119) 14 (EU)*

If a company has the resources to have a hotline that can meet the number of justifications required, then the problem is solved as follows:

S believes *p*; *p* might be true; *S* can obtain justification from a human.

This will work if:

- The number of requests is lower than the capacity of the hotline to answer them.
- The hotline has the capacity to train and make AI experts available.

As AI expands, a better approach would be to:

- Implement XAI as much as possible to avoid consuming human resources.
- Make human support available only when necessary.

In this section, we saw that justifications make an explanation clearer for the users.

We will now add *sensitivity* to our counterfactual explanation method.

Sensitivity

Sensitivity is an essential concept for counterfactual explanations. It will take the explanations to the core of the method.

In the *Belief* section, belief could be compromised; see the following:

If *p* is false, *S* cannot believe *p*.

This assertion can rapidly lead to more doubts:

If this p is false, S cannot believe any other p.

This negative assertion does not solve the problem. Not believing in p only expresses doubt, not the truth, and doesn't provide any justification. Truth can determine whether or not p is true. Justification can provide interesting rules. Sensitivity will bring us closer to the explanation we are looking for.

Let p be a false negative prediction for a person who was, in fact, smiling but was classified as not smiling.

Let X_{tp} be the data points in the dataset that are true positives of people who are smiling:

$$X_{tp} = \{x_1, x_2, x_3, ..., x_n\}$$

Our goal will be to find data points that have a set of features that are the closest to p, such as in the following example:

Figure 9.18: Visualizing sensitivity

In this section, we went through the key concepts of counterfactual explanations: belief, trust, justification, and sensitivity.

We will now select the best distance functions for counterfactual explanations.

The choice of distance functions

WIT uses a distance function for its visual representation of data points.

If you click on the information symbol (**i**) next to **Nearest counterfactual**, WIT shows the three distance function options available:

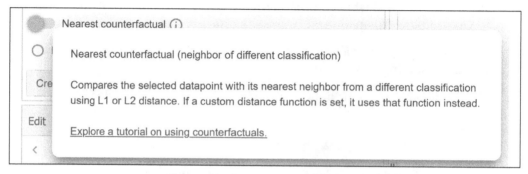

Figure 9.19: Choosing a distance function

In this section, we will go through these options, starting with the L1 norm:

- The L1 norm
- The L2 norm
- Custom distance

The L1 norm

The L1 norm is the Manhattan or taxicab norm because it calculates distances in a way that resembles the blocks in Manhattan. The following diagram shows a grid like the blocks of buildings in Manhattan, New York City:

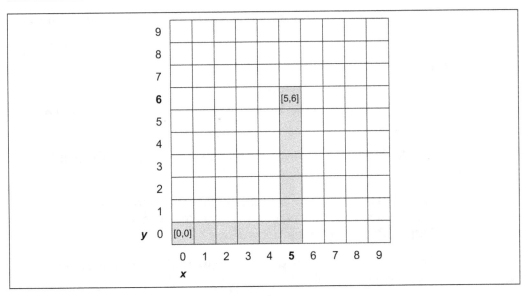

Figure 9.20: Manhattan distance

Suppose you take a cab at point [0, 0] and want to go to point [5, 6]. The driver will go 5 blocks in a straight line (see the blocks in gray) and will then turn to the left and drive 6 blocks (see the path in gray). You will pay a distance of 5 + 6 blocks = 11 blocks, represented as follows:

Distance to pay = 5 blocks + 6 blocks = 11 blocks

If we now translate this expression into a mathematical expression of the L1 norm, we obtain the following:

$$|X| = |x| + |y|, \text{ or in this case, } |X| = 5 + 6 = 11$$

This value is the distance for one data point.

We can also translate our taxicab expression in the least deviations function. The variables are:

- Y_i: The target values
- $p(X_i)$: The predicted values produced by the ML model
- S: The sum of the absolute differences between the target values and the predicted values

Y_i can be compared to the shortest way for the taxicab driver to get to the point we want to get to.

$p(X_i)$ can be compared to a cab driver who does not take the shortest path to the point we want to go to and takes us a longer way. This could be the cab driver's first day on the job with a GPS system that is not working.

S is the absolute difference between the distance we wanted to pay, the shortest one, and the longer distance the cab took.

The mathematical expression to measure all of the n paths a cab took in one day for all customers, for example, is as follows:

$$S = \sum_{i=1}^{n} |y_i - p(x_i)|$$

There are variations of L1 in which you can divide the sum of the values by other statistical values. A simple variation is to divide the result by the number n of cab fares in the day, in our example, to obtain a mean deviation for this cab driver.

At the end of the day, we might find the mean deviation of this cab driver is the total deviations/number of fares = mean deviation. This is only one variation.

In any case, the goal in ML is to minimize the value of L1 to improve the accuracy of a model.

This explanation captures the essence of L1, a robust and reliable distance function.

The L2 norm is also widely used as a distance function.

The L2 norm

The L2 norm calculates the shortest path between two points. Unlike the Manhattan method, it can go straight through the buildings. Imagine the L2 norm as "a bird's distance" from one point to another:

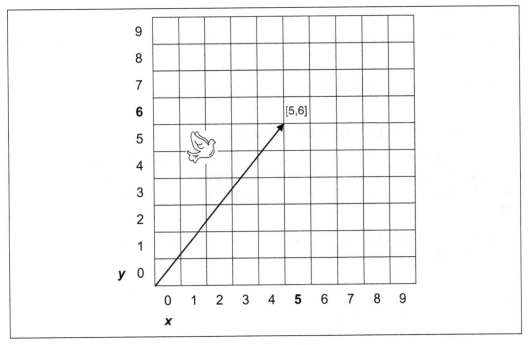

Figure 9.21: Euclidean distance

L2 uses the Euclidean distance between two points.

y_i represents the $t(x)$ and $t(y)$ coordinates of the target prediction and $p(x_i)$ represents the $p(x)$ and $p(y)$ coordinates of a prediction.

The Euclidean distance can be expressed as follows:

$$d_i = \sqrt{y_i^2 - p(x_i)^2} = \sqrt{\left(t(x_i) - p(x_i)\right)^2 + \left(t(y_i) - p(y_i)\right)^2}$$

In our taxicab case, $t(x) = 0$ and $t(y) = 0$ at the point of origin. The Euclidean distance is as follows:

$$d_i = \sqrt{\left(t(x_i) - p(x_i)\right)^2 + \left(t(y_i) - p(y_i)\right)^2} = \sqrt{(0-5)^2 + (0-6)^2}$$

$$= \sqrt{(25 + 36)} = 7.81$$

The goal in ML is, as for L1, to minimize the value of L2 to improve the accuracy of a model.

We can also use a custom distance function for WIT.

Custom distance functions

WIT's custom function for this image dataset uses `numpy.linalg.norm`, which provides a range of parameters and options, more information about which can be found at `https://docs.scipy.org/doc/numpy/reference/generated/numpy.linalg.norm.html`.

In this case, we can see that the distance function calculates the current distance to the average color of the images:

```
# Define the custom distance function that compares the
# average color of images
def image_mean_distance(ex, exs, params):
    selected_im = decode_image(ex)
    mean_color = np.mean(selected_im, axis=(0, 1))
    image_distances = [np.linalg.norm(mean_color -
        np.mean(decode_image(e), axis=(0, 1))) for e in exs]
    return image_distances
```

We have gone through the counterfactual explanations' method and distance functions. We will now drill down into the architecture of the deep learning model.

The architecture of the deep learning model

In this section, we will continue the top-to-bottom, user-oriented approach. This drill-down method takes us from the top layer of a program down to the bottom layer. It is essential to learn how to perceive an application from different perspectives.

We will go from the user's point of view back to the beginning of the process in the following order:

- Invoking WIT
- The custom prediction function for WIT

We will first see how the visualization tool is launched.

Invoking WIT

You can choose the number of data points and the tool's height in the form just above WIT as shown in the following screenshot:

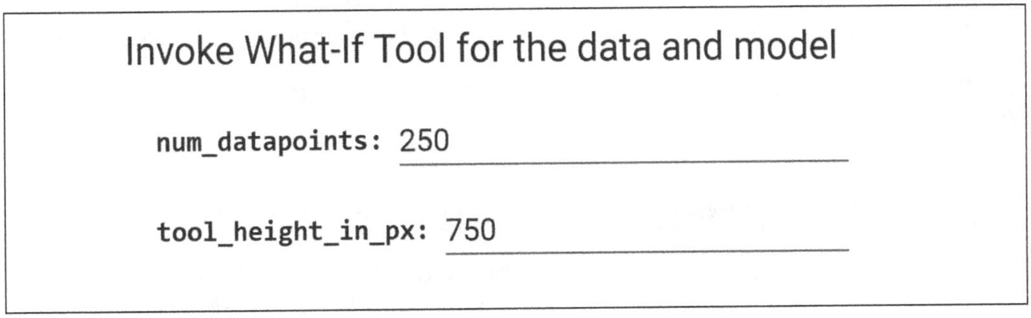

Invoke What-If Tool for the data and model

num_datapoints: 250

tool_height_in_px: 750

Figure 9.22: WIT parameters

The form is driven by the following code:

```
# Decode an image from tf.example bytestring
def decode_image(ex):
    im_bytes = ex.features.feature['image/encoded'].bytes_list.value[0]
    im = Image.open(BytesIO(im_bytes))
    return im
```

We already explored the custom distance function in *The choice of distance functions* section:

```
# Define the custom distance function that compares
# the average color of images
```

The program now sets the tool up with `WitConfigBuilder`, with `num_datapoints` defined in the form just above the cell, and the custom `image_mean_distance` function described in the custom distance function in *The choice of distance functions* section:

```
# Setup the tool with the test examples and the trained classifier
config_builder = WitConfigBuilder(
    examples[:num_datapoints]).set_custom_predict_fn(
        custom_predict).set_custom_distance_fn(image_mean_distance)
```

`WitWidget` now displays WIT, taking the height defined in the form above the cell into account:

```
wv = WitWidget(config_builder, height=tool_height_in_px)
```

WIT displays the interface explored in *The counterfactual explanations method* section.

Note that `config_builder` calls a custom prediction function for images named `custom_predict`, which we will now define.

The custom prediction function for WIT

WIT contains a custom prediction function for the image dataset of this notebook. The function extracts the `image/encoded` field, which is a key feature that contains an encoded byte list. The feature is read into `BytesIO` and decoded back to an image using **Python Imaging Library (PIL)**.

PIL is used for loading and processing images. PIL can load images and transform them into NumPy arrays. In this case, arrays of images are floats between `0.0` and `1.0`. The output is a NumPy array containing *n* samples and labels:

```
def custom_predict(examples_to_infer):
    def load_byte_img(im_bytes):
        buf = BytesIO(im_bytes)
        return np.array(Image.open(buf), dtype=np.float64) / 255.

    ims = [load_byte_img(
        ex.features.feature['image/encoded'].bytes_list.value[0])
            for ex in examples_to_infer]
    preds = model1.predict(np.array(ims))
    return preds
```

You can call this function from the interface. Note that the model, `model1`, is called in real time. First, click on a data point, then activate the **Nearest counterfactual** function, which will use the distance function to find the nearest counterfactual:

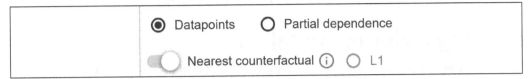

Figure 9.23: The nearest counterfactual function

The interface will display the factual and counterfactual data points and their attributes:

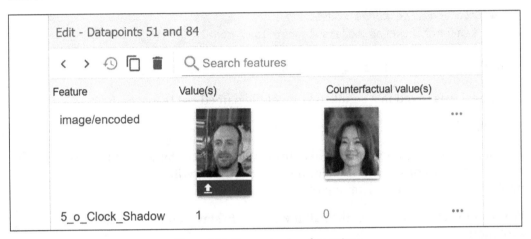

Figure 9.24: Comparing two data points

You might want to see what happens if you change the value of an attribute of the factual data point. For example, set `Arched_Eyebrows` to 1 instead of 0. Then click on the **Run inference** button to activate the prediction function that will update the prediction of this data point:

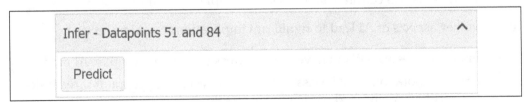

Figure 9.25: WIT's prediction function

The data point might change positions with a new visible prediction change. Activate **Nearest counterfactual** to see whether the nearest counterfactual has changed.

Take some time to experiment with changing data point attributes and visualizing the changes.

WIT relies on a trained Keras model to display the initial predictions.

Loading a Keras model

In this section, we will see how to load a Keras model and envision the future of deep learning.

In this notebook, TensorFlow uses `tf.keras.models.load_model` to load a pretrained model:

```
# @title Load the Keras models
from tensorflow.keras.models import load_model

model1 = load_model('smile-model.hdf5')
```

The model was saved in a serialized model file named `smile-model.hdf5`.

And that's it!

Only a few years ago, a notebook like this would have contained a full deep learning model such as a **convolutional neural network (CNN)** with its convolutional, pooling, and dense layers, among others.

We need to keep our eyes on the ball if we want to stay in tune with the rapid evolution of AI.

Our tour of counterfactual explanations in this chapter has shown us two key aspects of AI:

- XAI has become mandatory
- AI systems will continue to increase in complexity year on year

These two key aspects of AI lead to significant implications for AI projects:

- Small businesses will not have the resources to develop complex AI models
- Large corporations will be less inclined to invest in AI programs if ready-to-use certified AI and XAI models are available
- Certified cloud platforms will offer AI as a service that will be cost-effective, offering AI and legal XAI per region
- AI as a service will wipe out many bottom-to-top AI projects of teams that want to build everything themselves

- Users will load their data into cloud platform buckets and wait for AutoML to either provide the output of the model or at least provide a model that can be loaded like the one in this section

- These ready-to-use, custom-built models will be delivered with a full range of XAI tools

 Cloud platforms will provide users with AI and XAI as a service. In the years to come, AI specialists will master a broad range of AI and XAI tools that they will mostly implement as components and add customized development only when necessary.

We will now retrieve the dataset and model from this perspective.

Retrieving the dataset and model

Let's continue our top-to-bottom exploration with the future of AI in mind.

The remaining cells represent the functions that will be embedded in an AI as a service platform: retrieving the data and the pretrained model.

The data can be retrieved as a CSV file, as follows:

```
# @title Load the CSV file into a pandas DataFrame and process it
# for WIT
import pandas as pd
data = pd.read_csv('celeba/data_test_subset.csv')
examples = df_to_examples(data,
    images_path='celeba/img_test_subset_resized/')
```

The pretrained model is downloaded automatically so you can just focus on using XAI:

```
!curl -L https://storage.googleapis.com/What-If-tool-resources/smile-
demo/smile-colab-model.hdf5 -o ./smile-model.hdf5
!curl -L https://storage.googleapis.com/What-If-tool-resources/smile-
demo/test_subset.zip -o ./test_subset.zip
!unzip -qq -o test_subset.zip
```

This section paved the way for the future of AI. XAI will replace trying to explain a black box model. AI models will become components buried in AutoML applications.

XAI will be the white box of an AI architecture.

The last cell of the notebook lists some more exploration ideas. You can also go back and explore *Chapter 6, AI Fairness with Google's What-If Tool (WIT)*, for example, with the counterfactual explanation method in mind.

A whole world of AI innovations remains ahead of us!

Summary

In this chapter, we approached XAI with a top-to-bottom method. We learned that the counterfactual explanations method analyzes the output of a model *unconditionally*. The explanation goes beyond explaining why a prediction is true or not. The model does not come into account either. The counterfactual explanations method is based on four key pillars: belief, trust, justification, and sensitivity.

A user must first believe a prediction. Belief will build trust in an AI system. However, even if a user believes a prediction, it must be true. A model can produce a high accuracy rate on a well-designed dataset, which shows that it should be true.

The truth alone will not suffice. A court of law might request a well-explained justification of a prediction. A defendant might not agree with the reasons provided by a bank to refuse a loan based on a decision made by an AI system.

Counterfactual explanations will provide a unique dimension: sensitivity. The method will find the nearest counterfactual data point, which will display the distance between the two data points. The features of each data point will show whether or not the model's prediction is justified. If a loan is refused to one person with an income of x units of currency, but granted to a person with an income of $x + 0.1\%$, we could conclude that the bank's thresholds are arbitrary.

We saw that good practice should lead to working on counterfactual explanations before the model is released to market. A rule base could represent some best-practice rules that would limit the number of errors.

Finally, we examined the innovative architecture of the deep learning model, which minimized the amount of code and resources necessary to implement the AI system.

Counterfactual explanations take us another step forward in the expansion of our understanding of AI, XAI, and AutoML.

In the next chapter, *The Contrastive Explanation Method (CEM)*, we will discover how to identify minimal features that justify a classification.

Questions

1. A true positive prediction does not require a justification. (True | False)
2. Justification by showing the accuracy of the model will satisfy a user. (True | False)
3. A user needs to believe an AI prediction. (True | False)
4. A counterfactual explanation is unconditional. (True | False)
5. The counterfactual explanation method will vary from one model to another. (True | False)
6. A counterfactual data point is found with a distance function. (True | False)
7. Sensitivity shows how closely a data point and its counterfactual are related. (True | False)
8. The L1 norm uses Manhattan distances. (True | False)
9. The L2 norm uses Euclidean distances. (True | False)
10. GDPR has made XAI de facto mandatory in the European Union. (True | False)

References

- The reference code for counterfactual explanations can be found at `https://colab.research.google.com/github/PAIR-code/What-If-tool/blob/master/WIT_Smile_Detector.ipynb`
- The reference document for counterfactual explanations can be found at *Counterfactual explanations without opening the black box: Automated decisions and the GDPR*. Wachter, S., Mittelstadt, B., and Russell, C. (2017). `https://arxiv.org/abs/1711.00399`

Further reading

- For more on the CelebA dataset, visit `http://mmlab.ie.cuhk.edu.hk/projects/CelebA.html`
- For more on GDPR, visit `https://eur-lex.europa.eu/legal-content/EN/TXT/PDF/?uri=CELEX:32016R0679`

10
Contrastive XAI

Explainable AI (**XAI**) tools often show us the main features that lead to a positive prediction. SHAP explains a prediction with features having the highest marginal contribution, for example. LIME will explain the key features that locally had the highest values in the vicinity of an instance to prediction. In general, we look for the key features that push a prediction over the true or false boundary of a model.

However, IBM Research has come up with another idea: explaining a prediction with a missing feature. The **contrastive explanations method** (**CEM**) can explain a positive prediction with a feature that is absent. For example, Amit Dhurandhar of IBM Research suggested that a tripod could be identified as a table with a missing leg.

At first, we might wonder how we can explain a prediction by focusing on what is missing and not highlighting the highest contributions of the features in the instance. It might seem puzzling. But within a few minutes, we understand that we make critical decisions based on contrastive thinking.

In this chapter, we will begin by describing the CEM.

We will then get started with Alibi. We will use the Alibi Python open source library to create a program that will illustrate CEM interpretations of images. The MNIST dataset will be implemented in an innovative way to find missing features to identify a number, for example.

The program will make predictions with a **convolutional neural network** (**CNN**) that will be trained and tested.

The program will then create an autoencoder to verify whether the output images remain consistent with the original images.

We will see how to create a CEM explainer to detect pertinent positives and negatives. Finally, we will display visual explanations made by the CEM.

This chapter covers the following topics:

- Defining the CEM
- Getting started with Alibi
- Preparing the MNIST dataset for the CEM
- Defining the CNN model
- Training and saving the CNN model
- Testing the accuracy of the CNN
- Defining and training an autoencoder
- Comparing the original images with the decoder
- Creating the CEM explainer
- Defining CEM parameters
- Visual explanations of pertinent negatives
- Visual explanations of pertinent positives

Our first step will be to explore the CEM with an example.

The contrastive explanations method

IBM Research and the University of Michigan researchers define the CME in the publication you can find in the *Further reading* section of this chapter.

The title of the publication is self-explanatory: *Explanations based on the Missing: Toward Contrastive Explanations with Pertinent Negatives*.

The contrastive method can be summed up as follows:

- x is an input to classify
- y is the class the model predicted for x
- $F = \{f_p, ..., f_n\}$ are features that are present

- $M = \{f_{m_1}, \ldots, f_n\}$ are features that are missing
- x is classified in y because F and M are true

One of the examples the authors of the publication describe in their paper is a classic example used to illustrate a decision-making process: estimating the health condition of a patient.

We will hence make use of the diagnosis process described in *Chapter 1, Explaining Artificial Intelligence with Python,* and in *Chapter 3, Explaining Machine Learning with Facets.*

In this section, we will expand the representations of these two chapters with contrastive explanations. We will explain how a missing feature can lead to the conclusion that a patient has a cold, the flu, pneumonia, or the West Nile virus.

We could, but will not, include the diagnosis of the COVID-19 2020 pandemic for ethical reasons. We cannot create an educational model representing a tragedy for humanity that is happening while writing this chapter. Let's go back to the case study in *Chapter 1* and its initial dataset:

```
     colored_sputum  cough  fever  headache  class
0               1.0    3.5    9.4       3.0    flu
1               1.0    3.4    8.4       4.0    flu
2               1.0    3.3    7.3       3.0    flu
3               1.0    3.4    9.5       4.0    flu
4               1.0    2.0    8.0       3.5    flu
..              ...    ...    ...       ...    ...
145             0.0    1.0    4.2       2.3   cold
146             0.5    2.5    2.0       1.7   cold
147             0.0    1.0    3.2       2.0   cold
148             0.4    3.4    2.4       2.3   cold
149             0.0    1.0    3.1       1.8   cold
```

We will apply a contrastive explanation to the dataset to determine whether a patient has the flu or pneumonia. Examine these two sets of features for two instances of x to classify:

$x_1 = \{\text{cough, fever}\}$

$x_2 = \{\text{cough, colored sputum, fever}\}$

We will also add the number of days a patient has a fever with Facets as implemented in *Chapter 3*:

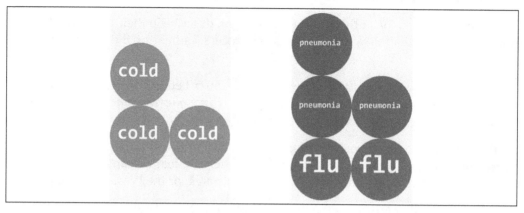

Figure 10.1: Facets representation of symptoms

The number of days is the x axis. If a patient has had a high fever for several days, a general practitioner will now have additional information. Let's add the number of days a patient has had a fever as the final feature of each instance:

x_1 = {cough, fever, 5}

x_2 = {cough, colored sputum, fever, 5}

We can now express the explanation of a doctor's diagnosis in CEM terms.

x_1 most likely has the flu because feature {colored sputum) is absent, and {cough, fever, 5} are present.

x_2 most likely has pneumonia because {Chicago}, one of the symptoms of the West Nile virus seen in *Chapter 1*, is absent, and {cough, colored sputum, fever, 5} are present. It must be noted that the West Nile virus can infect the patient without the colored sputum symptom.

We can sum CEM up as follows:

if FA absent and FP present, then prediction = True

In this section, we described contrastive explanations using text classification. In the next section and the remainder of this chapter, we will explore a Python program that explains images with CEM.

Getting started with the CEM applied to MNIST

In this section, we will install the modules and the dataset. The program will also prepare the data for the CNN model.

Open the CEM.ipynb program that we will use in this chapter.

We will begin by installing and importing the modules we need.

Installing Alibi and importing the modules

We will first install Alibi by trying to import Alibi:

```
# @title Install Alibi
try:
  import alibi
except:
  !pip install alibi
```

If Alibi is installed, the program will continue. However, when Colaboratory restarts, some libraries and variables are logs. In this case, the program will install Alibi.

We will now install the modules for the program.

Importing the modules and the dataset

In this section, we will import the necessary modules for this program. We will then import the data and display a sample.

Open the CEM.ipynb program that we will use in this chapter.

We will first import the modules.

Importing the modules

The program will import two types of modules: TensorFlow modules and the modules Alibi will use to display the explainer's output.

The TensorFlow modules include the Keras modules:

```
# @title Import modules
import tensorflow as tf
tf.logging.set_verbosity(tf.logging.ERROR) # suppress
                                     # deprecation messages
from tensorflow.keras import backend as K
from tensorflow.keras.layers import Conv2D, Dense, Dropout, Flatten,
MaxPooling2D, Input, UpSampling2D
from tensorflow.keras.models import Model, load_model
from tensorflow.keras.utils import to_categorical
```

The Alibi explainer requires several modules for processing functions and displaying outputs:

```
import matplotlib
import matplotlib.pyplot as plt
import numpy as np
import os
from time import time
from alibi.explainers import CEM
```

We will now import the data and display a sample.

Importing the dataset

The program now imports the MNIST dataset. It splits the dataset into training data and test data:

```
# @title Load and prepare MNIST data
(x_train, y_train), (x_test, y_test) =
    tf.keras.datasets.mnist.load_data()
```

The dataset is now split and ready:

- x_train contains the training data
- y_train contains the training data's labels
- x_test contains the test data
- y_test contains the test data's labels

We will now print the shape of the training data and display a sample:

```
print('x_train shape:', x_train.shape, 'y_train shape:',
      y_train.shape)
plt.gray()
plt.imshow(x_test[15]);
```

The program first displays the shapes of the training data and its labels:

```
x_train shape: (60000, 28, 28) y_train shape: (60000,)
```

Then, the program displays a sample:

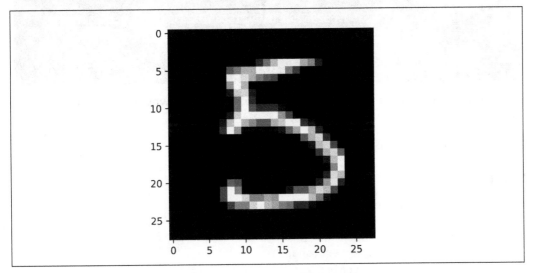

Figure 10.2: Displaying a CEM sample

The image is a grayscale image with values between [0, 255]. The values cover a wide range.

We will squash these values when we prepare the data.

Preparing the data

The data will now be scaled, shaped, and categorized. These phases will prepare the data for the CNN.

Scaling the data

The program first scales the data:

```
# @title Preparing data: scaling the data
x_train = x_train.astype('float32') / 255
x_test = x_test.astype('float32') / 255
print(x_test[1])
```

When we print the result of a sample, we will obtain squashed values in low dimensions that are sufficiently similar for the CNN to train and test its model:

```
[ 0.          0.          0.          0.          0.          0.
  0.          0.          0.68235296 0.99215686 0.99215686 0.99215686
  0.99215686 0.99215686 0.99215686 0.99215686 0.99215686 0.99215686
  0.99215686 0.99215686 0.9764706  0.96862745 0.96862745 0.6627451
  0.45882353 0.45882353 0.22352941 0.          ]
```

The original values of an image were in a [0, 255] range. However, when divided by 255, the values are now in a range of [0, 1].

Let's now shape the data.

Shaping the data

We still need to shape the data before sending it to a CNN:

```
# @title Preparing data: shaping the data
print("Initial Shape", x_test.shape)
x_train = np.reshape(x_train, x_train.shape + (1,))
x_test = np.reshape(x_test, x_test.shape + (1,))
print('x_train shape:', x_train.shape, 'x_test shape:', x_test.shape)
```

The output shows that a dimension has been added for the CNN:

```
Initial Shape (10000, 28, 28)
x_train shape:(60000, 28, 28, 1) x_test shape: (10000, 28, 28, 1)
```

We are almost ready to create the CNN model. We now have to categorize the data.

Categorizing the data

We need to categorize the data to train the CNN model:

```
# @title Preparing data: categorizing the data
y_train = to_categorical(y_train)
y_test = to_categorical(y_test)
print('y_train shape:', y_train.shape, 'y_test shape:', y_test.shape)

xmin, xmax = -.5, .5
x_train = ((x_train - x_train.min()) /
    (x_train.max() - x_train.min())) * (xmax - xmin) + xmin
x_test = ((x_test - x_test.min()) /
    (x_test.max() - x_test.min())) * (xmax - xmin) + xmin
```

The output now displays perfectly shaped data for the CNN model:

```
y_train shape: (60000, 10) y_test shape: (10000, 10)
```

We are now ready to define and train the CNN model.

Defining and training the CNN model

A CNN will take the input and transform the data into higher dimensions through several layers. Describing artificial intelligence, machine learning, and deep learning models is not within the scope of this book, which focuses on explainable AI.

However, before creating the CNN, let's define the general concepts that determine the type of layers it will contain:

- The *convolutional* layer applies random filters named *kernels* to the data; the data is multiplied by weights; the filters are optimized by the CNN weight optimizing function.
- The *pooling* layer groups features. If you have {1, 1, 1, 1, 1, ..., 1, 1, 1} in an area of the data, you can group them into a smaller representation such as {1, 1, 1}. You still know that a key feature of the image is {1}.

- The *dropout* layer literally drops some data out. If you have a blue sky with millions of pixels, you can easily take 50% of those pixels out and still know that the sky is blue.
- The *flatten* layer transforms the data into a long vector of numbers.
- The *dense* layer connects all the neurons.

Layer by layer, the CNN model will transform a large amount of data into a very high dimension of few values that represent the prediction as shown in the following output of the CNN model we are creating in this section:

```
Model: "model"

Layer (type)                 Output Shape              Param #
=================================================================
input_1 (InputLayer)         [(None, 28, 28, 1)]       0

conv2d (Conv2D)              (None, 28, 28, 64)        320

max_pooling2d (MaxPooling2D) (None, 14, 14, 64)        0

dropout (Dropout)            (None, 14, 14, 64)        0

conv2d_1 (Conv2D)            (None, 14, 14, 32)        8224

max_pooling2d_1 (MaxPooling2 (None, 7, 7, 32)          0

dropout_1 (Dropout)          (None, 7, 7, 32)          0

flatten (Flatten)            (None, 1568)              0

dense (Dense)                (None, 256)               401664

dropout_2 (Dropout)          (None, 256)               0

dense_1 (Dense)              (None, 10)                2570
=================================================================
```

Figure 10.3: Structure representation of the model generated by TensorFlow

Let's now create the CNN model.

Creating the CNN model

We first create a function that adds the layers we described in the previous section to the model:

```python
# @title Create and train CNN model
def cnn_model():
    x_in = Input(shape=(28, 28, 1))
    x = Conv2D(filters=64, kernel_size=2, padding='same',
               activation='relu')(x_in)
    x = MaxPooling2D(pool_size=2)(x)
    x = Dropout(0.3)(x)

    x = Conv2D(filters=32, kernel_size=2, padding='same',
               activation='relu')(x)
    x = MaxPooling2D(pool_size=2)(x)
    x = Dropout(0.3)(x)

    x = Flatten()(x)
    x = Dense(256, activation='relu')(x)
    x = Dropout(0.5)(x)
    x_out = Dense(10, activation='softmax')(x)
```

x_out contains the precious classification information we are looking for. The CNN model's function is called with the input data: inputs=x_in:

```python
    cnn = Model(inputs=x_in, outputs=x_out)
    cnn.compile(loss='categorical_crossentropy', optimizer='adam',
                metrics=['accuracy'])
    return cnn
```

The model will be compiled and ready to be trained and tested.

Training the CNN model

Training the CNN model can take a few minutes. A form was added to skip the training process once the model has been saved:

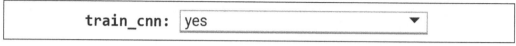

train_cnn: | yes ▼

Figure 10.4: CNN training options

The first time you run the program, you must set `train_cnn` to yes.

The CNN model will be called, trained, and saved in a file named `mnist_cnn.h5`:

```
train_cnn = 'no' # @param ["yes","no"]
if train_cnn == "yes":
  cnn = cnn_model()
  cnn.summary()
  cnn.fit(x_train, y_train, batch_size=64, epochs=3, verbose=0)
  cnn.save('mnist_cnn.h5')
```

`cnn.summary()` will display the structure of the CNN, as shown in the introduction of this section.

If you wish to keep this model and not have to train it each time you run the program, download it using the Colaboratory file manager.

First, click on the file manager icon on the left of the notebook's page:

Figure 10.5: File manager button

`mnist_cnn.h5` will appear in the list of files:

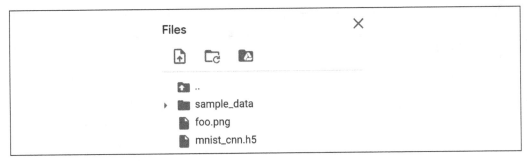

Figure 10.6: List of temporary files

Right-click on `mnist_cnn.h5` and download it.

When Colaboratory restarts, it deletes local variables. To upload the file to avoid training the CNN, upload the file by clicking on **Upload**:

Figure 10.7: Uploading the file

We will now load and test the accuracy of the model.

Loading and testing the accuracy of the model

The program trained and saved the CNN model in the previous cell of the program. It is now ready to be loaded and trained:

```
# @title Load and test accuracy on test dataset
cnn = load_model('/content/mnist_cnn.h5')
cnn.summary()
score = cnn.evaluate(x_test, y_test, verbose=0)
print('Test accuracy: ', score[1])
```

`cnn.summary()` displays the summary of the model and the test score:

```
Model: "model"

Layer (type)                    Output Shape              Param #
=================================================================
input_1 (InputLayer)            [(None, 28, 28, 1)]       0

conv2d (Conv2D)                 (None, 28, 28, 64)        320

max_pooling2d (MaxPooling2D)    (None, 14, 14, 64)        0

dropout (Dropout)               (None, 14, 14, 64)        0

conv2d_1 (Conv2D)               (None, 14, 14, 32)        8224

max_pooling2d_1 (MaxPooling2     (None, 7, 7, 32)          0

dropout_1 (Dropout)             (None, 7, 7, 32)          0

flatten (Flatten)               (None, 1568)              0

dense (Dense)                   (None, 256)               401664

dropout_2 (Dropout)             (None, 256)               0

dense_1 (Dense)                 (None, 10)                2570
=================================================================
Total params: 412,778
Trainable params: 412,778
Non-trainable params: 0


Test accuracy:   0.9867
```

Figure 10.8: Summary of the model and test score

The test accuracy is excellent.

We will now define and train the autoencoder.

Defining and training the autoencoder

In this section, we will create, train, and test the autoencoder.

An autoencoder will encode the input data using a CNN with the same type of layers as the CNN we created in the *Defining and training the CNN model* section of this chapter.

However, there is a fundamental difference compared with the CNN:

An autoencoder encodes the data and then decodes the result to match the input data.

We are *not* trying to classify the inputs. We are finding a set of weights that guarantees that if we apply that set of weights to a *perturbation* of an image, we will remain close to the original.

The perturbations are ways to find the missing feature in an instance that produced a prediction. For example, in the *The contrastive explanation method* section of this chapter, we examined the following possible symptoms of the patient described as features:

Features for label 1 = {cough, fever, number of days=5}

The label of the diagnosis is flu.

The closest other label is pneumonia, with the following features:

Features for label 2 = {cough, colored sputum, fever, number of days=5}

Take a close look and see which feature is missing for the flu label.

For contrastive explanations, flu is pneumonia without colored sputum.

Perturbations will change the values of the features to find the missing feature — the **pertinent negative (PN)**. If it finds a feature that would change a diagnosis if it were missing, it would be a **pertinent positive (PP)**.

Alibi uses the autoencoder as an input to make sure that when the CEM explainer changes the values of the input to find the PN and PP features, it does not stray too far from the original values. It will *stretch* the input, but not much.

With this in mind, let's create the autoencoder.

Creating the autoencoder

The autoencoder is created in a function as described in the introduction of this section:

```
# @title Define and train autoencoder
def ae_model():
    x_in = Input(shape=(28, 28, 1))
    x = Conv2D(16, (3, 3), activation='relu', padding='same')(x_in)
    x = Conv2D(16, (3, 3), activation='relu', padding='same')(x)
    x = MaxPooling2D((2, 2), padding='same')(x)
    encoded = Conv2D(1, (3, 3), activation=None, padding='same')(x)

    x = Conv2D(16, (3, 3), activation='relu',
            padding='same')(encoded)
```

```
x = UpSampling2D((2, 2))(x)
x = Conv2D(16, (3, 3), activation='relu', padding='same')(x)
decoded = Conv2D(1, (3, 3), activation=None, padding='same')(x)

autoencoder = Model(x_in, decoded)
autoencoder.compile(optimizer='adam', loss='mse')

return autoencoder
```

The optimizer in the autoencoder guarantees that the output will match the input with a loss function that measures the distance between the original inputs and the weighted outputs.

We will visualize the outputs when we test the autoencoder.

Training and saving the autoencoder

In this section, we will train and save the autoencoder:

```
train_auto_encoder = 'no' # @param ["yes","no"]

if train_auto_encoder == "yes":
  ae = ae_model()
  # ae.summary()
  ae.fit(x_train, x_train, batch_size=128, epochs=4,
         validation_data=(x_test, x_test), verbose=0)
  ae.save('mnist_ae.h5', save_format='h5')
```

You can choose to train and save the autoencoder by selecting **yes** in the autoencoder form:

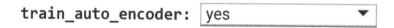

Figure 10.9: Autoencoder options

You can also select **no** in the form to skip the training phase of the autoencoder if you have already trained it. In that case, you download the `mnist_ae.h5` file that has been created:

Figure 10.10: Saved autoencoder model

You can upload this file if you want to skip the training, as described in the *Training the CNN model* section of this chapter.

We will now load the autoencoder and visualize its performance.

Comparing the original images with the decoded images

In this section, we will load the model, display the summary, and compare the decoded images with the encoded ones:

First, we load the model and display the summary:

```
# @title Compare original with decoded images
ae = load_model('/content/mnist_ae.h5')
ae.summary()
```

The summary of the model is displayed:

```
Model: "model_1"

Layer (type)                   Output Shape            Param #
=================================================================
input_2 (InputLayer)           [(None, 28, 28, 1)]     0

conv2d_2 (Conv2D)              (None, 28, 28, 16)      160

conv2d_3 (Conv2D)              (None, 28, 28, 16)      2320

max_pooling2d_2 (MaxPooling2   (None, 14, 14, 16)      0

conv2d_4 (Conv2D)              (None, 14, 14, 1)       145

conv2d_5 (Conv2D)              (None, 14, 14, 16)      160

up_sampling2d (UpSampling2D)   (None, 28, 28, 16)      0

conv2d_6 (Conv2D)              (None, 28, 28, 16)      2320

conv2d_7 (Conv2D)              (None, 28, 28, 1)       145
=================================================================
Total params: 5,250
Trainable params: 5,250
Non-trainable params: 0
```

Figure 10.11: Summary of the model generated by TensorFlow

The model now uses the autoencoder model to predict the output of an encoded image. "Predicting" in this case means reconstructing an image that is as close as possible to the original image:

```
decoded_imgs = ae.predict(x_test)
```

The decoded images are now plotted:

```
n = 5
plt.figure(figsize=(20, 4))
for i in range(1, n+1):
    # display original
    ax = plt.subplot(2, n, i)
    plt.imshow(x_test[i].reshape(28, 28))
    ax.get_xaxis().set_visible(False)
    ax.get_yaxis().set_visible(False)
    # display reconstruction
    ax = plt.subplot(2, n, i + n)
    plt.imshow(decoded_imgs[i].reshape(28, 28))
    ax.get_xaxis().set_visible(False)
    ax.get_yaxis().set_visible(False)
plt.show()
```

We first display the original images on the first line, and the second line shows the reconstructed images:

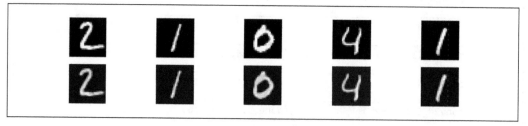

Figure 10.12: Controlling the output of the autoencoder

The autoencoder has been loaded and tested. Its accuracy has been visually confirmed.

Pertinent negatives

In this section, we will visualize the contrastive explanation for a pertinent negative.

For example, the number 3 could be an 8 with a missing half:

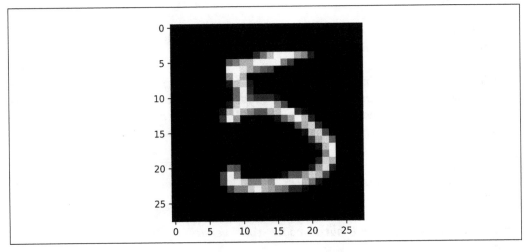

Figure 10.13: 3 is half of 8!

We first display a specific instance:

```
# @title Generate contrastive explanation with pertinent negative
# Explained instance
idx = 15
X = x_test[idx].reshape((1,) + x_test[idx].shape)
plt.imshow(X.reshape(28, 28));
```

The output is displayed as follows

Figure 10.14: An instance to explain

We now check the accuracy of the model:

```
# @title Model prediction
cnn.predict(X).argmax(), cnn.predict(X).max()
```

We can see that the prediction is correct:

```
(5, 0.9988611)
```

We will now create a pertinent negative explanation.

CEM parameters

We will now set the parameters of the CEM explainer.

The Alibi notebook explains each parameter in detail.

I formatted the code in the following text so that each line of code is preceded by the description of each parameter of Alibi's CEM open source function:

```
# @title CEM parameters
# 'PN' (pertinent negative) or 'PP' (pertinent positive):
mode = 'PN'

# instance shape
shape = (1,) + x_train.shape[1:]

# minimum difference needed between the prediction probability
# for the perturbed instance on the class predicted by the
# original instance and the max probability on the other classes
# in order for the first loss term to be minimized:
kappa = 0.

# weight of the L1 loss term:
beta = .1

# weight of the optional autoencoder loss term:
gamma = 100

# initial weight c of the loss term encouraging to predict a
# different class (PN) or the same class (PP) for the perturbed
# instance compared to the original instance to be explained:
c_init = 1.
```

```
# nb of updates for c:
c_steps = 10

# nb of iterations per value of c:
max_iterations = 1000

# feature range for the perturbed instance:
feature_range = (x_train.min(),x_train.max())

# gradient clipping:
clip = (-1000.,1000.)

# initial learning rate:
lr = 1e-2

# a value, float or feature-wise, which can be seen as containing
# no info to make a prediction
# perturbations towards this value means removing features, and
# away means adding features for our MNIST images,
# the background (-0.5) is the least informative, so
# positive/negative perturbations imply adding/removing features:
no_info_val = -1.
```

We can now initialize the CEM explainer with these parameters.

Initializing the CEM explainer

We will now initialize the CEM explainer and explain the instance. Once you understand this set of parameters, you will be able to explore other scenarios if necessary.

First, we initialize the CEM with the parameters defined in the previous section:

```
# @title initialize CEM explainer and explain instance
cem = CEM(cnn, mode, shape, kappa=kappa, beta=beta,
          feature_range=feature_range,gamma=gamma, ae_model=ae,
          max_iterations=max_iterations, c_init=c_init,
          c_steps=c_steps, learning_rate_init=lr, clip=clip,
          no_info_val=no_info_val)
```

Then, we create the explanation:

```
explanation = cem.explain(X)
```

We will now observe the visual explanation provided by the CEM explainer.

Pertinent negative explanations

The innovative CEM explainer provides a visual explanation:

```
# @title Pertinent negative
print('Pertinent negative prediction: {}'.format(
      explanation.PN_pred))
plt.imshow(explanation.PN.reshape(28, 28));
```

It shows the pertinent negative prediction, that is, portions of 3:

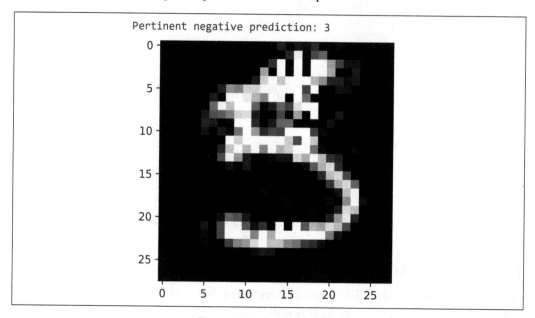

Figure 10.15: Explaining a PN

Pertinent positive explanations are displayed in the same way. You may notice that images are sometimes fuzzy and noisy. That is what is going on inside the inner workings of machine learning and deep learning! The CEM explainer runs in a cell and produces an explanation for a pertinent positive instance:

```
# @title Pertinent positive
print('Pertinent positive prediction: {}'.format(
      explanation.PP_pred))
plt.imshow(explanation.PP.reshape(28, 28));
```

The pertinent positive explanation is displayed:

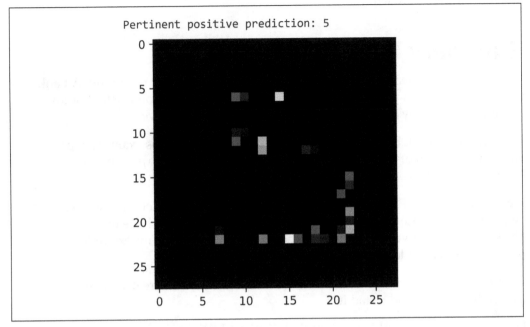

Figure 10.16: Explaining PP

We can see that the image obtained vaguely resembles the number 5.

In this section, we visualized CEM explanations and can reach the following conclusions:

- A prediction can be made by removing features to explain a prediction. This is a pertinent negative (PN) approach. For example, you can, depending on the font, describe the number 3 as the number 8 with a missing half. The opposite can be true leaning to the pertinent positive (PP) approach.
- When making perturbations in inputs to reach a PN, we remove features.
- When making perturbations in inputs to reach a PP, we add features.
- For example, adding and removing information can be done by removing a white (replaced by black) pixel or by adding a white pixel.
- The perturbations are made without any knowledge of the model's prediction.

The CME adds another tool to your explainable AI toolkit with its innovative missing feature approach.

Summary

In this chapter, we learned how to explain AI with human-like reasoning. A bank will grant a loan to a person because their credit card debt is non-existent or low. A consumer might buy a soda because it advertises low sugar levels.

We found how the CEM can interpret a medical diagnosis. This example expanded our representation of the XAI process described in *Chapter 1, Explaining Artificial Intelligence with Python*.

We then explored a Python program that explained how predictions were reached on the MNIST dataset. Numerous machine learning programs have used MNIST. The CEM's innovative approach explained how the number 5, for example, could be predicted because it lacked features that a 3 or an 8 contain.

We created a CNN, trained it, saved it, and tested it. We also created an autoencoder, trained it, saved it, and tested it.

Finally, we created a CEM explainer that displayed PNs and PPs.

Contrastive explanations shed new light on explainable AI. At first, the method seems counter-intuitive. XAI tools usually explain the critical features that lead to a prediction.

The CEM does the opposite. Yet, human decisions are often based on a missing feature as represented. Many times, a human will say, *it cannot be x, because there is no y*.

We can see that XAI tools will continue to add human reasoning to help a user relate to AI and understand a model's predictions.

In the next chapter, *Anchors XAI*, we will add more human reasoning to machine learning explanations.

Questions

1. Contrastive explanations focus on the features with the highest values that lead to a prediction. (True | False)

2. General practitioners never use contrastive reasoning to evaluate a patient. (True | False)

3. Humans reason with contrastive methods. (True | False)

4. An image cannot be explained with CEM. (True | False)

5. You can explain a tripod using a missing feature of a table. (True | False)

6. A CNN generates good results on the MNIST dataset. (True | False)

7. A pertinent negative explains how a model makes a prediction with a missing feature. (True | False)

8. CEM does not apply to text classification. (True | False)

9. The CEM explainer can produce visual explanations. (True | False)

References

- Reference code for the CEM: https://docs.seldon.io/projects/alibi/en/stable/examples/cem_mnist.html

- Reference documents for the CEM: https://docs.seldon.io/projects/alibi/en/stable/methods/CEM.html

- *Contrastive Explanations Help AI Explain Itself by Identifying What Is Missing* (Amit Dhurandhar): https://www.ibm.com/blogs/research/2018/05/contrastive-explanations/

Further reading

For more on the CEM:

- *Explanations Based on the Missing: Toward Contrastive Explanations with Pertinent Negatives*, by Amit Dhurandhar, Pin-Yu Chen, Ronny Luss, Chun-Chen Tu, Paishun Ting, Karthikeyan Shanmugam, and Payel Das: https://arxiv.org/abs/1802.07623

- The AI Explainability 360 toolkit contains the definitive implementation of the contrastive explanations method, and can be found at http://aix360.mybluemix.net/

11

Anchors XAI

The **explainable AI** (**XAI**) tools we have explored up to now are model-agnostic. They can be applied to any **machine learning** (**ML**) model. The XAI tools we implemented come from solid mathematical theory and Python modules. In *Chapter 8, Local Interpretable Model-Agnostic Explanations (LIME)*, we even ran several ML models to prove that LIME, for example, was model-agnostic.

We can represent model-agnostic (*ma*) tools as a function of *ML(x)* algorithms in which *ma(x) -> Explanations*. You can read the function as a model-agnostic tool that will generate explanations for any ML model.

However, the opposite is not true! *Explanations(x) -> ma* is false. You can read the function as an explanation of any ML model that can be obtained by any model-agnostic tool *x*. A model-agnostic XAI tool can technically work with an ML model *x*, but the results may not be satisfactory.

We can even say that an XAI tool might work with an ML algorithm and that *ma(x)* is true. But if we change the dataset and goals of an AI project, the same *ma(x)* will be inaccurate. We must add the dataset *d* to our analysis. *ma(x(d)) -> Explanations* now takes the dataset into account. A dataset *d* that contains very complex images will not be as simple to explain as a dataset containing simple images.

We think we can choose an XAI tool by first analyzing the dataset. But there is still another problem we need to solve. A "simple" dataset containing words might also contain so many words that we may find that in the true and false predictions, it confuses the XAI tool! We now need to add the instance *i* of a dataset to our analysis of XAI tools, expressed as *ma(x(d(i))) -> Explanations*.

In *Chapter 8, Local Interpretable Model-Agnostic Explanations (LIME)*, we saw that LIME focuses on $ma(x(d(i)))$, a specific instance of a dataset, to explain the output of the model by examining the vicinity, the features around the core of the prediction. LIME took us down to one prediction and its local interpretable environment. We might think that there is nothing left to do.

However, LIME (from Ribeiro, Singh, and Guestrin) found that though their tool could be *locally accurate*, some of the explanatory features did not influence the prediction as planned. LIME would work with some datasets and not others.

Ribeiro, Singh, and Guestrin have introduced high-precision rules, anchors, to increase the efficiency of the explanation of a prediction. The explanatory function now becomes $ma(x(d(i)))$ -> high-precision anchor explanations using rules and thresholds to explain a prediction. Anchors take us deep into the core of XAI.

In this chapter, we will begin by examining anchor AI explanations through examples. We will use text examples to define anchors, which are high-precision rules.

We will then build a Python program that explains ImageNet images with anchors.

By the end of the chapter, you will have reached the core of XAI.

This chapter covers the following topics:

- High-precision rules – anchors
- Anchors in text classification
- An example of text classification with LIME and anchors
- The productivity of anchors
- The limits of LIME in some cases
- The limits of anchors
- A Python program to explain ImageNet images with anchors
- Implementing an anchors explanation function in Python
- Visualizing anchors in an image
- Visualizing all the superpixels of an image

Our first step will be to explore the anchors explanation method with examples.

Anchors AI explanations

Anchors are high-precision model-agnostic explanations. An anchor explanation is a rule or a set of rules. The rule(s) will anchor the explanations locally. Changes to the rest of the feature values will not matter anymore for a specific instance.

The best way to understand anchors is through examples. We will define anchor rules through two examples: predicting income and classifying newsgroup discussions.

We will begin with an income prediction model.

Predicting income

In *Chapter 5, Building an Explainable AI Solution from Scratch*, we built a solution that could predict income levels.

We found a ground truth that has a strong influence on income: age and level of education are critical features that determine the income level of a person.

The first key feature we found was that age is a key factor when predicting the income of a person, as shown in the following chart:

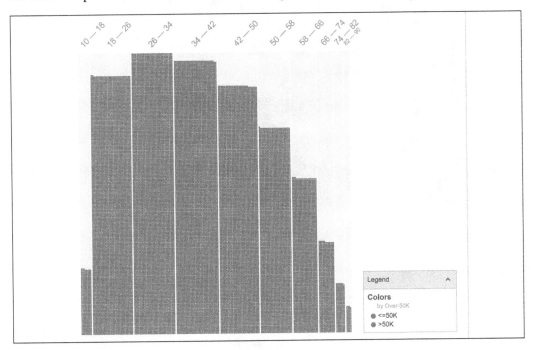

Figure 11.1: Income by age

The red (shown in the color image) values form the top section of each bar and represent people with a level of income >50K. The blue (shown in the color image) values form the bottom sections of the bars and represent people with a level of income <=50K.

Universal principles clearly appear:

- A ten-year-old person earns less than a person that is 30 years old
- A person that is over 70 years old is more likely than not to be retired and have a lower income than a person that is 40 years old
- The income curve increases from childhood to adulthood, reaches a peak, and then goes slowly down with age

The feature we found was the level of education. When we binned the age categories and included the level of education, we obtained a realistic income chart:

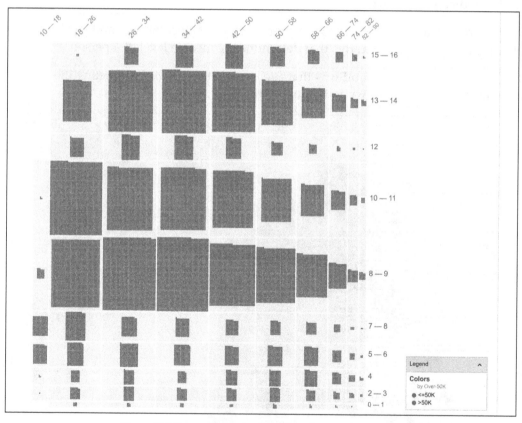

Figure 11.2: Income by age and number of years of education

We conclude that several additional universal principles appear:

- The longer a person studies, the more that person will earn
- The longer a person gains experience in work, the more that person will earn
- Learning can be acquired through experience
- After a few years of experience, a person with higher education will make more
- The age factor is intensified by education and experience, which explains why the higher-income portion of the bars increases in a significant way starting at age 30, for those having between 13 and 17 years of education for example

Let's now suppose that the anchors explanations tool used the same dataset as we did in *Chapter 5, Building an Explainable AI Solution from Scratch*. We used a version of the U.S. census dataset that was transformed into an international legal and ethical dataset. The idea was to predict whether a person earned more or less than 50K.

The anchor explainer would probably come up with the following anchor explanation:

```
IF Country = United States AND 34 <= Age <= 42
AND Number of years of education >= 14
THEN PREDICT Income > USD50K
```

The anchor explanation is very strongly "anchored." It will most likely remain constant even if other values are changed. Naturally, this explanation will not be 100% true in every instance, but it is highly precise and efficient.

The beauty of anchor explanations is that they are high-precision explanations that we can all understand.

The wonder of anchor explanations is that they are produced automatically!

Let's now see why anchors can produce better results than LIME in some cases.

Classifying newsgroup discussions

In *Chapter 8, Local Interpretable Model-Agnostic Explanations (LIME)*, we implemented LIME to classify newsgroup discussions into two categories: "electronics" and "space."

We built a LIME explainer that produced a visual explanation for each instance. Let's examine the following LIME explanation, for instance:

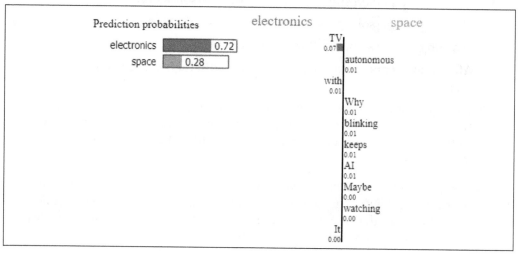

Figure 11.3: LIME explanation

We can see that the prediction was **electronics** based on the left side of the explanation:

- **TV**
- **with**
- **It**

However, the features for **space** include the following:

- **watching**
- **Why**
- **keeps**

We can see that the word "TV" can guarantee a prediction for electronics, for example.

In another instance, if we see "watching" and "TV" on the electronics side, it will make the prediction even more probable.

We can now imagine a highly precise anchor explanation:

```
IF feature x = "TV"
AND feature y = "watching"
THEN PREDICT category = electronics
```

We can only admire the way anchor explanations were designed to provide such clear and precise explanations.

In this section, we went through anchors for text classification. If you wish to further explore text classification with anchors, you can consult the following example applied to movie reviews: `https://docs.seldon.io/projects/alibi/en/stable/examples/anchor_text_movie.html`

You could then compare the method used with anchors with the SHAP program we created for movie reviews in *Chapter 4, Microsoft Azure Machine Learning Model Interpretability with SHAP*.

We will now build a Python program to explain ImageNet images with anchors. It will be interesting to discover how anchor explanations of images are visualized.

Anchor explanations for ImageNet

In this section, we will build a Python Alibi program that will produce anchors for images. Alibi is a library that contains several XAI resources.

We will use images from ImageNet to run the explainer.

We will build the program in the following order:

1. Installing Alibi and importing the modules
2. Loading an `InceptionV3` model
3. Downloading an image to explain
4. Processing the image and making predictions
5. Creating the anchor image explainer and displaying the visual explanations

Let's first install Alibi and import the modules.

Installing Alibi and importing the modules

To get started, open the `Image_XAI_Anchor.ipynb` notebook for this chapter. This notebook is in the chapter directory of this book.

We will first install Alibi as follows:

```
# @title Install Alibi
try:
    import alibi
except:
    !pip install alibi
```

If Alibi is installed, the program will continue. However, when Colaboratory restarts, some libraries and variables are lost. In this case, the program will install Alibi.

We will now install the modules for the program.

We will first import the necessary modules for this program. We will then import the data and display a sample.

The program will import two types of modules: TensorFlow modules and modules that Alibi will use to display the explainer's output.

```
# @title Importing modules
import tensorflow as tf
# tf.logging.set_verbosity(tf.logging.ERROR) # suppress deprecation
                                             # messages
import matplotlib
%matplotlib inline
import matplotlib.pyplot as plt
import numpy as np
from tensorflow.keras.applications.inception_v3 import InceptionV3,
preprocess_input, decode_predictions
from alibi.datasets import fetch_imagenet
from alibi.explainers import AnchorImage
```

Let's now load the InceptionV3 model.

Loading an InceptionV3 model

In this section, we will load a pretrained InceptionV3 model. InceptionV3 is an image recognition model. It produces acceptable results on the ImageNet dataset.

By *acceptable*, I mean that XAI tools, as well as AI models, are not dataset-agnostic, as we will see in the *Building the anchor image explainer* subsection in this section.

The model contains image processing layers such as convolutions, pooling, dropouts, and dense layers.

The model is loaded with the following code:

```
# @title Load InceptionV3 model pretrained on ImageNet
model = InceptionV3(weights='imagenet')
```

Let's now download the images to train on and explain them.

Downloading an image

ImageNet contains 1,000 classes of labeled images that you can consult at `https://gist.github.com/yrevar/942d3a0ac09ec9e5eb3a`.

The list contains a variety of categories, as shown in the following excerpt:

```
1: 'goldfish, Carassius auratus',
2: 'great white shark, white shark, man-eater, man-eating shark,
Carcharodon carcharias',
3: 'tiger shark, Galeocerdo cuvieri',
4: 'hammerhead, hammerhead shark',
5: 'electric ray, crampfish, numbfish, torpedo',
6: 'stingray',
7: 'cock',
8: 'hen',
9: 'ostrich, Struthio camelus',
10: 'brambling, Fringilla montifringilla',
```

Alibi has focused on a limited number of ImageNet categories that are listed in `datatsets.py`, an Alibi backend program for downloading ImageNet images:

```
mapping = {'Persian cat': 'n02123394',
           'volcano': 'n09472597',
           'strawberry': 'n07745940',
           'centipede': 'n01784675',
           'jellyfish': 'n01910747'}
```

A form was added to the program to choose a category of images to explain:

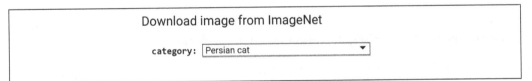

Figure 11.4: Selecting a category

Once a category is selected, the program sets the image shape. Then it retrieves the data and the corresponding labels of the images:

```
# @title Download image form ImageNet
category = 'Persian cat' # @param ["Persian cat", "volcano",
#                                  "strawberry", "centipede",
#                                  "jellyfish"]
image_shape = (299, 299, 3)
```

```
data, labels = fetch_imagenet(category, nb_images=25,
                              target_size=image_shape[:2],
                              seed=2, return_X_y=True)
print('Images shape: {}'.format(data.shape))
```

The images are downloaded and ready to be processed to make predictions.

Processing the image and making predictions

The program now processes the images and makes predictions with the pretrained InceptionV3 model:

```
# @title Process image and make predictions
images = preprocess_input(data)
preds = model.predict(images)
label = decode_predictions(preds, top=3)
print(label[0])

# @title Define prediction model
predict_fn = lambda x: model.predict(x)
```

We are now all set. We imported, processed, and made predictions on the images. We can now build the anchor image explainer and visualize the explanations.

Building the anchor image explainer

In this section, we will build the anchor image explainer and display the visual explanations.

The Alibi anchor image explainer has scikit-learn's built-in segmentation methods. In this notebook, the `slic` segmentation function is selected:

```
# @title Initialize anchor image explainer
segmentation_fn = 'slic'
kwargs = {'n_segments': 15, 'compactness': 20, 'sigma': .5}
explainer = AnchorImage(predict_fn, image_shape,
                        segmentation_fn=segmentation_fn,
                        segmentation_kwargs=kwargs,
                        images_background=None)
```

`slic` uses k-means clustering in color space to segment an image. Alibi has built the function in its module. However, the key parameters are standard in the `kwargs` argument:

- `n_segments` represents the number of labels in the segmented output image.
- `compactness` will produce superpixel shapes by balancing color proximity and space proximity. The explainer will use these superpixels.
- `sigma` is the size of the Gaussian smoothing kernel. The kernel will preprocess each dimension of the image.

The explainer is initialized with the variables we prepared up to this point:

- `predict_fn = model.predict(x)`
- `image_shape = (299, 299, 3)`
- `segmentation_fn = 'slic'`
- `segmentation_kwargs = kwargs`
- `(images_background=None)` is not initialized at this point

The explainer is now ready to produce outputs.

The program will now display the image:

```
i = 0
plt.imshow(data[i]);
```

The output displays the image:

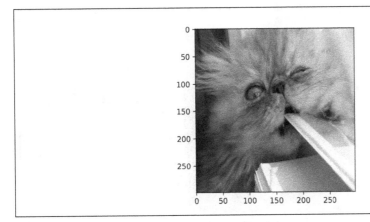

Figure 11.5: Persian cat

You can change i = 0 to another image to display within the range of nb_images=25 defined in the download function of this program. You can also increase the value of nb_images if you wish to explore more visual anchors.

The program now produces the anchor explanation:

```
# @title Anchor explanation
image = images[i]
np.random.seed(0)
explanation = explainer.explain(image, threshold=.95,
                                p_sample=.5, tau=0.25)
```

The parameters of explanation are as follows:

- Image is images[i].
- threshold=.95 is the minimum fraction of samples to take into account.
- p_sample=.5 is the portion of superpixels that are changed. They can be averaged, for example.
- tau=0.25 is the convergence level. If the value is high, convergence will be reached faster but with fewer anchor constraints.

The program now displays the superpixels in the anchor:

```
# @title Superpixels in the anchor
plt.imshow(explanation.anchor);
```

The output is a visual explanation that contains the anchors:

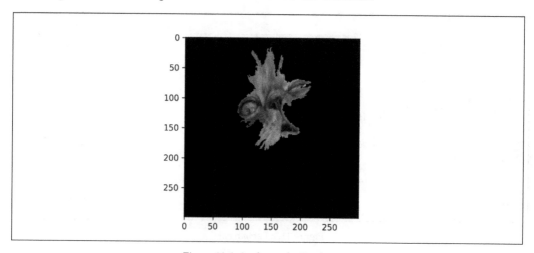

Figure 11.6: Anchors of a Persian cat

We have a visual anchor explanation.

The program will also display all the superpixels (there may be slight variations of color) so that we can see the segments in the image:

```
# @title All superpixels
plt.imshow(explanation.segments);
```

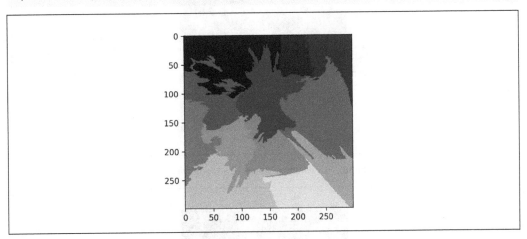

Figure 11.7: Displaying all the superpixels

We have implemented the anchor explanation process. Let's visualize more explanations.

Explaining other categories

Go back to the category selection form and choose **strawberry** from the dropdown list:

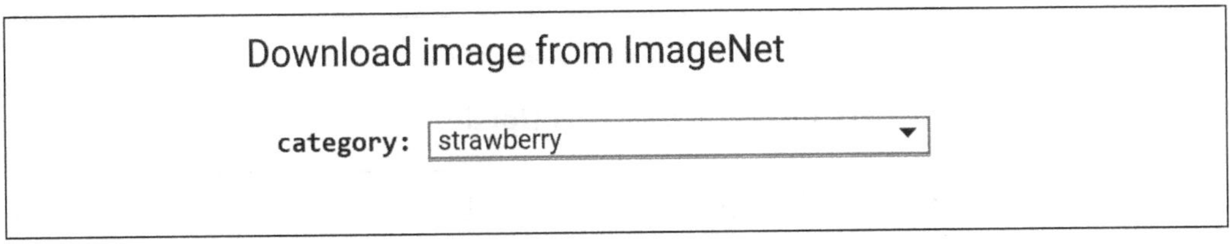

Download image from ImageNet

category: strawberry

Figure 11.8: Selecting a category

Then run the program, and you will visualize the superpixels and the anchor. The first image is the original image, and the second one shows the anchor:

Figure 11.9: Original image of strawberries

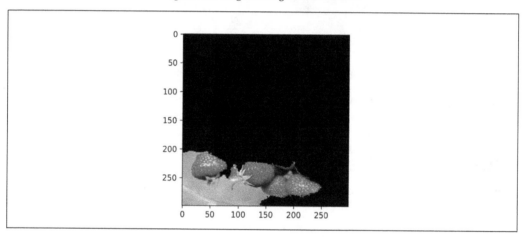

Figure 11.10: Anchor explanations

Now go back to the category form and select **centipede**:

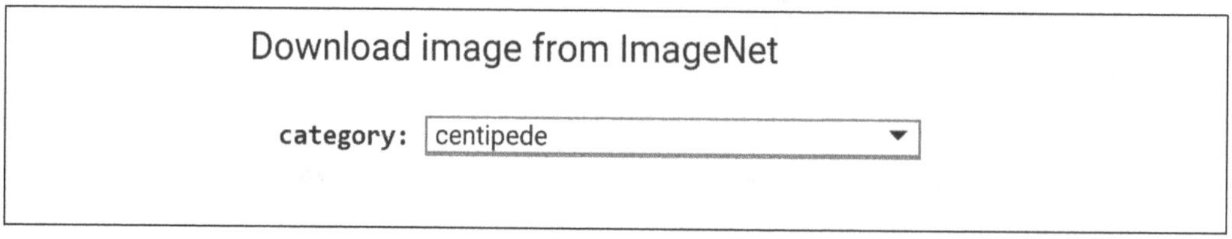

Download image from ImageNet

category: centipede ▼

Figure 11.11: Selecting a category

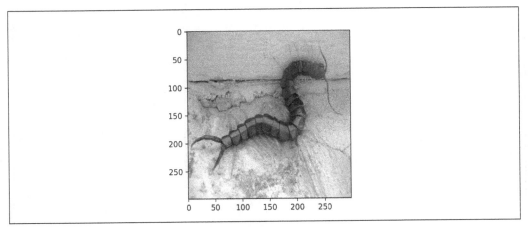

Figure 11.12: Our centipede image

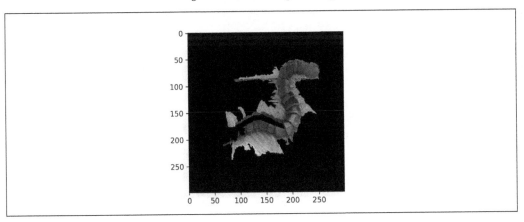

Figure 11.13: Anchor explanations

You can select other images within the categories to visualize anchors from different perspectives depending on the image.

As always, there are limitations to this XAI tool, as we will see now.

Other images and difficulties

The categories we have chosen up to now lead to good visual anchor explanations.

However, if you select `jellyfish`, the superpixels may be detected, and maybe the anchor too. The first image is the original one.

But the explanation with the superpixels in the anchor is not displayed, as you can see in the second image that follows:

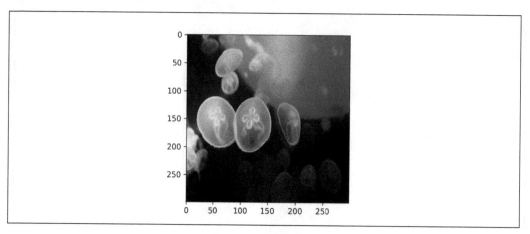

Figure 11.14: Jellyfish

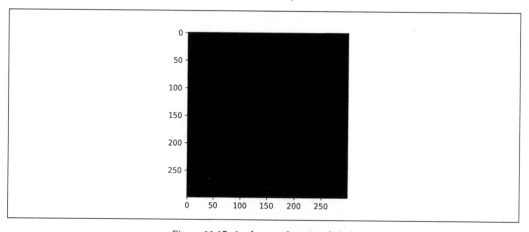

Figure 11.15: Anchor explanation failed

This black image requires an investigation. It could be a limit of the explainer, it could be that the parameters need to be changed through trial and error, it could be the choice of image, or a problem with `InceptionV3`.

In any case, in this notebook, when I tried the categories, the anchor explanation statuses were as follows:

- persian cat = OK
- jellyfish = failed
- volcano = failed
- strawberry = OK
- centipede = OK

In this section, we confirmed that anchors can also be applied to images. We built a Python program and produced anchor explanations for ImageNet images. We also discovered the natural limitations of any XAI tool.

These limitations should encourage us to get involved in open source XAI tool projects to help improve the programs. It also shows that we might need to change XAI tools when we reach the limits of a specific XAI method.

Summary

In this chapter, we explored the boundaries of XAI tools. We found that an XAI tool, though model-agnostic, is not dataset-agnostic! An XAI tool might work well for text classification and not for images. An XAI tool might even work with some text classification datasets and not others.

We first described how a model-agnostic XAI tool cannot be dataset-agnostic. We used the knowledge gathered in the previous chapters to explain the limitations of an XAI tool when it reaches the boundaries of a prediction.

We saw how the interception function developed in *Chapter 4, Microsoft Azure Machine Learning Model Interpretability with SHAP*, introduced samples containing pseudo-anchors in the IMDb dataset. SHAP then interpreted these values as anchors and provided a SHAP explanation.

We transformed the prediction process of the model built in *Chapter 6, AI Fairness with Google's What-If Tool (WIT)*, into an anchor explanation.

We also used the LIME explanations from *Chapter 8, Local Interpretable Model-Agnostic Explanations (LIME)*, to illustrate the limits of LIME and how to improve the explanation with anchors.

Finally, we ran a program in Python to explain images with anchors. The anchor explainer detected superpixels in an image to produce explanations.

Anchor explanations can thus be sets of rules with thresholds that apply to text classification as well as image-based predictions.

In the next chapter, *Cognitive XAI*, we will continue to explore how to explain AI with rules. We will see how to build human-made rules to explain AI.

Questions

1. LIME explanations are global rules. (True | False)
2. LIME explains a prediction locally. (True | False)
3. LIME is efficient on all datasets. (True | False)
4. Anchors detect the ML model used to make a prediction. (True | False)
5. Anchors detect the parameters of an ML model. (True | False)
6. Anchors are high-precision rules. (True | False)
7. High-precision rules explain how a prediction was reached. (True | False)
8. Anchors do not apply to images. (True | False)
9. Anchors can display superpixels on an image. (True | False)
10. A model-agnostic XAI tool can run on many ML models. However, not every ML model is compatible with an XAI tool for specific applications. (True | False)

References

- The reference code repositories for anchors can be found at the following links:

  - `https://github.com/SeldonIO/alibi/blob/524d786c81735ed90da2d2c 68851c1145fa1b595/examples/anchor_image_imagenet.ipynb`

  - `https://github.com/SeldonIO/alibi/tree/524d786c81735ed90da2d2c 68851c1145fa1b595`

  The reference documentation for anchors can be found at `https://docs. seldon.io/projects/alibi/en/stable/methods/Anchors.html`

- The reference documentation for scikit-learn segmentation methods can be found at `https://scikit-image.org/docs/dev/api/skimage.segmentation. html`

Further reading

- For more on anchors, see the paper *Anchors: High-Precision Model-Agnostic Explanations* by Ribeiro, Singh, and Guestrin, available at `https://homes. cs.washington.edu/~marcotcr/aaai18.pdf`

- For more on Alibi, see the documentation at `https://docs.seldon.io/ projects/alibi/en/stable/index.html`

- For more on the `InceptionV3` model, check out the following two links:

  - `https://cloud.google.com/tpu/docs/inception-v3-advanced`

  - `https://github.com/tensorflow/models/tree/master/research/ inception`

12

Cognitive XAI

Machines compute, humans construe. Humans interpret what they perceive. AI makes fabulous mathematical representations of the world. Humans *conceptualize ideas*. Machines still lack consciousness. Humans have *self-awareness*. Machines can outperform humans in many fields. Humans can reduce machines to dust with *ethics*. Machine intelligence takes raw data, makes sense of it, and will produce predictions. Humans take raw data, interpret it, and make careful decisions to avoid conflicts.

Everything goes well as long as these two forms of intelligence work converge. When they collide, the machine, or rather its owner, will have a tremendous price to pay. In the United States, *punitive damages* award mind-blowing levels of financial compensation to plaintiffs well beyond the actual damage caused by a defendant. In the European Union, the **General Data Protection Regulation (GDPR)** summons a corporation to explain an automatic process with human intervention. The sanctions applied can reach 4% of the global revenue of a cloud giant.

A human court of law will construe (interpret) *machine intelligence damage* to an individual as a severe violation of the law. We can avoid these situations by helping a human to understand AI through XAI.

We have explored a whole new world of AI through explainable AI tools in this book. This wide range of tools can explain AI. SHAP provides the marginal contribution of a feature. Facets can display data in an interpretable manner. We can make simulations with WIT. The **contrastive explanation method's (CEM)** unconditionality shows how far one prediction is from another. LIME explains a prediction locally. Contrastive explanations show why the absence or presence of a feature is critical. Anchors offer the extraordinary tool of context, the connection between words.

Cognitive explanations cannot replace the power of the XAI tools we have explored, but they will help a human understand XAI's machine reasoning.

Cognitive human-oriented explanations will bridge the gap between explanations, and initiate the moment when somebody says, "Right, now I get it! Thanks for the explanation."

We will begin the chapter by defining cognitive rule-based explanations. We will create a cognitive Python application to help a user understand the SHAP program we built in *Chapter 4, Microsoft Azure Machine Learning Model Interpretability with SHAP.*

Then, we will use our human-centered reasoning power to help a human understand and improve the LIME-WIT project in *Chapter 8, Local Interpretable Model-Agnostic Explanations (LIME).*

Finally, we will add human cognitive reasoning to improve the use of the vectorizer for the CEM project in *Chapter 9, The Counterfactual Explanations Method.*

As humans, throughout the chapter, we will use the concepts of all of the XAI tools in this book to express cognitive XAI in words a user will understand.

This chapter covers the following topics:

- Defining a cognitive rule
- Defining a cognitive rule base
- Building a cognitive XAI method in Python
- Building a cognitive dictionary
- Building a cognitive sentiment analysis function
- The marginal contribution of a feature from a human perspective
- A mathematical expression of a marginal cognitive contribution
- A Python function to measure marginal cognitive contributions
- Analyzing a vectorizer from a machine's perspective
- Analyzing a vectorizer from a cognitive AI perspective
- How to help a machine to accelerate its machine learning process with a cognitive perspective

Our first step will be to explore cognitive rule-based explanations in theory and practice.

Cognitive rule-based explanations

Machine intelligence can produce formidable algorithms and explainable AI tools.

However, it takes the self-awareness of human consciousness to understand.

Cognitive XAI adds a layer of understanding for a user to reduce the need for human intervention.

In *Chapter 7, A Python Client for Explainable AI Chatbots*, we designed the first steps of an XAI chatbot. Cognitive XAI will bring explainable AI to chatbots in the future to reduce the need for human resources and hotlines.

Cognitive XAI will by no means replace machine intelligence XAI. Cognitive XAI is not yet model-agnostic. You can imagine as many approaches as necessary for each project.

The goal in this section and chapter is to think like a human when explaining AI to a user who needs to understand a system in order to trust it.

The first step is to go from XAI tools to XAI concepts.

From XAI tools to XAI concepts

In this section, we will list some of the XAI tools we explored in this book and conceptualize the essence of their methods. We will then use some of the concepts as humans in cognitive XAI explanations:

1. **SHapley Additive exPlanations (SHAP)** to find the marginal contribution of a feature.
2. Facets to explain data and predictions from various angles, such as focusing on a set of features.
3. Google's **What-If Tool (WIT)** displays data points. One key feature is to be able to visualize the distance between a data point and its counterfactual prediction.
4. The CEM to identify a feature that is absent or present in a prediction.
5. **Local Interpretable Model-agnostic Explanations (LIME)** explore a prediction locally to see what contributed to an outcome.
6. Anchors show how features are connected and how to find specific features of a prediction based on if-then rules named "anchors" that are produced automatically. For example, "good" and "bad" are visible classification features. However, "not" could be in both categories as "not good" and "not bad." Anchors solve this problem.

We will be using these concepts in this chapter to describe cognitive processes.

We will now define cognitive XAI explanations.

Defining cognitive XAI explanations

Historically, a cognitive AI explanation relies on a list of human-designed assertions, such as:

Assertions = {*a house has a roof, a house has windows, a house has rooms,
a house has walls, is a home, ..., a house has floors*}

There are many ways to express them that are beyond the scope of this book. We just want to understand how a cognitive assertion-based or rule-based system works.

Explaining how such a system concludes can be controlled by the author of the system. Suppose the system needs to justify its process. A decision process can be described as follows:

- *has walls* => still cannot decide what it is
- *has floors* => could be several possible objects: garage, concert hall, house, other
- *has windows* => could be several possible objects: garage, concert hall, house, other
- *has rooms* => rooms will not be found in the garage and concert hall assertion list => could be a house
- *is a home* => bingo! It's a house

This decision process can be expressed in many forms. But they all can be summed up as having a list of assertions and rules. Then, wait until events are fed into the system, and enough true positives or true negatives lead to a decision.

These systems take quite some time to build but are easy to explain to a human user who will immediately understand the process.

It is important to note that in *Chapter 11, Anchors XAI*, we used if-then rules named anchors. However, anchors are machine-made, whereas cognitive rules are human-made.

We will now design one of the possible cognitive methods to understand sentiment analysis.

We will start from a user's perspective, trying to believe, trust, and understand the explanations provided by an AI system.

In *Chapter 4, Microsoft Azure Machine Learning Model Interpretability with SHAP*, we trained an ML model to predict whether a movie review was positive or negative. We used a notebook named SHAP_IMDB.ipynb. Then, we explained how the model reached a decision by displaying the Shapley values, the key features that led to a prediction.

If you take some time to look at the following excerpt of a movie review, the number of words to analyze, it is difficult to make sense of the content:

```
"The fact is; as already stated, it's a great deal of fun. Wonderfully
atmospheric. Askey does indeed come across as over the top, but it's
a great vehicle for him, just as Oh, Mr Porter is for Will hay. If
you like old dark house movies and trains, then this is definitely for
you.<br /><br />Strangely enough it's the kind of film that you'll want
to see again and again. It's friendly and charming in an endearing sort
of way with all of the nostalgic references that made great wartime
fare. The 'odd' band of characters simply play off each other as they
do in many another typical British wartime movie. It would have been
wonderful to have seen this film if it had been recorded by Ealing
studios . A real pity that the 1931 original has not survived intact"
```

Furthermore, the labels are provided from the start by IMDb. The model thus knows how to find True and False values to train.

The sample contains quite an amount of information:

```
TRAIN: The sample of length 20000 contains 9926 True values and 10074
False values
```

Somebody that looks at such an amount of data without labels or AI training might wonder how AI can make sense of these texts.

In *Chapter 4, Microsoft Azure Machine Learning Model Interpretability with SHAP*, SHAP_IMDB.ipynb offers the following SHAP explanation for a prediction:

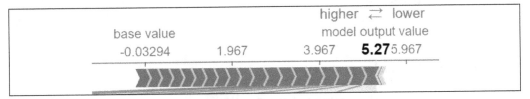

Figure 12.1: SHAP visual explanations

We then extracted the features involved, which produced an interesting list of words involved in the prediction.

Although the explanation is perfect for AI specialists or veteran software users, not everybody will understand how the model reached this prediction.

If you are involved in a significant AI project or have been required to explain how such systems reach a decision, a cognitive XAI method will undoubtedly help a user understand the process.

A cognitive XAI method

In this section, we will describe one way in which a human user would approach a movie review classification problem. Other methods are available.

In any case, you must be prepared to explain AI in a way that an impatient user or court of law will understand.

We will now build a model in the way a human would.

Importing the modules and the data

The program requires SHAP even though we will explain the output at a human cognitive level.

We just need SHAP to import the exact data that we used for our model in `SHAP_IMDB.ipynb` in *Chapter 4, Microsoft Azure Machine Learning Model Interpretability with SHAP*. We must justify our approach with the same dataset.

In this section and chapter, we will use `Cognitive_XAI_IMDB_12.ipynb`, which has been reduced to the cognitive functions we wish to explore.

Open `Cognitive_XAI_IMDB_12.ipynb`.

The program first checks whether SHAP is installed:

```
#@title SHAP installation
try:
  import shap
except:
  !pip install shap
```

Then, the program imports the necessary modules:

```
# @title Import modules
import sklearn
from sklearn.feature_extraction.text import TfidfVectorizer
from sklearn.model_selection import train_test_split
```

```
import numpy as np
import random
import shap
```

The program then loads the same dataset as in `SHAP_IMDB.ipynb`:

```
# @title Load IMDb data
corpus, y = shap.datasets.imdb() # importing the data
```

We now want to explain how a user makes an IMDb review in a training dataset by splitting it:

```
# @title Split data
sp = 0.2 # sample proportion
corpus_train, corpus_test, y_train, y_test = train_test_split(corpus,
    y, test_size=sp, random_state=7)
```

In this section, we imported the data and modules that we need. Now, we will create the cognitive XAI policy.

The dictionaries

The dictionaries contain words that anybody would use to describe a movie. You could ask around at a dinner table; note these words for positive and negative opinions when describing a movie. They do not come from any form of machine learning algorithm. They just come from common sense.

We begin by entering the features that tend to push a prediction toward a positive value:

```
# @title Cognitive XAI policy
pdictionary = ["good", "excellent", "interesting", "hilarious",
            "real", "great", "loved", "like", "best", "cool",
            "adore", "impressive", "happy", "awesome",
            "inspiring", "terrific", "extraordinary", "beautiful",
            "exciting", "fascinating", "fascinated", "pleasure",
            "pleasant", "pleasing", "pretty", "talent",
            "talented", "brilliant", "genius", "bright",
            "creative", "fantastic", "interesting", "recommend",
            "encourage", "go", "admirable", "irrestible",
            "special", "unique"]
```

Note that words such as "not," "in," and "and" are excluded since they could be found in both true (positive) or false (negative) reviews.

The program stores the length of `pdictionary`:

```
pl = len(pdictionary)
```

We now enter the features that tend to push a prediction toward a negative value:

```
ndictionary = ["bad", "worse", "horrible", "terrible", "pathetic",
               "sick", "hate", "horrific", "poor", "worst", "hated",
               "poorest", "tasteless"]
```

The program stores the length of `ndictionary`:

```
threshold = len(ndictionary)
```

In this section, we intuitively created two dictionaries based on everyday experience expressing views on movies. No calculation was involved, along with no machine learning program, and no statistics.

We created the two dictionaries with words any human user can relate to.

The program requires a number of global parameters.

The global parameters

The program has several parameters:

```
threshold = len(ndictionary)
y = len(corpus_train)
print("Length", y, "Positive contributions", pl,
      "Negative contributions", threshold)

tc = 0 # true counter
fc = 0 # false counter
```

These parameters will be used by the system to make predictions and measure its performance:

- `threshold = len(ndictionary)` represents the number of negative words to be found in a movie review

- `y = len(corpus_train)` represents the length of the dataset

- `tc = 0` represents a counter that will find the number of `True` values in the dataset

- `fc = 0` represents a counter that will find the number of `False` values in the dataset

The program now counts the number of `True` and `False` values in the dataset:

```
for i in range(0, y):
  if y_train[i] == True:
    tc += 1
  if y_train[i] == False:
    fc += 1
print("TRAIN: The sample of length", y, "contains", tc,
      "True values and", fc, "False values")
```

The output provides information on the dataset that the cognitive function will use to measure its performance:

```
Length 20000 Positive contributions 40 Negative contributions 12
TRAIN: The sample of length 20000 contains 9926 True values and 10074
False values
```

The program now enters its cognitive explanation function.

The cognitive explanation function

In this section, we will describe a function that requires hardly any AI experience, and practically no knowledge of algorithms or even of linguistics.

We will build a basic common-sense cognitive explanation function. Building an explanation with a dictionary and a what-if approach can conceptually be associated with the anchors method, which we explored in *Chapter 11, Anchors XAI*. Anchors are human user-centered and a good basis for understanding cognitive methods.

We create a function named `cognitive_xai(y,pl,threshold)` that will receive three parameters:

- y, which is the length of the dataset
- pl is the number of positive words
- threshold is the number of negative words

The function is called with those three variables:

```
# @title Cognitive XAI feature contribution
def cognitive_xai(y, pl, threshold):
    pc = 0   # true counter of positive rule
    cc = 0   # control counter
    dc = 0   # display counter
    show = 0 # number of samples to display to control
```

Four variables control the results we are obtaining:

- pc = 0 is the number of true positives found by the cognitive function
- cc = 0 is the number of true and false positives detected by the cognitive function
- dc = 0 is the counter of the number of samples to display (maintenance)
- show = 0 is the maximum number of samples to view (maintenance)

The program will now go through the dataset and store each review in fstr:

```
for i in range(0, y):
    fstr = corpus_train[i]
```

The first set of rules detects whether one of the words in the positive dictionary of words, pdictionary, is contained in the review fstr:

```
include = 0
for inc in range(0, pl):
    if fstr.find(pdictionary[inc]) > 0:
        include = 1
if pl == 0:
    if fstr.find(pdictionary[0]) > 0:
        include = 1
```

If fstr.find(pdictionary[inc]) > 0, then a positive word has been found in the review, and it is regarded as a positive review and will be included as a positive review:

```
include = 1
```

If you think about this, the function is doing what anybody would think. If we see a positive word in a movie review, we believe it to be a positive review.

The second set of rules detects whether any of the words in the negative dictionary of words, ndictionary, are not contained in the review fstr:

```
exclude = 0;
for inc in range(0, threshold):
    if fstr.find(ndictionary[inc]) < 0:
        exclude += 1
```

If fstr.find(ndictionary[inc]) < 0, then not a single negative word has been found in the review, and it is regarded as a positive review.

All the negative words must be found, which is controlled by the counter exclude += 1. The number of negative words counted by exclude must reach threshold, which is the number of words contained in the negative word dictionary, ndictionary.

If you think about what this part of the cognitive function is doing, you can see it's common sense. If you see a negative word in a review, you begin to think it's a bad review.

Now, the cognitive functions make sure there is no contradiction, such as finding positive and negative words in the same review:

```
# if-then rules for true positives
if include == 1:
    if exclude >= threshold:
        cc += 1
        if (y_train[i] == True):
            pc += 1
            if dc < show:
                dc += 1;
                print(i, y_train[i], corpus_train[i]);
```

The reasoning process of if-then rules follows a common-sense approach:

- If include == 1, then a positive word was found in the review
- If exclude >= threshold, then no negative word was found in the review
- If (y_train[i] == True), then the function found a true positive
- pc += 1 is the true positive counter

The last line of code displays the statistics if show > 0 is necessary.

The last part of the function will display the statistics for the entire dataset:

```
print(mcc, "true positives", pc, "scores", round(pc / tc, 4),
      round(pc / cc, 4), "TP", tc, "CTP", cc)
return round(pc/tc,4)
```

We will obtain a result, such as the main part of the following one:

```
true positives 7088 scores 0.7141 0.6696 TP 9926
```

Let's have a look at these results:

- `true positives 7088`, found by the cognitive function out of 9926 TP, true positives in the dataset, which produces a performance of `0.7141`
- If we add the false positives, the score is `0.6696`

We have obtained a reasonably good result with a common-sense cognitive process using dictionaries that could have been noted at a dinner table.

If we spent more time on the dictionaries, we would most probably reach a very interesting score.

Human beings are hardwired to tell something positive from something negative very well. If that was not the case, we would not have survived up to now!

In any case, a user will understand this explanation. We can then say that machine learning does similar calculations, but on a larger scale.

Let's go further and explain the marginal contribution of a feature.

The marginal contribution of a feature

In *Chapter 4, Microsoft Azure Machine Learning Model Interpretability with SHAP*, we saw how Shapley values were calculated. In this section, we will first simplify the Shapley value approach and then build another common-sense cognitive function to measure the contribution of each feature.

A mathematical perspective

In *Chapter 4, Microsoft Azure Machine Learning Model Interpretability with SHAP*, we described the following Shapley value mathematical expression:

$$\varphi_i(N, v) = \frac{1}{N!} \sum_{S \subseteq N \setminus \{i\}} |S|! \, (|N| - |S| - 1)! \, (v(S \cup \{i\}) - v(S))$$

If necessary, you can consult the explanation of the expression in *Chapter 4, Microsoft Azure Machine Learning Model Interpretability with SHAP*. However, to help a user understand how we calculate marginal contributions, we are going to pull most of the expression out, which leaves us with the following:

$$\varphi_i(v) = \big(v(S \cup \{i\}) - v(S)\big)$$

This simplified expression can be explained as follows:

- $\varphi_i(v)$ is the marginal contribution of a word, i, that will be named `mcc` (marginal cognitive contribution) in the Python program of the next section.
- S is the entire dataset. The limit of this experiment is that not all of the possible permutations are calculated.
- $v(S)$ is the marginal cognitive contribution of all of the words preceding i in `pdictionary`, but not including i.
- $v(S \cup \{i\})$ is the prediction performance over the dataset when i is included.
- $\big(v(S \cup \{i\}) - v(S)\big)$ is the marginal value of i.

If we now express this in plain English, we obtain the following:

1. The Python function will take the first word it finds in `pdictionary`
2. It will consider that this is the only positive word to find in each review of the dataset
3. Naturally, the number of true positives the function finds will be low because it's only looking for one word
4. However, the performance of one word will be measured
5. Then, the Python program adds the second word in `pdictionary`, and the function obtains a better overall score
6. This new score is compared to the previous one and thereby provides the marginal contribution of the current word

We will not show this mathematical function to a user.

We will only show the Python program's outputs.

The Python marginal cognitive contribution function

The set of rules described in the previous section are applied in a marginal cognitive contribution function:

```
# @title Marginal cognitive contribution metrics
maxpl = pl
for mcc in range(0, pl):
  score = cognitive_xai(y, mcc, threshold)
  if mcc == 0:
    print(score, "The MCC is", score, "for", pdictionary[mcc])
    last_score = score
  if mcc > 0:
    print(score, "The MCC is",
          round(score - last_score, 4), "for", pdictionary[mcc])
    last_score = score
```

If we look at a random line of the output of the function, we see:

```
4 true positives 3489 scores 0.3515 0.6792 TP 9926 CTP 5137
0.3515 The MCC is 0.0172 for real
```

The first part of the output was displayed from the code of the main function described in the previous section:

```
def cognitive_xai(y, pl, threshold):
```

It can be interesting to go through the values again for maintenance reasons.

However, the key part to focus on is the sentence beginning with MCC.

In this example, the key phrase to observe is this one:

```
The MCC is 0.0172 for real
```

This means that when the word "real" was added to the list of words to find in a review, the accuracy of the system went up by a value of 0.0172.

All of the negative values are taken into account each time as a prerequisite.

With this in mind, observe the output of the whole marginal cognitive contribution process by reading the part of the output that states:

```
"The MCC is x for "word w"
```

You will see what each word adds to the performance of the model:

```
0 true positives 2484 scores 0.2503 0.667 TP 9926 CTP 3724
0.2503 The MCC is 0.2503 for good
1 true positives 2484 scores 0.2503 0.667 TP 9926 CTP 3724
0.2503 The MCC is 0.0 for excellent
```

```
2 true positives 2953 scores 0.2975 0.6938 TP 9926 CTP 4256
0.2975 The MCC is 0.0472 for interesting
3 true positives 3318 scores 0.3343 0.6749 TP 9926 CTP 4916
0.3343 The MCC is 0.0368 for hilarious
4 true positives 3489 scores 0.3515 0.6792 TP 9926 CTP 5137
0.3515 The MCC is 0.0172 for real
5 true positives 4962 scores 0.4999 0.6725 TP 9926 CTP 7378
0.4999 The MCC is 0.1484 for great
6 true positives 5639 scores 0.5681 0.685 TP 9926 CTP 8232
0.5681 The MCC is 0.0682 for loved
7 true positives 5747 scores 0.579 0.6877 TP 9926 CTP 8357
0.579 The MCC is 0.0109 for like
8 true positives 6345 scores 0.6392 0.6737 TP 9926 CTP 9418
0.6392 The MCC is 0.0602 for best
9 true positives 6572 scores 0.6621 0.6778 TP 9926 CTP 9696
0.6621 The MCC is 0.0229 for cool
10 true positives 6579 scores 0.6628 0.6771 TP 9926 CTP 9716
0.6628 The MCC is 0.0007 for adore
11 true positives 6583 scores 0.6632 0.6772 TP 9926 CTP 9721
0.6632 The MCC is 0.0004 for impressive
.../...
26 true positives 6792 scores 0.6843 0.6765 TP 9926 CTP 10040
0.6843 The MCC is 0.0016 for talented
27 true positives 6792 scores 0.6843 0.6765 TP 9926 CTP 10040
0.6843 The MCC is 0.0 for brilliant
28 true positives 6819 scores 0.687 0.6772 TP 9926 CTP 10070
0.687 The MCC is 0.0027 for genius
29 true positives 6828 scores 0.6879 0.6772 TP 9926 CTP 10082
0.6879 The MCC is 0.0009 for bright
30 true positives 6832 scores 0.6883 0.6771 TP 9926 CTP 10090
0.6883 The MCC is 0.0004 for creative
31 true positives 6836 scores 0.6887 0.677 TP 9926 CTP 10097
0.6887 The MCC is 0.0004 for fantastic
32 true positives 6844 scores 0.6895 0.677 TP 9926 CTP 10109
0.6895 The MCC is 0.0008 for interesting
33 true positives 6844 scores 0.6895 0.677 TP 9926 CTP 10109
0.6895 The MCC is 0.0 for recommend
34 true positives 6883 scores 0.6934 0.6769 TP 9926 CTP 10169
0.6934 The MCC is 0.0039 for encourage
35 true positives 6885 scores 0.6936 0.6769 TP 9926 CTP 10171
0.6936 The MCC is 0.0002 for go
36 true positives 7058 scores 0.7111 0.6699 TP 9926 CTP 10536
```

```
0.7111 The MCC is 0.0175 for admirable
37 true positives 7060 scores 0.7113 0.67 TP 9926 CTP 10538
0.7113 The MCC is 0.0002 for irresitible
38 true positives 7060 scores 0.7113 0.67 TP 9926 CTP 10538
0.7113 The MCC is 0.0 for special
39 true positives 7088 scores 0.7141 0.6696 TP 9926 CTP 10585
0.7141 The MCC is 0.0028 for unique
```

The performance of these words picked intuitively is enough to understand that the more words you observe, the better the result.

The next steps would be to generate all the possible permutations and improve the system by adding other words to the dictionaries. Also, we could develop an HTML or Java interface to display the results in another format on a user-friendly web page.

In this section, we selected key features with our human cognitive ability. Let's now see how to fine-tune vectorizers that can approach our observation qualities.

A cognitive approach to vectorizers

AI and XAI outperform us in many cases. This is a good thing because that's what we designed them for! What would we do with slow and imprecise AI?

However, in some cases, we not only request an AI explanation, but we also need to understand it.

In *Chapter 8, Local Interpretable Model-Agnostic Explanations (LIME)*, we reached several interesting conclusions. However, we left with an intriguing comment on the dataset.

In this section, we will use our human cognitive abilities, not only to explain, but to understand the third of the conclusions we made in *Chapter 8*:

1. LIME can prove that even accurate predictions cannot be trusted without XAI

2. Local interpretable models will measure to what extent we can trust a prediction

3. Local explanations might show that the dataset cannot be trusted to produce reliable predictions

4. Explainable AI can prove that a model cannot be trusted or that it is reliable

5. LIME's visual explanations can be an excellent way to help a user trust an AI system

Note that in conclusion 3, the wording is *might show*. We must be careful because of the number of parameters involved in such a model.

Let's see why by exploring the vectorizer.

Explaining the vectorizer for LIME

Open `LIME.ipynb`, which is the program we explored in *Chapter 8, Local Interpretable Model-Agnostic Explanations (LIME)*. We are going to go back to the vectorizer in that code.

In *Chapter 8*, we wanted to find the newsgroup a discussion belonged to.

As humans, we know that in the English language, we will find a very long set of words that can belong in any newsgroup, such as:

set A = words found in any newsgroup = {*in, out, over, under, to, the, a, these, those, that, what, where, how, ..., which*}

As humans, we also know that these words are more likely to appear than words bearing a meaning or that relate to a specific area, such as:

set B = words not found in any newsgroup = {*satellites, rockets, make-up, cream, fish, ..., meat*}.

As humans, we then conclude that the words of *set A* will have a higher frequency value in a text than the words of *set B*.

Scikit-learn's vectorizer has an option that will fit our human conclusion: `min_df`.

`min_df` will vectorize words with a frequency exceeding the minimum frequency specified. We will now go back to the vectorizer in the program and we can add the `min_df` parameter:

```
vectorizer = sklearn.feature_extraction.text.TfidfVectorizer(
    min_df=20, lowercase=False)
```

You can experiment with several `min_df` values to see how the LIME explainer reacts.

`min_df` will detect the words that appear more than 20 times and prune the vectors. The program will drop many words that blurred LIME's explainer, such as "in," "our," "out," and "up."

We can also comment the LIME feature dropping function and let the explainer examine a wider horizon since we have reduced the volume of features taken into account:

```
"""
# @title Removing some features
print('Original prediction:',
      rf.predict_proba(test_vectors[idx])[0, 1])
tmp = test_vectors[idx].copy()
tmp[0, vectorizer.vocabulary_['Posting']] = 0
tmp[0, vectorizer.vocabulary_['Host']] = 0
print('Prediction removing some features:',
      rf.predict_proba(tmp)[0, 1])
print('Difference:', rf.predict_proba(tmp)[0, 1] -
                rf.predict_proba(test_vectors[idx])[0, 1])
"""
```

If we run the program again and look at LIME's summary, the text of index 5 (random sampling may change this example), we obtain a better result:

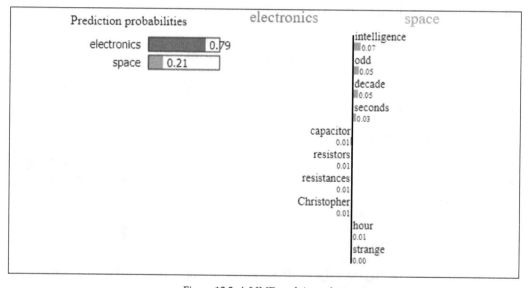

Figure 12.2: A LIME explainer plot

We can see that the prediction of 0.79 for electronics seems better, and the explanation has actually improved! Three features stand out for electronics:

electronics = {"capacitor", "resistors", "resistances"}

Note that the example might change from one run to another due to random sampling and the parameters you tweak.

We can now interpret one of the conclusions we made differently:

Local explanations might show that the dataset cannot be trusted to produce reliable predictions.

This conclusion can now be understood in light of our manual human cognitive brain's analysis:

Local explanations might show that the dataset contains features that fit both categories to distinguish. In that case, we must find the common features that blur the results and prune them with the vectorizer.

We can now make a genuine human conclusion:

Once a user has an explanation that doesn't meet expectations, the next step will be to involve a human to investigate and contribute to the improvement of the model. No conclusion can be made before investigating the causes of the explanations provided. No model can be improved if the explanations are not understood.

Let's apply the same method we applied to the vectorizer to a SHAP model.

Explaining the IMDb vectorizer for SHAP

In this section, we will use our knowledge of the vectorizer to see whether we can approach the human cognitive analysis of the IMDb dataset by pruning features.

In the *Cognitive rule-based explanations* section of this chapter, we created intuitive cognitive dictionaries from a human perspective.

Let's see how close the vectorizer's output and the human input can get to each other.

Open `Cognitive_XAI_IMDB_12.ipynb` again and go to the *Vectorize datasets* cell. We will add the `min_df` parameter, as we did in the previous section.

However, this time, we know that the dataset contains a massive amount of data. Intuitively, as in the previous section, we will prune the features accordingly.

This time, we set the minimum frequency value of a feature to `min_df = 1000`, as shown in the following code snippet:

```
# @title Vectorize datasets
# vectorizing
display = 1 # 0 no display, 1 display
vectorizer = TfidfVectorizer(min_df=1000, lowercase=False)
```

We now focus on fitting the training dataset:

```
X_train = vectorizer.fit_transform(corpus_train)
```

The program is now ready for our experiments.

We first retrieve the features' names and display some basic information:

```
# visualizing the vectorized features
feature_names = vectorizer.get_feature_names()
lf = (len(feature_names))
print("Number of features", lf)
if display == 1:
  for fv in range(0, lf):
    print(feature_names[fv], round(vectorizer.idf_[fv],5))
```

The output will produce the number of features and display them:

```
Number of features 434
Number of features 434
10 3.00068
After 3.85602
All 3.5751
American 3.74347
And 2.65868
As 3.1568
At 3.84909
But 2.55358
DVD 3.60509...
```

We did not need to limit the number of features to display since we pruned a large number of tokens (words). Only 434 features are left.

We will now add a function that will compare the human-made dictionary of *The dictionaries* section of this chapter with the feature names produced by the optimized vectorizer.

The program first looks for the positive contributions that are contained in both the human-made pdictionary and feature_names produced by the vectorizer:

```
# @title Cognitive min vectorizing control
lf = (len(feature_names))
if display == 1:
  print("Positive contributions:")
  for fv in range(0, lf):
```

```
      for check in range(0, pl):
        if (feature_names[fv] == pdictionary[check]):
          print(feature_names[fv], round(vectorizer.idf_[fv], 5),)
```

The program then looks for the negative contributions that are contained in both the human-made `ndictionary` and `feature_names` produced by the vectorizer:

```
    print("\n")
    print("Negative contributions:")
    for fv in range(0, lf):
      for check in range(0, threshold):
        if(feature_names[fv] == ndictionary[check]):
          print(feature_names[fv], round(vectorizer.idf_[fv], 5))
```

Some of our human-made words are not present in the vectorizer, although they contribute to a prediction. However, the ones in common with the vectorizer have high values:

```
Positive contributions:
beautiful 3.66936
best 2.6907
excellent 3.71211
go 2.84016
good 1.98315
great 2.43092
interesting 3.27017
interesting 3.27017
like 1.79004
pretty 3.1853
real 2.94846
recommend 3.75755
special 3.69865

Negative contributions:
bad 2.4789
poor 3.82351
terrible 3.95368
worst 3.46163
```

In *Chapter 4, Microsoft Azure Machine Learning Model Interpretability with SHAP*, the SHAP module in `SHAP_IMDB.ipynb` explained a prediction.

In this section, we compared what humans would intuitively do with SHAP's mathematical explanation. We first executed the process with a rules-based approach in the *Cognitive rule-based explanations* section of this chapter.

We have shown how to help a user go from machine intelligence explanations to human cognitive understanding.

We will now see how our human cognitive power can speed up a CEM result.

Human cognitive input for the CEM

In this section, we will use our human cognitive abilities to pick two key features out of tens of features inside a minute and solve a problem.

In *Chapter 9, The Counterfactual Explanations Method*, we used WIT to visualize the counterfactuals of data points. The data points were images of people who were smiling or not smiling. The goal was to predict the category in which a person was situated.

We explored Counterfactual_explanations.ipynb. You can go back and go through this if necessary. We found that some pictures were confusing. For example, we examined the following images:

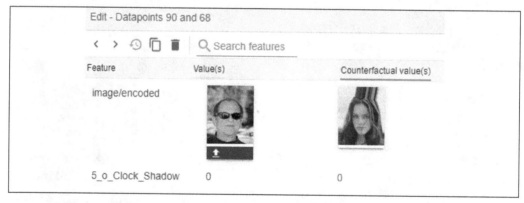

Figure 12.3: WIT interface displaying counterfactual data points

It is difficult to see whether the person on the left is smiling.

This leads us to find a cognitive explanation.

Rule-based perspectives

Rule bases can be effective when machine learning or deep learning models reach their explainable AI limits.

In this section, we will set out the ground for rule bases in datasets. Rule bases are based on cognitive approaches or other machine learning algorithms. In this case, we will create human-designed rules.

A productive approach, in our case, would be to control the AI system with a human-built rule base instead of letting the machine learning program run freely in its black box.

The advantage of this human-designed rule base is that it will alleviate the burden of mandatory human explanations once the program produces controversial outputs.

For example, take a moment to observe the column names of the CelebA dataset. Let's name the set of names C:

```
C = {image_id, 5_o_Clock_Shadow, Arched_Eyebrows, Attractive,
     Bags_Under_Eyes, Bald, Bangs, Big_Lips, Big_Nose, Black_Hair,
     Blond_Hair, Blurry, Brown_Hair, Bushy_Eyebrows, Chubby,
     Double_Chin, Eyeglasses, Goatee, Gray_Hair, Heavy_Makeup,
     High_Cheekbones, Male, Mouth_Slightly_Open, Mustache,
     Narrow_Eyes, No_Beard, Oval_Face, Pale_Skin, Pointy_Nose,
     Receding_Hairline, Rosy_Cheeks, Sideburns, Smiling,
     Straight_Hair, Wavy_Hair, Wearing_Earrings, Wearing_Hat,
     Wearing_Lipstick, Wearing_Necklace, Wearing_Necktie, Young}
```

We can see that there are quite a number of features! We might want to give up and just let a machine learning or deep learning algorithm do the work. However, that is what this notebook did, and it's still not clear how the program produced its predictions.

We can apply a cognitive approach to prepare for the mandatory justifications we would have to provide if required.

Let's now examine how a human would eliminate features that cannot explain a smile. We would strike through the features that do not come into account.

This is a basic, everyday, common-sense cognitive approach we could apply to the dataset in a few minutes:

```
C = {image_id, 5_o_Clock_Shadow, Arched_Eyebrows, Attractive,
     Bags_Under_Eyes, Bald, Bangs, Big_Lips, Big_Nose, Black_Hair,
     Blond_Hair, Blurry, Brown_Hair, Bushy_Eyebrows, Chubby,
     Double_Chin, Eyeglasses, Goatee, Gray_Hair, Heavy_Makeup,
     High_Cheekbones, Male, Mouth_Slightly_Open, Mustache,
     Narrow_Eyes, No_Beard, Oval_Face, Pale_Skin, Pointy_Nose,
     Receding_Hairline, Rosy_Cheeks, Sideburns, Smiling,
     Straight_Hair, Wavy_Hair, Wearing_Earrings, Wearing_Hat,
     Wearing_Lipstick, Wearing_Necklace, Wearing_Necktie, Young}
```

A human would only take these features into account to see whether somebody is smiling. However, these three features are simply potential features until we go a bit further.

We will name the set of features a human would take into account to determine whether a person is smiling *J*. If we exclude irrelevant features, or features that are difficult to interpret, the column headers, we can retain:

$C \cap J$ = the intersection between the column names C and J, the features a human would expect to see when a person is smiling.

The result could be as follows:

```
C ∩ J = {Mouth_Slightly_Open, Narrow_Eyes, Smiling}
```

We will exclude `Smiling`, which is a label of a class, not a real feature.

We will exclude `Narrow_Eyes`, which many humans have.

We are left with the following:

```
C ∩ J = {Mouth_Slightly_Open}
```

First, run the program we used in *Chapter 9, The Counterfactual Explanations Method*: Counterfactual_explanations.ipynb.

Now, we verify the conclusion we reached in WIT:

- Select **Mouth_Slightly_Open** in the **Binning | X-Axis** dropdown list:

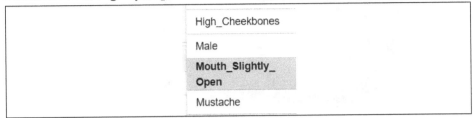

Figure 12.4: Selecting a feature

- Select **Inference score** in the **Color By** dropdown list:

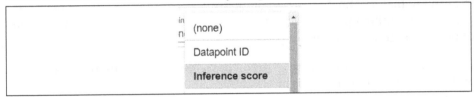

Figure 12.5: Selecting the inference score

- Select **Inference value** in the **Label By** dropdown list:

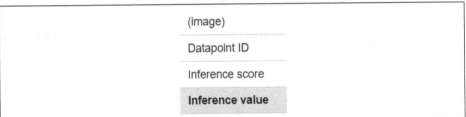

Figure 12.6: Selecting a label name

The binning divides the data points into two bins. The one on the left shows data points that do not contain our target feature.

The one on the right contains our target feature:

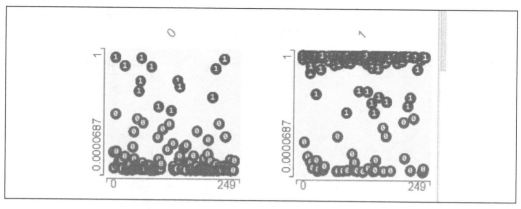

Figure 12.7: Visualizing a feature in bins

We can see that the bin on the right contains a significant amount of positive predictions (smiling people). The bin on the left only contains a sparse amount of positive predictions (smiling people).

In the bin on the left, the negative predictions (people who are not smiling) are dense and sparse in the bin on the right.

A justification rule that would filter the prediction of the AI system could be the following:

p is true if `Mouth_Slightly_Open` is true

However, many smiles are made with a closed mouth, such as the following true positive (the person is smiling):

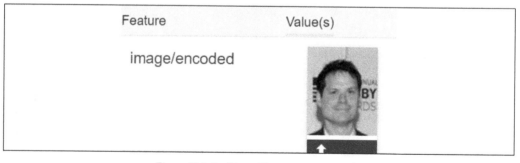

Figure 12.8: Smiling without an open mouth

This means that `Mouth_Slightly_Open` is not the only rule a rule base would require. The second rule could be:

If lip corners are higher than the middle of the lips, the person could be smiling

This rule requires other rules as well.

The conclusions we can draw from this experiment are as follows:

- We took that program as it was, unconditionally
- The program was designed to make us think using WIT!
- We analyzed the data points
- We found that many features did not apply to an AI program that was detecting smiles
- We found that features were missing to predict whether a person was smiling
- In *Chapter 9, The Counterfactual Explanations Method*, we used the CEM to explain the distances between the data points
- In this chapter, we used everyday, common human cognitive sense to understand the problem
- This is an example of how explainable AI and cognitive human input can work together to help a user understand an explanation

In this section, we used human reasoning to go from explaining a machine learning output to understanding how the AI system arrived at a prediction.

Summary

In this chapter, we captured the essence of XAI tools and used their concepts for cognitive XAI. Ethical and moral perspectives lead us to create a cognitive explanation method in everyday language to satisfy users who request human intervention to understand AI-made decisions.

SHAP shows the marginal contribution of features. Facets displays data points in an XAI interface. We can interact with Google's WIT, which provides counterfactual explanations, among other functions.

The CEM tool shows us the importance of the absence of a feature as well as the marginal presence of a feature. LIME takes us right to a specific prediction and interprets the vicinity of a prediction. Anchors go a step further and explain the connections between the key features of a prediction.

In this chapter, we used the concepts of these tools to help a user understand the explanations and interpretations of an XAI tool. Cognitive AI does not have the model-agnostic quality of the XAI tools we explored. Cognitive AI requires careful human design. However, cognitive AI can provide human explanations.

We showed how cognitive AI could help a user understand sentiment analysis, marginal feature contributions, vectorizers, and how to grasp counterfactual models among the many other concepts of our XAI tools.

The XAI tools described in this chapter and book will lead to other XAI tools.

XAI will bridge the gap between the complexity of machine intelligence and the even more complex human understanding of the world.

The need for human intervention to explain AI will explode unless explainable and interpretable AI spreads. That's why XAI will spread to every area of AI.

In *Chapter 7, A Python Client for Explainable AI Chatbots*, we built the beginning of a human-machine relationship that will expand as the first level of XAI in a human-machine relationship. This relationship will involve AI, XAI, and connected smart objects and bots.

The human user will obtain personal assistant AI explanations at every moment to use the incredible technology that awaits us.

You will write the next chapter in your everyday life as a user, developer, or manager of AI and XAI!

Questions

1. SHapley Additive exPlanations (SHAP) compute the marginal contribution of each feature with a SHAP value. (True | False)

2. Google's What-If Tool can display SHAP values as counterfactual data points. (True | False)

3. Counterfactual explanations include showing the distance between two data points. (True | False)

4. The contrastive explanations method (CEM) has an interesting way of interpreting the absence of a feature in a prediction. (True | False)

5. Local Interpretable Model-agnostic Explanations (LIME) interpret the vicinity of a prediction. (True | False)

6. Anchors show the connection between features that can occur in positive and negative predictions. (True | False)

7. Tools such as Google Location History can provide additional information to explain the output of a machine learning model. (True | False)

8. Cognitive XAI captures the essence of XAI tools to help a user understand XAI in everyday language. (True | False)

9. XAI is mandatory in many countries. (True | False)

10. The future of AI is people-centered XAI that uses chatbots, among other tools. (True | False)

Further reading

For more on cognitive and human-machine (XAI) approaches, visit the following URL:

https://researcher.watson.ibm.com/researcher/view_group.php?id=7806

Answers to the Questions

Chapter 1, Explaining Artificial Intelligence with Python

1. **Understanding the theory of an ML algorithm is enough for XAI. (True | False)**

   False. Implementing an ML program requires more than theoretical knowledge.

   True. If a user just wants an intuitive explanation of an ML algorithm.

2. **Explaining the origin of datasets is not necessary for XAI. (True | False)**

   True. If a third party has certified the dataset.

   False. If you are building the dataset, you need to make sure you are respecting privacy laws.

3. **Explaining the results of an ML algorithm is sufficient. (True | False)**

   True. If a user is not interested in anything else but the result.

   False. If it is required to explain how a result was reached.

4. **It is not necessary for an end user to know what a KNN is. (True | False)**

   True. If the end user is satisfied with results.

   False. If the end user is a developer that is deploying the program and must maintain it.

5. **Obtaining data to train an ML algorithm is easy with all the available data online. (True | False)**

   True. If we are training an ML with ready-to-use datasets.

   False. If we need to collect the data ourselves. It can take months to find the right way to collect the data and build meaningful samples.

6. **Location history is not necessary for a medical diagnosis. (True | False)**

   True. When a disease does not depend on where a patient traveled.

   False. When the patient was infected in a location before going to another location where the disease is not present.

7. **Our analysis of the patient with the West Nile virus cannot be applied to other viruses. (True | False)**

   False. Viruses usually start in a location and then travel. It many cases, it is vital to know about the virus, where it came from, and how a patient was infected. The whole process explored in this chapter can save lives.

8. **A doctor does not require AI to make a diagnosis. (True | False)**

   True. For a simple disease.

   False. When the diagnosis involves many parameters, AI can be a great help.

9. **It isn't necessary to explain AI to a doctor. (True | False)**

   False. A doctor needs to know why an ML algorithm reached a critical decision.

10. **AI and XAI will save lives. (True | False)**

    True. This is 100% certain. Humans that work with AI and understand AI will obtain vital information to reach a diagnosis quickly in life and death situations.

Chapter 2, White Box XAI for AI Bias and Ethics

1. **The autopilot of an SDC can override traffic regulations. (True | False)**
   True. Technically it is possible.
   False. Though possible, it is not legal.

2. **The autopilot of an SDC should always be activated. (True | False)**
   False. The simulations in this chapter prove that it should be avoided in heavy traffic until autopilots can deal with any situation.

3. **The structure of a decision tree can be controlled for XAI. (True | False)**
   True. Modifying the size and depth of a decision tree is a good tool to explain the algorithm.

4. **A well-trained decision tree will always produce a good result with live data. (True | False)**

   True. If the training reached an accuracy of 1.

   False. New situations might confuse the algorithm.

5. **A decision tree uses a set of hardcoded rules to classify data. (True | False)**

   False. A decision tree learns how to decide.

6. **A binary decision tree can classify more than two classes. (True | False)**

   False. A binary decision tree is designed for two classes.

7. **The graph of a decision tree can be controlled to help explain the algorithm. (True | False)**

   True. Explaining ML by visualizing different sizes and depths of a decision tree is efficient.

8. **The trolley problem is an optimizing algorithm for trollies. (True | False)**

   False. The trolley problem applies to a runaway trolley that can potentially kill pedestrians.

9. **A machine should not be allowed to decide whether to kill somebody or not. (True | False)**

   True. Ethics should forbid machines from doing this, although we don't know if we can stop the use of autopilot weapons.

10. **An autopilot should not be activated in heavy traffic until it's totally reliable. (True | False)**

    True. Autopilots progress each day. In the meantime, we should be careful when using autopilots in heavy traffic.

Chapter 3, Explaining Machine Learning with Facets

1. **Datasets in real-life projects are rarely reliable. (True | False)**

   True. In most cases, the datasets require a fair amount of quality control before they can be used as input data for ML models. In rare cases, the data is perfect in some companies that constantly check the quality of their data.

2. **In a real-life project, there are no missing records in a dataset. (True | False)**

   False. In most cases, data is missing.

   True. In some critical areas, such as aerospace projects, the data is clean.

3. **The distribution distance is the distance between two data points. (True | False)**

   False. The distribution distance is measured between two data distributions.

4. **Non-uniformity does not affect an ML model. (True | False)**

   False. Non-uniformity has profound effects on the outputs of an ML model. However, in some cases, non-uniform datasets reflect the reality of the problem we are trying to solve, and the challenge is to find a solution!

5. **Sorting by feature order can provide interesting information. (True | False)**

   True. You can design your dataset so that the features appear in the order or display the reasoning you wish to convey.

6. **Binning the x axis and the y axis in various ways offers helpful insights. (True | False)**

   True. By binning different features, you can visualize how each feature influences the outcome of the machine learning model.

7. **The median, the minimum, and the maximum values of a feature cannot change an ML prediction. (True | False)**

   False and *True.* If the median divides a set of values of a feature into two very different feature values, you might have an unstable feature.

   However, this could also be a key aspect of the dataset to take into account.

8. **Analyzing training datasets before running an ML model is useless. It's better to wait for outputs. (True | False)**

   False. Quality control of a dataset comes first. Building an ML model using unreliable data will lead to a waste of time and resources.

9. **Facets Overview and Facets Dive can help fine-tune an ML model. (True | False)**

   True. By visualizing your datasets, you can see where your ML model needs fine-tuning. You might find missing data, zeros, non-uniform data distributions, and more problems that will help you improve your datasets and ML model.

Chapter 4, Microsoft Azure Machine Learning Model Interpretability with SHAP

1. **Shapley values are model-dependent. (True | False)**

   False. Shapley values are particularly interesting because they are not ML model dependent.

2. **Model-agnostic XAI does not require output. (True | False)**

   False. The output of an ML model is necessary to analyze the contributions of each feature to a result.

3. **The Shapley value calculates the marginal contribution of a feature in a prediction. (True | False)**

   True.

4. **The Shapley value can calculate the marginal contribution of a feature for all of the records in a dataset. (True | False)**

   True. Each feature can then be compared to the marginal contribution of other features when analyzing the output of an ML model.

5. **Vectorizing data means that we transform data into numerical vectors. (True | False)**

   True. This is a key function before running an ML algorithm.

6. **When vectorizing data, we can also calculate the frequency of a feature in the dataset. (True | False)**

   True. Calculating the frequency of a feature in a dataset can help explain ML model outputs.

7. **SHAP only works with logistic regression. (True | False)**

   False. SHAP is model-agnostic. It can be used to explain many types of ML models.

8. **One feature with a very high Shapley value can change the output of a prediction. (True | False)**

   True. One feature can change a result.

   False. Many other features can also have high Shapley values. In this case, the features can form a coalition of features to influence the outcome of a prediction, for example.

9. **Using a unit test to explain AI is a waste of time. (True | False)**

   False. In some cases, the results are challenging to explain an ML model. Isolating samples to run a unit test can save a lot of time.

   True. If an ML model is easy to explain with SHAP, for example, creating a unit test is useless.

10. **Shapley values can show that some features are mispresented in a dataset. (True | False)**

    True. If an ML model keeps producing errors, SHAP can help track them using SHAP's numerical and visual tools.

Chapter 5, Building an Explainable AI Solution from Scratch

1. **Moral considerations mean nothing in AI as long as it's legal. (True | False)**

   False. You have conflicts with people that are offended by AI solutions that do not take moral considerations into account.

2. **Explaining AI with an ethical approach will help users trust AI. (True | False)**

   True. An ethical approach will make your AI programs and explanations trustworthy.

3. **There is no need to check whether a dataset contains legal data. (True | False)**

   False. You must verify if the data used is legal or not.

4. **Using machine learning algorithms to verify datasets is productive. (True | False)**

   True. ML can provide automated help to check datasets.

5. **Facets Dive requires an ML algorithm. (True | False)**

   False. You can load and analyze raw data without running an ML algorithm first.

6. **You can anticipate ML outputs with Facets Dive. (True | False)**

   True. In some cases, you can anticipate what the ML algorithm will produce.

   False. In other cases, the number of parameters and the amount of data will be overwhelming. ML will be required.

7. **You can use ML to verify your intuitive predictions. (True | False)**

   True. This is an essential aspect of explainable AI and AI.

8. **Some features in an ML model can be suppressed without changing the results. (True | False)**

   True. Yes, in some cases, this will work.

   False. In other cases, the results will be either inaccurate or biased.

9. **Some datasets provide accurate ML labels but inaccurate real-life results. (True | False)**

   True. In some cases, an ML algorithm will produce good results from a metrics perspective and produce false predictions. In this case, you must check the data and the model in detail.

10. **You can visualize counterfactual datapoints with WIT. (True | False)**

    True. This is one of the excellent functions provided by WIT.

Chapter 6, AI Fairness with Google's What-If Tool (WIT)

1. **The developer of an AI system decides what is ethical or not. (True | False)**

   True. The developer is accountable for the philosophy of an AI system.

   False. Each country has legal obligation guidelines.

2. **A DNN is the only estimator for the COMPAS dataset. (True | False)**

   False. Other estimators would produce good results as well, such as decision trees or linear regression models.

3. **Shapley values determine the marginal contribution of each feature. (True | False)**

   True. The values will show if some features are making the wrong contributions, for example.

4. **We can detect the biased output of a model with a SHAP plot. (True | False)**

   True. We can visualize the contribution of biased data.

5. **WIT's primary quality is "people-centered." (True | False)**

   True. People-centered AI systems will outperform AI systems that have no human guidance.

6. **A ROC curve monitors the time it takes to train a model. (True | False)**

   False. ROC stands for "receiver operating characteristic." It displays true and false positives.

7. **AUC stands for "area under convolution." (True | False)**

   False. AUC stands for "area under curve." If the area under the true positive curve is small, then the true positive curve is failing to approach an accuracy of 1.

8. **Analyzing the ground truth of a model is a prerequisite in ML. (True | False)**

   True. If the goal of the model, the ground truth, is false, the model is false.

9. **Another ML program could do XAI. (True | False)**

   True. Technically, yes. This would be a personal decision to accept bias.

   False. Another machine learning program would need to go through human moral and ethical control, which brings us back to people-centered AI. Legal constraints will most certainly slow the distribution of the AI system down.

10. **The WIT "people-centered" approach will change the course of AI. (True | False)**

    True. Human intelligence added to machine intelligence will contribute to the wide distribution of AI in all fields based on accuracy and trust.

Chapter 7, A Python Client for Explainable AI Chatbots

1. **It is possible to create a dialog with Python and Dialogflow. (True | False)**

   True. The Google Python client can communicate with Dialogflow.

2. **You can customize your XAI dialog with a Python client. (True | False)**

   True. Yes, a chatbot can help to interestingly explain AI.

3. **You do not need to set anything up in Dialogflow if you use a Python client. (True | False)**

   False. You must configure Dialogflow.

4. **Intents are optional in Dialogflow. (True | False)**

   False. Intents contain training phrases and responses.

5. **A training phrase is a response in a dialog. (True | False)**

   False. A training phase contains a question or phrase, not the response.

6. **Context is a way of enhancing an XAI dialog. (True | False)**

   True. It is a good way of improving a dialog by remembering the previous exchanges.

7. **A follow-up question is a way of managing the context of a dialog. (True | False)**

   True. A follow-up question continues a dialog.

8. **Small talk improves the emotional behavior of a dialog. (True | False)**

   True. Introducing some small talk makes the dialog less technical and cold.

9. **Small talk can be directly set up in Dialogflow. (True | False)**

   True. Yes. There is a small talk feature in Dialogflow.

Chapter 8, Local Interpretable Model-Agnostic Explanations (LIME)

1. **LIME stands for Local Interpretable Model-agnostic Explanations. (True | False)**

   True.

2. **LIME measures the overall accuracy score of a model. (True | False)**

   False. LIME's unique approach measures the truthfulness of a prediction locally.

3. **LIME's primary goal is to verify if a local prediction is faithful to the model. (True | False)**

   True.

4. **The LIME explainer shows why a local prediction is trustworthy or not. (True | False)**

   True.

5. **If you run a random forest model with LIME, you cannot use the same model with an extra trees model. (True | False)**

   False. LIME's algorithm is model-agnostic.

6. **There is a LIME explainer for each model. (True | False)**

   False. LIME's explainer applies to a range of models.

7. **Prediction metrics are not necessary if a user is satisfied with predictions. (True | False)**

   False. The predictions might seem accurate, but the global accuracy of a model must be displayed and explained.

8. **A model that has a low accuracy score can produce accurate outputs. (True | False)**

   True. Even a poor model can produce true positives and true negatives. However, the model is globally unreliable.

9. **A model that has a high accuracy score provides correct outputs. (True | False)**

   True. But the same model might produce false positives and negatives as well. A model might be accurate but requires constant monitoring.

10. **Benchmarking models can help choose a model or fine-tune it. (True | False)**

    True. A model might not fit a specific dataset for several reasons. First, try to refine the model and check the datasets. If not, perhaps another model might produce better predictions.

Chapter 9, The Counterfactual Explanations Method

1. **A true positive prediction does not require a justification. (True | False)**
   False. Any prediction should be justified, whether it is true or false.

2. **Justification by showing the accuracy of the model will satisfy a user. (True | False)**

   False. A model can be accurate but for the wrong reasons, whatever they may be.

3. **A user needs to believe an AI prediction. (True | False)**

   True. A user will not trust a prediction without a certain amount of belief.

   False. In some cases, such as a medical diagnosis, some truths are difficult to believe.

4. **A counterfactual explanation is unconditional. (True | False)**

   True.

5. **The counterfactual explanation method will vary from one model to another. (True | False)**

   False. A counterfactual explanation is model-agnostic.

6. **A counterfactual data point is found with a distance function. (True | False)**

   True.

7. **Sensitivity shows how closely a data point and its counterfactual are related. (True | False)**

   True.

8. **The L1 norm uses Manhattan distances. (True | False)**

   True.

9. **The L2 norm uses Euclidean distances. (True | False)**

   True.

10. **GDPR has made XAI de facto mandatory in the European Union. (True | False)**

    True. Furthermore, explaining automatic decisions will eventually become mainstream as consumer suits will challenge controversial choices made by bots.

Chapter 10, Contrastive XAI

1. **Contrastive explanations focus on the features with the highest values that lead to a prediction. (True | False)**

   False. CEM focuses on the missing features.

2. **General practitioners never use contrastive reasoning to evaluate a patient. (True | False)**

   False. General practitioners often eliminate symptoms when assessing a patient's condition.

3. **Humans reason with contrastive methods. (True | False)**

   True.

4. **An image cannot be explained with CEM. (True | False)**

   False. CEM can use the output of a CNN and an autoencoder to produce explanations.

5. **You can explain a tripod using a missing feature of a table. (True | False)**

   True. It is the example given by the IBM Research team.

6. **A CNN generates good results on the MNIST dataset. (True | False)**

   True.

7. **A pertinent negative explains how a model makes a prediction with a missing feature. (True | False)**

   True.

8. **CEM does not apply to text classification. (True | False)**

   False.

9. **The CEM explainer can produce visual explanations. (True | False)**

   True.

Chapter 11, Anchors XAI

1. **LIME explanations are global rules. (True | False)**

   False. LIME explanations explain predictions locally.

2. **LIME explains a prediction locally. (True | False)**

   True.

3. **LIME is efficient on all datasets. (True | False)**

   False. An XAI tool is model-agnostic but not dataset-agnostic.

4. **Anchors detect the ML model used to make a prediction. (True | False)**

   False. Anchors are model-agnostic.

5. **Anchors detect the parameters of an ML model. (True | False)**

   False. Anchors are model-agnostic.

6. **Anchors are high-precision rules. (True | False)**

   True.

7. **High-precision rules explain how a prediction was reached. (True | False)**

   True.

8. **Anchors do not apply to images. (True | False)**

   False.

9. **Anchors can display superpixels on an image. (True | False)**

   True.

10. **A model-agnostic XAI tool can run on many ML models. However, not every ML model is compatible with an XAI tool for specific applications. (True | False)**

    True. You must carefully choose the XAI tools you will use for a specific database for a specific ML model.

Chapter 12, Cognitive XAI

1. **SHapley Additive exPlanations (SHAP) compute the marginal contribution of each feature with a SHAP value. (True | False)**

   True.

2. **Google's What-If Tool can display SHAP values as counterfactual data points. (True | False)**

   True.

3. **Counterfactual explanations include showing the distance between two data points. (True | False)**

   True.

4. **The contrastive explanations method (CEM) has an interesting way of interpreting the absence of a feature in a prediction. (True | False)**

   True.

5. **Local Interpretable Model-agnostic Explanations (LIME) interpret the vicinity of a prediction. (True | False)**

   True.

6. **Anchors show the connection between features that can occur in positive and negative predictions. (True | False)**

   True.

7. **Tools such as Google Location History can provide additional information to explain the output of a machine learning model. (True | False)**

    True.

8. **Cognitive XAI captures the essence of XAI tools to help a user understand XAI in everyday language. (True | False)**

    True.

9. **XAI is mandatory in many countries. (True | False)**

    True.

10. **The future of AI is people-centered XAI that uses chatbots, among other tools. (True | False)**

    True.

Other Books You
May Enjoy

If you enjoyed this book, you may be interested in these other books by Packt:

Artificial Intelligence By Example - Second Edition

Denis Rothman

ISBN: 9781839211539

- Apply k-nearest neighbors (KNN) to language translations and explore the opportunities in Google Translate
- Understand chained algorithms combining unsupervised learning with decision trees
- Solve the XOR problem with feedforward neural networks (FNN) and build its architecture to represent a data flow graph

- Learn about meta learning models with hybrid neural networks
- Create a chatbot and optimize its emotional intelligence deficiencies with tools such as Small Talk and data logging
- Building conversational user interfaces (CUI) for chatbots
- Writing genetic algorithms that optimize deep learning neural networks
- Build quantum computing circuits

Advanced Deep Learning with TensorFlow 2 and Keras - Second Edition

Rowel Atienza

ISBN: 9781838821654

- Use mutual information maximization techniques to perform unsupervised learning
- Use segmentation to identify the pixel-wise class of each object in an image
- Identify both the bounding box and class of objects in an image using object detection
- Learn the building blocks for advanced techniques - MLPs, CNN, and RNNs
- Understand deep neural networks - including ResNet and DenseNet
- Understand and build autoregressive models – autoencoders, VAEs, and GANs
- Discover and implement deep reinforcement learning methods

Leave a review - let other readers know what you think

Please share your thoughts on this book with others by leaving a review on the site that you bought it from. If you purchased the book from Amazon, please leave us an honest review on this book's Amazon page. This is vital so that other potential readers can see and use your unbiased opinion to make purchasing decisions, we can understand what our customers think about our products, and our authors can see your feedback on the title that they have worked with Packt to create. It will only take a few minutes of your time, but is valuable to other potential customers, our authors, and Packt. Thank you!

Index

CPSIA information can be obtained
at www.ICGtesting.com
Printed in the USA
FSHW011447130820
72936FS